More Than Meets the Ear

MORE THAN MEETS THE EAR

❧

How Symphony Musicians Made Labor History

Julie Ayer

SYREN BOOK COMPANY
Minneapolis

Most Syren Books are available at special quantity discounts for bulk purchases for sales promotions, premiums, fund-raising, and educational needs. For details, write

Syren Book Company
Special Sales Department
5120 Cedar Lake Road
Minneapolis, MN 55416

Published by
Syren Book Company
5120 Cedar Lake Road
Minneapolis, MN 55416

Printed in the United States of America on acid-free paper

ISBN-13: 978-0-929636-43-6
ISBN-10: 0-929636-43-0

LCCN 2005924967

Cover design by Kyle G. Hunter
Book design by Wendy Holdman

To order additional copies of this book see the form
at the back of this book or go to www.itascabooks.com

This book is dedicated to those visionary leaders who conceived of and formulated what ultimately became ICSOM, the International Conference of Symphony and Opera Musicians.

It is hoped that their activism will inspire present and future generations of symphony musicians, teachers, patrons, historians, and music lovers everywhere.

Nothing has really happened until it has been recorded.

Virginia Woolf

Contents

Appendixes

Preface

Snaring topflight musicians is easy, because people who push
brooms are treated better than symphony players.

*Dr. Wilfred Bain, legendary dean of the
Indiana University School of Music, who built its
extraordinary music faculty beginning in the 1960s*

*T*HIS BOOK IS A CHRONICLE of symphony musicians' historic
struggle toward improving and enriching their professional
lives. The countless anecdotes and stories that were told again and again
among colleagues, family, and friends in the late 1950s, '60s, and early
'70s have become part of the collective folklore, informing and often
entertaining each new generation. My Minneapolis colleagues related
countless stories of orchestra life and the challenges of contract negotiations: the behind-the-scenes dramas that even then many musicians
took for granted. I learned that notwithstanding the professional artistic
fulfillment of orchestral involvement, they had found lives of financial
hardship, no job security, difficult working conditions, grueling tours,
dictatorial conductors, and a nonrepresentational union.

I came to realize that the background to these stories was an important part of the musicians' labor history that was evaporating with the
passage of time. There was no cohesive documentation of the real drama
of the grassroots labor movement that had transformed the lives of professional orchestra musicians.

I thought I had heard it all from my colleagues in Minneapolis, and
other orchestras, until I met my brother-in-law, Rudy Nashan, member
of the Chicago Symphony Orchestra from 1950 to 1963, a committee
and union activist, and one of the founders of ICSOM, the International
Conference of Symphony and Opera Musicians. His experiences with

Musicians Union president James C. Petrillo, his committee and union work, and the personal and professional hardships and accomplishments that resulted, reflected a major turning point in the history of labor relations in American symphony orchestras.

This book is not intended as an exposé. Conductors, managers, and union leaders are mentioned anecdotally and in the context of contractual issues. The musicians' activism had a profound effect on their professional lives as well.

Nor is this book intended as a definitive history of ICSOM. Archivist Tom Hall, a member of the Chicago Symphony, has assembled *Forty Years of ICSOM* for all of the member orchestras. I do not presume to offer that kind of detail here.

On a summer day in 1997, I began to document the movement that had led to the formation, thirty-five years previously, of ICSOM. My husband, Carl Nashan, and I—both violinists with the Minnesota Orchestra—had organized a gathering of former and current members of the Chicago Symphony Orchestra (the CSO). We met at Ravinia, the CSO's summer home. The third host of the reunion, Carl's brother, Rudy, moderated the discussion and conversations among the assembled musicians, some of whom had not seen each other for many years.

As I listened and took notes, the musicians began to reminisce and recall the historic meeting of the representatives from twelve major symphony and opera orchestras who had, at their own expense, convened in Chicago in May 1962 to discuss issues of mutual concern. That meeting, which had produced ICSOM, signified the transition to a major era in labor relations and in the symphony orchestra profession. The gathering at Ravinia gave me personal insight into the significance of it all. Putting their stories together, the Chicago musicians began to sort out details not only of the May 1962 meeting but also of the events leading up to it. As the day progressed, their conversations became livelier.

Their remarkable stories, their vivid anecdotes, and their passionate language changed my intentions that day. Originally thinking that I could help new generations of symphony musicians understand and appreciate their collective history, I now realized that my CSO colleagues were telling the story of a unique grassroots labor movement that had meaning for a much broader audience. Their story can continue to inspire us all.

The crucial role of a few visionary militants of the Chicago and Cleveland orchestras in this national story derived from their willingness to do battle at great personal risk with the formidable adversaries of their orchestra managements and with Musicians Union president James C. Petrillo, one of the most powerful union leaders in America. In the end, they succeeded in deposing Petrillo, and Chicago became one of the last orchestras in the country to form a musicians representative committee—a basic union right that had long eluded symphony musicians.

In the post–World War II era, orchestra musicians in locals across the United States and Canada waged their own union battles. They had begun to discover common problems, and in Chicago the movement ignited. What happened next was revolutionary.

In my work on many committees in two major symphony orchestras, nothing prepared me more to write this book than the actual experience of contract negotiations, as difficult and trying as they can be. The contract becomes a living force, with a human history. Since human nature disposes us to take many things for granted, we tend to pay close attention only to those things that affect us personally. Writing this book has given me the chance to record and credit the human history and personal stories of those committed and principled people who created the chain of symphony orchestra contracts that bring so many benefits to symphony musicians today. We dare not take those benefits for granted.

I have connected with so many people who encouraged and inspired me, particularly current and retired colleagues from many orchestras, some of whom, sadly, have not lived to see the publication of their stories. Others who offered invaluable help and resources include labor lawyers; ICSOM leaders, their spouses and children; historians and archivists; authors; union leaders; and symphony orchestra staff members and managers. All were fascinated with the documentation of this story and supportive of my telling it.

Acknowledgments

*M*Y DEEPEST GRATITUDE to the members of all past and present negotiating committees of the Minnesota Orchestra (individual names are listed in Chapter 10), whose time and efforts contributed valuable information for this book through written and oral interviews, correspondence, and personal archives. In addition, my thanks go to:

Gary Andrews, Michael Anthony, Edward Arian, Ron Balazs, Wayne Barrington, Bunny Beckerman, Susan Borenstein, Dr. Alice Brandfonbrenner, Russell Brodine, Sandi Brown, Brad Buckley, Court Burns, Monique Buzzarte, Evelina Chao, Richard Cisek, Robert Coleman, Leslie Czechowski, Sandy Date, Sam Denov, Doriot Dwyer, J. Michelle Edwards, Lea Foli, Martin Foster, Roger Frisch, Myron Gannon, E. B. Gill, Joseph Golan, Paul Gunther, Julie Haight-Curran, Barbara Haws, Dr. Frank Heller, Sara Honen, Janet Horvath, David J. Hyslop, Clifton Jackson, Clifford Johnson, Paul Judy, Nathan Kahn, Michele Kort, Walfrid Kujala, Leonard Leibowitz, Robert Levine, Kurt Loebel, Richard Lottridge, Joan Mainzer, Gary Matts, Michelle Mattson, Mrs. Jess Meltzer, Carl Nashan, Rudy Nashan, Florence Nelson, Debbie Newmark, Idell Nissila-Stone, Ray Niwa, Robert Olson, William Osborne, Gwen Pappas, Charles Pinto, Gino Raffaelli, Lavette Rainer, Elster Rheinhardt, Ron Ricketts, Ronald Rollins, Carl Schiebler, Charles Schlueter, Marsha Schweitzer, Morris Secon, Richard Simon, I. Philip Sipser, Wayne Sivertson, Ray Still, Herman Straka, Christine Sweet, Dace Taube, Dyan Valdes, Clement Volpe, Eric Wahlin, Lew Waldeck, Kirke Walker, David Waters, Serena Williams, Mele Willis, Vera Willis, Amy Yen, Marl Young, Erica Zazofsky, Steve Zellmer, Fred Zenone.

And gratitude to those readers who offered valuable suggestions, support, and encouragement about the manuscript as it took shape:

Stephanie Arado, Nina Archabal, Brad Eggen, Mary Ann Feldman, Henry Fogel, Gwendolyn Freed, Laurel Green, Keith Gunderson, Tom Hall, Jim Klobuchar, Sara de Luca, Virginia Martin, Anne Montague, Erica Nashan, Jeffrey Nashan, Brian Newhouse, Joanne Opgenorth, Karl Reichert, Dr. James Snyder, Janis Snyder, Carol Spindel, Michael Steinberg, John Swanson, Christine Sweet, Kathy Timmerman, Sande Turner, Tom Turner, Margaret Vaillancourt, Bonnie West, Dr. Karen Winer.

Special affection to my husband and soulmate, Carl Nashan, whose humor, love, and support helped me keep my sanity throughout this amazing and sometimes agonizing journey.

To my dearest friend, Sandra Hyslop, I extend my deepest appreciation for her help, insight, and enthusiasm for this project. Through her expertise these historic events were brought into focus.

The book has ended, but the stories continue.

My Story

"Darling, let your fingers travel without clutching tightly. It will make the fingerboard seem half as long. . . . I want to hear a soprano, and then a tenor singing in response—imagine a song with words to it. And here there's a little bit of a sigh: don't be afraid to slide—it gives the violin a wonderful chance to sing."

Josef Gingold

$\mathscr{B}$Y THE TIME I BEGAN taking violin auditions in the mid-1970s, many major American symphony orchestras were offering full-time employment, or nearly so, including the benefits of job security, insurance, and a small pension. Even as a young, idealistic student, I could imagine a profession in an orchestra, and I was determined to achieve economic independence and professional fulfillment.

I had grown up in Spokane, Washington (population 161,721), in midcentury America, at the time when most major orchestras performed twenty-four to twenty-six weeks annually and paid barely a living wage to their musicians. *The Lawrence Welk Show, The Ed Sullivan Show,* and *The Huntley-Brinkley Report* were the favorite family television programs, and hometown boy Bing Crosby was my mother's favorite crooner.

Music filled our home. My older brother, Larry, played the clarinet and, in his first major experiment playing records and tinkering with electronics (which became his profession), loudly cranked out Les Paul and Mary Ford, and Chet Atkins, on 78 RPM vinyl discs on the 1939 Seeburg Classic jukebox in our basement. He remembers getting yelled at from upstairs, above the din of our roller skates, to turn it down. My sister, Jane, was advancing quickly on the violin, and my father played the guitar as a hobby. My mother, a professional violinist, proved the most steadfast and patient influence on my own musical development. Both parents made it clear to Jane and me (I was easily distracted) from an early age that they would not force us to practice, but costly private instruction depended upon our commitment to a daily practice regimen and regular preparation for our weekly lessons.

As a beginning student, I looked forward to my violin lessons at the home of Harold Paul Whelan, the founding conductor of the Spokane Symphony Orchestra and a loving teacher. He imparted to his students the joy of music and the fundamentals of the violin, as well as a vision for Spokane's musical future.

The Spokane Philharmonic, as it was known then, had been established in 1945, with my mother one of its founding members. Listening and watching her perform were some of the greatest pleasures of my childhood. When my family moved to Spokane after World War II, she found work playing with dance bands and for radio shows. The Evelyn Ayer Trio played for dinners, weddings, style shows, and other social events popular in the 1940s, '50s, and '60s. But joining a symphony orchestra drawn from the local community of fellow musicians was her dream come true, and it remained a source of great pride and joy all her life.

In an interview with the local newspaper in 1949, my mother stated, "As a member of the Spokane Philharmonic Orchestra for the last four years, my greatest pleasure and benefit has been in learning and playing the works of the great composers. Most housewives need and maintain an interest outside of home and daily duties and participation in the Philharmonic is, to me, a very happy diversion, and makes possible my greater enjoyment of the fine symphonic music presented over the radio networks by the great orchestras of the country." Her words reflected the attitudes of many women of that time. Her actions, on the other hand, provided me with a role model that inspired my own goals and represented the highest professional standards. I admired how much the Spokane Symphony meant to her and to my sister; for several years they were stand partners and even roommates on tours. Yet, somehow, even as a child, I knew I wanted more from music than a "happy diversion."

Spokane provided ample opportunities for music students to play in youth orchestras, hear symphony concerts, and enter competitions. My older sister and I did it all, for one year overlapping as members of the Spokane Junior Symphony. During EXPO '74, my mother, my sister, and I all performed together in a concert of the Spokane Symphony (the name had changed in 1962).

In my last year of high school, the Spokane Symphony hired me as an extra, or substitute, player for youth concerts and Spokane Chamber Orchestra tours. This initial professional experience gave me an appreciation for the high quality of Young People's Concerts presented by the Spokane Symphony and its new conductor, Donald Thulean. Modeled after the New York Philharmonic's popular televised Young People's Concerts, created and hosted by Leonard Bernstein beginning in the late 1950s, the Spokane Symphony's youth concert series brought an important musical dimension to our community's children, who delighted in the commentary, conversation, interaction, humor, and musical excerpts.

My parents supported my interest in performance—and eventually a career in a major symphony orchestra—but their practical side encouraged me to pursue a degree in education. In the late 1960s, even the major orchestras barely provided full-time employment, and teaching provided much more job security. Unconvinced that I could devote my energies to two extremely demanding professions—or that I wanted to—I nevertheless acquiesced to their wishes. I continued with music education courses, but my fervent desire to play in a major symphony orchestra was my overriding priority.

As an undergraduate at the University of Washington in Seattle, I studied with Russian violin pedagogue Emanuel Zetlin. A teacher from the old school, he gave lessons that mixed pure terror, on the one hand, and musical inspiration, on the other. Zetlin had an intense passion for the violin and music, and he could not tolerate mistakes, inattention, or even an inkling of laziness. I respected and loved him and learned a great deal in the four years I worked with him, before he retired.

I began my career in Seattle, unsettled about my future and continuing to split my energies between teaching music part-time in public schools and working as a freelance violinist. By that time, I had experienced the horror of the assassinations of President John F. Kennedy, Senator Robert F. Kennedy, and the Reverend Martin Luther King Jr., as well as the Vietnam War and civil rights protests. These events and the resulting campus turmoil of the late 1960s and early '70s made a huge impression on me and on my generation.

At a personal and professional crossroads, I made a bold move. I left the Pacific Northwest and public school teaching in order to further my studies with Josef Gingold, professor of violin at Indiana University in Bloomington. The very name Gingold had become legendary in my household, not only because of Mr. Gingold's great professional reputation, but also because of a close personal connection. In the 1920s, my mother had been Gladys Anderson's classmate and friend at Washington State College (now known as Washington State University) in Pullman. An accomplished violinist, Gladys Anderson performed in a college string quartet and other chamber ensembles with my mother, and in 1934 she married Josef Gingold.

As a concertmaster, first of the Detroit Symphony and then of the Cleveland Orchestra in the 1940s and '50s—and, earlier, as a member of the NBC Symphony Orchestra under Arturo Toscanini—Gingold had established an international reputation as a respected leader and outstanding violinist. Joining the faculty of the Indiana University School of Music in 1960, he left his orchestra career to devote himself fully to his first love, teaching. Until his death in 1995 at the age of eighty-five, he delighted in passing along his vast knowledge to new generations of string players. He established a reputation as one of the most renowned violin pedagogues in the world.

Gingold's first class in 1960 comprised a relatively few—ten to thirteen—students. Eager to teach and finding extra time to do so, he would circle the Music School third floor or drop by the lounge looking for his students, to whom he would impulsively offer extra lessons. "Come on, let's go!" he would say, and those fortunate students might receive two or three lessons weekly.

In 1972 I proudly joined his international class of forty-four students. Violin students from throughout the world flocked to his small studio in Bloomington, the Lake Wobegon of Brown County, Indiana. Lessons consisted of much more than learning violin technique. In addition to conveying to his students how to shape a musical phrase with vibrato speed or an expressive slide, Gingold imparted his love of the violin and

The 1972 Indiana University School of Music violin class of Josef Gingold (seated front row, second from left) included the author (third row, standing third from right; not all students are represented) (Collection of the author).

music with great joy, humor, and compassion. He loved telling anecdotes and stories of his relationships with some of the major musicians of the early twentieth century. From his personal experiences with such renowned violinists as his beloved teacher Eugène Ysaÿe and the legendary Fritz Kreisler, conductors Toscanini and George Szell, and many other musicians, he passed along to his students a priceless musical legacy.

Weekly master classes often included mock auditions. Gingold's expertise in the violin repertoire—solo, chamber, and orchestral music—was unlimited, and he encouraged students to follow their own passions. Those who wanted an orchestral career, he encouraged to take auditions. (He compiled and edited an invaluable three-volume edition of violin repertoire for audition purposes, published by the International Music Company as *Orchestral Excerpts from the Symphonic Repertoire*.) For others, he equally supported their desires to teach or to pursue solo careers. Many of his students have joined major American and European orchestras, several as concertmasters. Others have become respected teachers, international soloists, and chamber musicians.

"It's a wonderful life," Gingold often declared, referring to a career as an orchestra musician, and he encouraged his students preparing for auditions. Artistically, it was indeed a wonderful life. In spite of the fact that in his lifetime orchestra musicians lived without job security, adequate salaries, or fringe benefits, he truly believed in the honor and beauty of the profession. I would soon learn about the financial hardships, difficult working conditions, job insecurity, lack of benefits and pensions, grueling tours, dictatorial conductors, and nonrepresentational unions of that life. Although professional orchestra musicians had made some progress in these areas since the 1960s, I was only peripherally aware of what, why, or how it had occurred.

When I joined the Houston Symphony Orchestra in the winter of 1976, I had no idea of the problems ready to erupt there. During my brief membership in that orchestra, my eyes were opened to the basic principles of musicians' committee involvement, the importance of speaking with one voice, unanimity of purpose, and strong representative leadership. I realized quickly that no amount of violin practice or freelance experience could have prepared me for all of the nonperformance obligations in an orchestra. Through the impressive example of the Houston musicians, I began to understand the fundamentals of organization, committee work, and labor negotiations. I also began to learn of the history of this labor struggle, not only for the Houston musicians, but for musicians all over the United States and Canada. Six months after my first concert, the Houston Symphony Orchestra management locked out the musicians in a bitter labor dispute. I regretfully left the orchestra to resume auditioning.

In September 1976, I joined the Minnesota Orchestra (formerly known as the Minneapolis Symphony). I settled quickly into the routine of the orchestra's life—four rehearsals and four concerts each week, Young People's Concerts, Pops Concerts, summer season, and a few years later, Sommerfest, as well as run-outs and tours away from the Twin Cities. Several former IU classmates were now members of the orchestra, including friends from Professor Gingold's and cellist Janos Starker's classes.

Among them was violinist Carl Nashan, one of the lucky members of the 1960 violin class to whom Gingold had given extra lessons in his first year at Indiana University. Carl and I met when I joined the orchestra in 1976, and we married in 1979.

The older musicians of the Minnesota Orchestra had experienced tumultuous times during the past several decades. The orchestra I had just joined—with its audition committees and improved working conditions, salary, and pension—seemed a world apart from their experiences just a few years earlier. Many important labor issues, including the establishment of ICSOM (the International Conference of Symphony and Opera Musicians), had found resolution by the late 1970s. (Much later, I would serve as the Minnesota Orchestra's ICSOM representative for three years, an invaluable experience I would highly recommend to my colleagues.)

> To tell what has transpired since 1962 should become a part of new member orientation. It must be emphasized that ICSOM is an investment and it must be protected. Perhaps an occasional reminder of difficulties that had to be dealt with is in order, along with the admonition that history can surely repeat itself where complacency becomes the order of the day.
>
> *Henry Shaw, Cincinnati Symphony,* Senza Sordino *(April 1977)*

In spite of dramatic changes in the music profession, several aspects of musicians' lives have remained constant, regardless of age, ethnicity, or gender. The arduous path to a chair in a major symphony orchestra usually begins in childhood, with costly private studies on an instrument (sometimes more than one), and continues for at least fifteen years—usually more. Invaluable experience in youth orchestras prepares students for the grueling audition process, as does study at a conservatory or university music school, with expensive instrumental instruction added to the tuition bill. By the time they set out to take symphony orchestra auditions, musicians compete with sometimes as many as a hundred or more other musicians for a single vacancy. Young musicians also face the cost of precious instruments—a financial burden that has, for years, compared favorably with a home mortgage.

Like professional athletes, symphony orchestra musicians experience the physical stress of lifelong practice and performance, and most of them will eventually suffer a wide range of injuries. Even the use of the word *playing* in reference to performing on an instrument conveys a common misconception. Audience members frequently ask about the "fun" of working as a musician; although we love the music and dedicate ourselves to high-quality performance standards, we cannot describe the workplace as "fun." To achieve beauty in performance, we undertake a profession that requires physical stamina and risks a wide range of possible serious injuries.

The typical orchestra musician's week of professional obligations includes, first of all, time for private practice and care of his or her instrument(s). The musician must practice consistently and regularly in preparation for rehearsals with the orchestra. The typical week includes seven to nine orchestral "services" (a service being defined as a rehearsal or a performance of approximately two-and-a-half hours' length), including subscription concerts of many kinds, children's concerts, conductor auditions, family concerts, pops concerts, recordings, tours, and other contractual committee obligations.

Few people realize that orchestral musicians belong to a union until labor negotiations raise public awareness—and, along with it, frequent misunderstandings. The public's lack of knowledge leads to questions such as, "What does the union have to do with musicians?"—not an unusual or infrequent query. Most people do not correlate the performing artist and the union member until pickets, leaflets, and press releases appear at contract negotiation time.

The past forty years have seen a dramatic transformation in the profession, both on and off the stage. A landmark Ford Foundation $80.2 million grant for symphony orchestras in 1966 coincided with the growing strength of ICSOM, enabling the musicians to negotiate for wages and benefits never thought obtainable by previous generations. Without the support and generosity of countless individuals, corporations, and foundations throughout the United States, no amount of negotiating would have brought about the financial stability and security that symphonic musicians would achieve by the early twenty-first century. Ironically, some of these very supportive community forces have also formed the orchestra boards of directors with whom the musicians have struggled over the years.

This is the story of an intense and protracted labor struggle—unique in labor history. The important terms of today's master agreements in the symphony orchestra world, such as contract ratification, lawyer representation, players committees, pension, sick leave, insurance, and benefits *didn't just happen*. All resulted from a struggle between the musicians, their union—the American Federation of Musicians (AFM)—and orchestra managements and boards of directors.

The very existence of "the committee," musician representatives elected by their colleagues to fulfill various obligations spelled out in the master agreement, is a basic workers' right that the musicians' own union did not allow until the musicians demanded change. They achieved it through the establishment of their own networking organization, which became ICSOM. Before the establishment of ICSOM in 1962, the union did not provide the help or support needed by symphony musicians, and in some cases opposed the very people it was supposed to represent. Representatives of the local musicians union and the orchestra's board or management conducted negotiations behind closed doors, without musician participation.

Before ICSOM, the conductor held all the power to hire and fire, with no recourse for the musician. Deeply engrained paternalism and autocracy characterized the top-heavy relationship between the conductor and "his" musicians, and the general public—including members of symphony orchestra boards and audiences—supported the cult of glamorous, temperamental, godlike podium giant. (See the sidebar for a fine example of the patronizing attitude that for many generations informed the behavior of most conductors.) The musicians' movement changed conductors' lives forever; and they, too, have made adjustments to a changing workplace. Gone are the days of the conductor who could hire and fire at will.

Gone, too, are the poor working and tour conditions of the pre-ICSOM era, and with them has disappeared the practice of hiring musicians on the basis of gender, race, and cronyism. ICSOM orchestra musicians are universally protected against discrimination on the basis of sex, race, age, and union activity.

Other major achievements of the past forty years include the establishment of the following provisions:

- Rights for all orchestra members to ratify their employment contracts (by American Federation of Musicians bylaws amendment);
- Legal representation for musicians;
- Players', audition, dismissal review, and artistic advisory committees of orchestra musicians;
- Tenure systems;
- Pension benefits;
- Sick leave regulations and benefits;
- Health, life, disability, dental insurance;
- Maternity and paternity leave;
- Strike funds;
- Formal process for conductor evaluation by musicians;
- Year-round contracts;
- AFM Symphony Department; and
- Recording, audiovisual, and Internet agreements and revenue sharing.

The American Federation of Musicians (AFM) now recognizes ICSOM as a vital partner and force for change. The struggles still continue, and differences will always exist, but the musicians' relationships with both the AFM and the orchestra managements and boards have improved in most cases. The basic committee principle—what happens to you, happens to me—forms the foundation for the past, present, and future. The continuity of understanding and knowledge of this labor history empowers each new generation to continue to make informed choices.

In the following chapters I will show how these elements developed as issues that demanded resolution and how the existence of ICSOM— thanks to the great symphony orchestra pioneers of the mid-twentieth century—helped consolidate the orchestra profession and raise its standards.

As every artist represents an individuality, how is one to reconcile the various points of view of the artists, often conflicting with that of the conductor, in the course of the rehearsal? To accomplish that is the real secret of the conductor's success. Here innumerable factors must work together: Magnetism, power of suggestion, experience of life, the way one comes into contact with the performers, powers of persuasion, and even humor. One must understand the members of the orchestra. Difficult as this task may appear, the experienced conductor has his sure way of accomplishing it.

Each instrumental group must be handled differently. But it is not at all necessary to know the artists personally. As the calling makes the man, so the instrument played upon makes the musician. The most sensitive and "touchy," for example, are the oboeists and the fagottists [bassoonists], and that is easily explained. These gentlemen have to blow upon a thin pipe with the chest pumped full of air, and then they slowly and carefully give out the breath. That causes a rush of blood to the brain and produces nervousness. Therefore they must be fondled so to speak.

With the gentlemen who play basses and the big wind instruments it is quite a different matter. From their instruments they derive healthy strength, peacefulness, gemütlichkeit. They can stand a good deal from the conductor. Now the clarinet player inclines to sentimentality, and must be spoken to in a gentle way, or, so as not to disturb his mental equilibrium, humorously.

If one has a capacity for researches of that sort, one recognizes that the character of the individual musician may be traced back to mechanical causes, whose effects are so uniform and inevitable that one seldom makes a mistake in handling the artists. The conductor must, in a way, have an entire orchestra on the tip of his tongue, to play to each artist a different instrument—and then his purpose is attained.

His tactics succeed perfectly when every artist is made to believe that the latter's original ideas are adhered to, whereas, in fact, he is in full accord with the interpretation of the conductor.

Attributed to the famous conductor Artur Nikisch
and published in the February 1912 issue of The Violinist

Definitions, Acronyms, Unions, Guilds

AAC   Artistic Advisory Committee

AFM   American Federation of Musicians, founded 1896
AFM Symphony Department established 1970
AFM Symphonic Services Division established 1982
AFM Local 802: The musicians local of members working
     in and around New York City; the largest union local
     of professional musicians in the world

AGMA   American Guild of Musical Artists (Founded in 1936 as
an organization of solo musical artists working to eliminate unfair practices in the music profession, AGMA
now represents, in addition, performers in opera, dance,
oratorio, concert, choral, and recital fields)

ASCAP   American Society of Composers, Authors and Publishers
(performance rights organization)

ASOL   American Symphony Orchestra League (which refers to
itself as "The League" in order to avoid the unfortunate-
sounding pronunciation of the acronym A-S-O-L)

BMI   Broadcast Music, Inc. (performance rights organization)

BSO   Boston Symphony Orchestra

CMUD   Chicago Musicians for Union Democracy, spearheaded
by Chicago Symphony musicians in 1961 in opposition
to autocracy of Chicago Local 10

Committee   Orchestra, members, or players committee—elected
representatives of a symphony orchestra who deal with
contractual matters

CSO   Chicago Symphony Orchestra

EMG   Electronic media guarantee—fixed amount paid to each
               musician, which includes radio, television, film, record-
               ings, cable television, and any other services involving
               electronic media

IAWM   International Alliance for Women in Music

IBB   Interest-based bargaining—a consensus-based style of
               collective bargaining

ICSOM   International Conference of Symphony and Opera Musi-
               cians, founded 1962

Landrum-   Established in 1959, guaranteeing each member of every
Griffin Act   labor organization the right to "express any view, argu-
               ment or opinion about the conduct of the union's affairs"

Lea Act   Also known as the "anti-Petrillo" act, passed in 1946;
               made it a criminal offense for a union to use coercion to
               force observance of its rules

MAF   Music Assistance Fund for talented minority musicians,
               established 1965

Master   Agreement between the orchestral association, referred
contract   to as the "Employer," a nonprofit corporation, and the
               musicians local of the AFM, referred to as the "Union"

MD   Music director

MGA   Musicians Guild of America (1956–1962)—an AFM rival
               union established by recording musicians and dissolved
               when goals of ratification and fair compensation were
               achieved

MOA   Minnesota Orchestral Association

MOMC   Minnesota Orchestra Members Committee

MPTF   Music Performance Trust Fund, established 1948

NEA   National Endowment for the Arts, established 1965

NLRB	National Labor Relations Board
OCSOM	Organization of Canadian Symphony and Opera Musicians, established 1974
PAMA	The Performing Arts Medicine Association
Parity	The quality or state of being equal or equivalent
Personal or individual contract	Personal contract entered into with individual musicians and consistent with the terms of the master contract
RMA	Recording Musicians Association
ROPA	Regional Orchestra Players' Association, founded 1984
Rotation	Variable with every orchestra; term refers to a periodic change of string players' seating, with only the titled players having fixed positions
Service	Traditionally used as either rehearsal or concert
SOI	Symphony Orchestra Institute
SPCO	Saint Paul Chamber Orchestra
SSD	Symphonic Services Division—the branch of the AFM that serves the needs of symphony orchestra musicians within the union; established 1982
TMA	Theater Musicians Association, an official player conference of the AFM that unites professional theater musicians throughout the United States and Canada
TMI	Three Mile Island—site of the most serious accident in US commercial nuclear power plant operating history, Middleton, Pennsylvania, 1979
VPO	Vienna Philharmonic
WPA	Works Progress Administration, established in 1935
YP	Young People's (children) Concerts

More Than Meets the Ear

MAJOR SYMPHONY ORCHESTRA SURVEY — 1952-1953

THIS SURVEY COVERS EMPLOYMENT BY SYMPHONY ORCHESTRAS WHOSE MEMBERS ARE EMPLOYED BY THE WEEK

CITY	STATE	NAME OF ORCHESTRA	Number of Men Regular Season	Number of Men Summer Season	Number of Importa-tions	No. of Weeks Regular Season	No. of Weeks Summer Season	Minimum Scale Regular Season	Minimum Scale Summer Season	Seasonal Budget
Boston	Massachusetts	BOSTON SYMPHONY Conductor, Charles Munch	105	105	7	30	16	$125.00	$105.00	$1,826,565.00
New York	New York	NEW YORK PHILHARMONIC Conductor, Dimitri Mitropoulos	106	0	0	30	0	140.00	0	1,241,500.00
Philadelphia	Pennsylvania	PHILADELPHIA SYMPHONY Conductor, Eugene Ormandy	104	91	0	32	6	135.00	112.50	1,200,000.00
Chicago	Illinois	CHICAGO SYMPHONY Conductor, Rafael Kubelik	102	98	0	28	6	132.50		1,015,027.53
Cleveland	Ohio	CLEVELAND SYMPHONY Conductor, George Szell	95	70	20	30	6	98.00	55.00	679,000.00
Los Angeles	California	LOS ANGELES PHILHARMONIC Conductor, Alfred Wallenstein	100	88	0	22½	8	100.00	100.00	572,000.00
Detroit	Michigan	DETROIT SYMPHONY Conductor, Paul Paray	102	86	11	22	12	100.00	70.00	571,692.67
Pittsburgh	Pennsylvania	PITTSBURGH SYMPHONY Conductor, William Steinberg	87	0	27	25	0	100.00	0	514,928.76
Cincinnati	Ohio	CINCINNATI SYMPHONY Conductor, Thor Johnson	88	0	1	28	0	95.00	0	501,398.77
Minneapolis	Minnesota	MINNEAPOLIS SYMPHONY Conductor, Antal Darati	89	0	16	26	0	100.00	0	487,551.25
Washington	D.C.	NATIONAL SYMPHONY Conductor, Howard Mitchell	86	0	26	26	0	80.00	0	479,644.93
San Francisco	California	SAN FRANCISCO SYMPHONY Guest Conductors	96	0	0	22	0	100.00	0	450,000.00
Rochester	New York	ROCHESTER PHILHARMONIC Conductor, Eric Leinsdorf	45	0	0	30	0	88.00	0	400,000.00
Houston	Texas	HOUSTON SYMPHONY Conductor, Efrem Kurtz	85	46	25	24	8	90.00	50.00	400,000.00
San Antonio	Texas	SAN ANTONIO SYMPHONY Victor Alessandro	73	0	46	21	0	70.00	0	330,000.00
Dallas	Texas	DALLAS SYMPHONY Conductor, Walter Hendl	72	0	26	20	0	80.00	0	320,000.00
Toronto	Ontario	TORONTO SYMPHONY Conductor, Sir Ernest MacMillan	86	0	1	26	0	70.00	0	285,000.00
St. Louis	Missouri	ST. LOUIS SYMPHONY Conductor, Vladimir Golschmann	85	0	25	23	0	96.25	0	280,000.00
Baltimore	Maryland	BALTIMORE SYMPHONY Conductor, Massimo Freccia	85	0	45	20	0	70.00	0	280,000.00
New Orleans	Louisiana	NEW ORLEANS PHILHARMONIC SYMPHONY Conductor, Alexander Hilsberg	82	0	43	20	0	65.00	0	258,280.50
Indianapolis	Indiana	INDIANAPOLIS SYMPHONY Conductor, Fabien Sevitzky	83	0	40	20	0	70.00	0	252,500.00
Kansas City	Missouri	KANSAS CITY PHILHARMONIC Conductor, Hans Schwieger	79	0	41	20	0	78.00	0	230,593.97
Atlanta	Georgia	ATLANTA SYMPHONY Conductor, Henry Sopkin	85	0	34	22	0	55.00	0	164,000.00
Oklahoma City	Oklahoma	OKLAHOMA CITY SYMPHONY Conductor, Guy Frazier Harrison	69	0	20	22	0	60.50	0	161,000.00
Denver	Colorado	DENVER SYMPHONY Conductor, Saul Caston	80	70	20	20	6	65.00	60.00	160,000.00
Buffalo	New York	BUFFALO PHILHARMONIC Conductor, Isler Soloman	80	40	19	21	10	82.50	15.00 per concert	150,000.00
Portland	Oregon	PORTLAND SYMPHONY Conductor, James Sample	67	0	4	22	0	50.00	0	140,000.00
Salt Lake City	Utah	UTAH SYMPHONY Conductor, Maurice Abravanel	80	35	4	18	3	42.50	42.50	125,000.00
Vancouver	British Columbia	VANCOUVER SYMPHONY Conductor, Irwin Hoffman	70	0	0	12	0	54.00	0	114,483.32
Raleigh	North Carolina	NORTH CAROLINA SYMPHONY Conductor, Benjamin F. Swalin	60	0	55	17	0	62.00	0	105,000.00
Orlando	Florida	FLORIDA SYMPHONY Conductor, Yves Chardon	68	0	57	12	0	60.00	0	104,000.00
Chicago	Illinois	GRANT PARK SYMPHONY Conductor, Nicolai Malko	75	75	0	8	8	88.00	88.00	85,000.00
		TOTALS	2,269	804	613	719½	89			$13,884,166.70

(Compiled by American Federation of Musicians)

1952 AFM survey (first known survey of wages and working conditions) (April 4, 1977 Senza Sordino).

One

American Orchestras Create a European Tradition in Their Own Fashion

> First oboe or first clarinet on part-time basis; willing to work in other employments.
>
> *From the Classified Section*
> *of a 1952* International Musician

*L*IKE ALL PROFESSIONAL symphony orchestra musicians in the United States, during my career I have had many contacts with colleagues throughout the world. In addition, I exchanged with a violinist from the Sydney (Australia) Symphony Orchestra, which gave me further insights into the structure and practices of symphony orchestras outside the United States. It also gave me good insight into the issues we face in the United States.

Having such perspective gave me a better understanding of the labor history of U.S. symphony orchestras, and I could devote an entire book to comparing and contrasting our orchestra world with those of Europe and Asia. However, that is not my purpose here. In order to sketch the history of American musicians' efforts to achieve fair recognition and remuneration for their contributions to their own society, I will confine myself to pointing out in simple terms how the institutions differ *fundamentally*. The details will have to wait for another book.

I believe it is most important to know and keep in mind that although European and U.S. orchestras aspire to the same artistic standards, their fundamental social, economic, and organizational structures differ radically. The two societies (Europe and the United States, to use a broad generalization) produced symphony orchestra cultures from widely different root stock.

European orchestras trace their origins to the opera house, whose roots, in turn, were planted and nourished almost entirely by royal patronage. Such a well-known ensemble as the Leipzig Gewandhaus Orchestra, whose music directors have included such notable conductors as the composer Felix Mendelssohn, was an exception that proved the rule.

The American symphony orchestra, by contrast, traces its origins to the concert hall as an entity separate from the opera house. All American orchestras were founded by the coming together of musicians and conductors who wanted to perform the symphonic repertoire (rather than serving as pit orchestras for opera houses), and private citizens who wanted to listen—and were willing to pay for the privilege. To be sure, American opera houses, like their European counterparts, have developed very fine orchestras. But they have, by and large, stayed in the opera house (today's Metropolitan Opera Orchestra under James Levine is a rare exception) and have left the symphonic repertoire to the freestanding world of the symphony orchestras in their concert halls. American orchestras are rooted firmly in the base of their communities, supported by local resources friendly to their own concert halls.

This is not to say that European and American orchestras are utterly different, or that they have not shared the same concerns about salary and working conditions. Even in Mozart's time, when royal courts supported their own opera houses and musicians, the musicians frequently had to supplement their incomes with other work. Mozart's friend Joseph Leutgeb, for instance, the virtuoso for whom he wrote his horn concertos, had to run a delicatessen on the side. And we regard as remarkable the fact that Beethoven could earn a living as a composer independent of the Austrian emperor's patronage. The fact remains that throughout the nineteenth century, and well into the twentieth, many of the musicians of Europe counted on the opera house for their orchestral careers. Their salaries came, traditionally, from the royal (later, the governmental) supporters of those houses.

While European composers and musicians created their strong music culture (significantly, during the eighteenth and nineteenth centuries, most of the composers of opera, symphony, and chamber music also performed as instrumentalists), European immigrants to American shores brought with them a respect for musical achievements and the desire to transplant what they knew of music to their new homeland. Some new Americans possessed a sophisticated knowledge of music composition and performance. Inevitably, however, their principal concerns had to do with the practical business of founding a home, a community, a government, and a nation.

Thomas Jefferson, for example, who played the violin, integrated music into his daily life through at-home chamber music performances. He had charge of a vast property—developing farm holdings at Monticello that required much skilled manual labor, including that of slaves. In a letter he wrote in 1778 to a colleague in France, Jefferson asked for help in employing a gardener, weaver, cabinetmaker, and stonecutter, stipulating that this person should also perform on the French horn, clarinet, oboe, and bassoon.

We see that Jefferson did not ask for a musician who could also perform skilled labor. At the same time the Esterházy family could hire Josef Haydn to provide music under full-time employment on its estate in Austro-Hungary, Jefferson faced the realities of pioneering life in a new land. While acknowledging the importance of music, he had gardens to plant, cloth to weave, cabinets to make, and stones to cut. At the end of the workday—with whatever energy he might summon—the gardener would join in the music making. One can only wonder at the sounds that resulted.

Jefferson's letter illustrates the origins of the American musician's Jack-of-all-trades status, which persisted from the time of the country's founding well into the mid-twentieth century. To find adequate employment, the American musician had to master a nonmusical trade or profession, in addition to learning musical skills. After more than fifty years of union representation and the establishment of all the major symphony orchestras, the professional symphony musician's part-time status remained unimproved. This 1952 musicians union magazine advertisement demonstrates how little had changed for the symphonic musician in 175 years: "The ——— Orchestra desires to contact musicians interested in combining symphony work with full-time industrial or business employment."

From Individual Worker-Musician to Union Member

The history of the American labor movement, an enormous topic, has been well documented throughout the years. With that general history as the necessary background, we will begin the discussion of the musicians' labor movement by pointing out a general principle of workers' status in the nineteenth century. In 1842 the Massachusetts Supreme Court countered a prevailing public view by ruling that labor unions were not illegal conspiracies.

Given the central position of workers' unions in the American economy for the past century, we may find it strange that the public should ever have considered such organizations illegal, or their members conspiratorial. Yet, such was the anti-union climate when the first American symphony orchestra was founded—coincidentally, the same year as the Massachusetts Supreme Court's ruling.

In 1842, musicians in New York formed a cooperative venture named the Philharmonic Society of New York (later to become the New York Philharmonic). Its musicians accepted responsibility for all management functions, including hiring personnel, conductors, and soloists, and selecting programs. The ethnic diversity of the orchestra reflected the thriving new immigrant community of New York City. English, French, Italian, and German musicians were seated side by side with those born on American soil. All willingly and eagerly took the responsibility of running their own performances and dividing the profits among themselves. At the conclusion of its first season, consisting of only three concerts, the Philharmonic Society was financially solvent, had paid a small dividend to its members, and was increasing its subscriptions for the following year.

The remainder of the nineteenth century saw the founding of orchestras in St. Louis (1880), Boston (1881), Chicago (1891), and Cincinnati and Portland, Oregon (1895). By the beginning of the twentieth century, civic leaders in Dallas, Honolulu, Minneapolis, Philadelphia, San Francisco, Cleveland, and many others had undertaken to organize and underwrite orchestras for their communities. But with the exception of the Boston Symphony, which formed its Boston Pops orchestra in 1885 and thereby provided year-round employment, symphony orchestra positions constituted part-time jobs that the musicians had to supple-

> ℘ It had been a tradition for the musicians to stand on the stage through-
> out their concerts, until the press noted that "aside from being uncom-
> fortable to them, this looks bad and impresses the spectators uncomfort-
> ably." By 1853 the musicians finally sat down, and were not asked to serve
> as ushers either, a custom which dissolved that same year, when paid
> ushers were employed.

ment with other work. Those who did not get jobs in the newly formed
orchestras worked in military and civilian bands, opera, theater, minstrel
shows, vaudeville, dance halls, riding academies, and skating rinks. And
many who did get jobs in the newly formed orchestras did the same.

Attempts to loosely organize musicians as worker groups had begun
in the middle of the nineteenth century. As early as 1857, Baltimore and
Chicago had mutual aid societies, which were mostly social organizations that provided some death benefits and financial assistance. These
early informal efforts at organization included a club in New York that
was limited at first to German-speaking members. The Aschenbroedel
Club, renamed the Musical Mutual Protective Union, soon found that
mere fraternity was not enough. In 1878 it amended its charter to provide for uniform fixed rates for the employment of its members, with
fines and expulsion from the club being the consequences for noncom-
pliant members.

Other cities followed New York's lead, including St. Louis, whose Musicians' Mutual Benefit Association (which later became Local 2 of the
American Federation of Musicians) was founded in 1885. From these
roots grew the first efforts at setting uniform fee scales for different types
of musical employment. The growth of independent local musicians'
unions, however, did not serve the purposes of its members that the
protection of a parent organization could provide.

Momentum for the trade union movement in general swelled across
America in the 1880s, with intensifying labor rallies. In Chicago, 350,000
workers demonstrated for the eight-hour workday, and that city's Hay-
market Square labor rally in 1886 was attacked by police, becoming a
riot that ended with violence and death.

These events led to the formation of the American Federation of Labor (AFL) in 1886. In the same year, the National League of Musicians (NLM) came into being. The NLM was invited to affiliate with the AFL, but the NLM refused. The AFL formed a rival musicians' organization, calling it the American Federation of Musicians (AFM), and Local 1 started up in the city of Cincinnati, where formal union activities had begun around 1881.

The competition between the two music unions did not help their members; in fact, it only drove down wages for all musicians. In 1896, the NLM was absorbed into the AFM, and by 1904 most musicians, including those who were Canadian citizens, were under AFM jurisdiction. The AFM, part of the AFL (now AFL-CIO), soon represented approximately three thousand musicians nationally, the beginning of the long road to union solidarity.

Many of the conductors of the fledgling American symphony orchestras were European-born (as many of them are to this day). At that time, the late nineteenth century, some were active musicians' union members (unlike the practice today, by which most conductors do not participate in union activities). Many chose to hire their orchestra musicians from the growing pool of talent that arrived from Europe onto U.S. shores daily.

The quality of the European players was generally of a high caliber. Except for a privileged few Americans whose families could send them to Europe for musical training, young music students did not have firsthand benefit of the extraordinary European teaching tradition that would in later years have such a marked influence on music performance standards in America. At the turn of the twentieth century, musicians from all parts of Europe had the competitive edge in the United States.

The first president of the American Federation of Musicians, in fact, was an immigrant clarinetist from a small village in the Austro-Hungarian Empire. The thirty-seven-year-old Joseph Weber became president in 1902 and held the office for forty years. His efforts to have musicians recognized as workers made him immensely popular with his membership. "We may be artists," he said, "but we still work for wages . . . We are exploited by our employers in the same manner as any other wage-earners who stand alone."

In 1885 Congress had passed the Alien Contract Labor Law, a bill forbidding employers to contract with alien laborers for importation into the United States.

In 1907 the law was amended to prohibit the importation of *skilled and unskilled* foreign laborers. But because musicians were not considered laborers, the "exception for artists" excluded them from the Alien Contract Labor Law, and conductors could continue to hire European rather than American musicians of equal capability.

Conductor Walter Damrosch tested importation restrictions several times during his tenure with the New York Symphony Orchestra (a significant rival to the Philharmonic Society of New York). In 1891 he persuaded the union to waive the six-month rule, the amount of time required of foreign musicians to reside in the United States before joining the union. Damrosch wanted to import Russian violinist Adolf Brodsky as concertmaster, and he succeeded without incident—the first time. But in 1893 his orchestra refused to play when a Danish cellist appeared onstage in its ranks. This constituted the first strike by an American orchestra.

Damrosch was threatened with expulsion from the union after this incident. Undeterred by the threats, he again stretched union regulations by importing five French musicians for his orchestra in 1905. The union charged that Damrosch had not properly advertised for American musicians, and he was forced to resign his membership. The union reinstated him after he paid a $1,000 fine, and the five European musicians were permitted to remain and to join the union.

Another of the earliest examples of conflict between imported and local musicians had involved the New York orchestra of conductor Theodore Thomas in 1885. Perhaps because of his personal fame, his great presence in American musical life, and his reputation as an otherwise fair employer, Thomas was able to ignore the union local's protests and he imported a Belgian oboist and many others of his choice from Europe in following years.

Born in Germany in 1835, Thomas had moved with his family to America when he was a child. He began conducting in the New York area in 1859 and attracted a great deal of attention with his innovative programming, including music of the great European masters. He presented more than one thousand concerts of great variety at New

York's Central Park Gardens from 1868 to 1875. The Theodore Thomas Orchestra began touring the nation as early as 1869, performing for isolated midwestern audiences and eventually traveling from coast to coast, tours that helped to educate the American people in a greater appreciation of symphonic music.

The Thomas Orchestra gave one or two series of concerts a season in Boston, Chicago, Philadelphia, Cleveland, Detroit, St. Louis, and Cincinnati. The musicians traveled by rail, performing six or seven times a week. In the pre-union era of the late nineteenth century, Thomas personally signed contracts with all of the players, never abandoning them on the road or when pay was due. His creative programming and tireless leadership were a role model for the next generation.

In 1891 a group of Chicago businessmen invited Thomas to establish a new orchestra in their city. Thomas brought many of his New York players with him to Chicago and continued to maintain his touring orchestra, even as it merged with the new Chicago Symphony. For the next fourteen years, until his death in 1905, Thomas reigned over the increasingly sophisticated musical life of his new home. Supporting his success, the Chicago Symphony Orchestral Association set the standard for an orchestral board of directors. Its members established a community-based system of donor support that kept the orchestra from dependence on only one wealthy individual, which became the model for orchestras across the country.

In 1900, a board of directors founded the Philadelphia Orchestra, directing and managing it themselves. For the first years they struggled with financial difficulties. Philadelphia music lovers favored the opera performances staged at the Academy of Music, built in 1885 and modeled after the La Scala Opera House in Milan. By the time of Leopold Stokowski's appointment as music director in 1912, the Philadelphia Orchestra board's financial problems had become critical. The public finally took notice of the orchestra's concerts when the Philadelphia Orchestra premiered Gustav Mahler's Eighth Symphony, the "Symphony of a Thousand," in 1916. The premiere created an unprecedented media event and drew attention to the power and excitement of orchestral music. That same year, the Philadelphia Orchestra established an endowment fund under the management of Arthur Judson, who would become legendary in American music as the manager of the New York Philharmonic and the Philadelphia Orchestra, as well as the founder of the performing artists management firm that became Columbia Artists Management, Inc.

Three years after Philadelphia, the Minneapolis Symphony Orchestra became the eighth major orchestra to be established in the United States. Conductor Emil Oberhoffer led its first performance on November 3, 1903. Following the Chicago and Philadelphia models, prominent Twin Cities business and community leaders formed a board of directors. They organized an inaugural season of six orchestral and four choral concerts and quickly raised a three-year guaranty fund of $10,000, proving strong community support in a city ranking only eighteenth in U.S. population. Lumberman Elbert L. Carpenter was named chairman of the board in 1905. During his forty-year association with the orchestra, Carpenter was a model of individual philanthropy and considered by many a dedicated, visionary community leader.

By the early twentieth century, orchestra musicians were members of the American Federation of Musicians, which represented them (badly, as we shall see) in salary negotiations. The lone exception was the Boston Symphony. Founded in 1881, it was the domain of a single benefactor, Boston financier Henry L. Higginson. He established financial guidelines that are still in use today, such as the first orchestral endowment fund and a percentage of income derived from ticket sales. But his paternalistic control over management, finances, conductors, and musicians, in conjunction with his adamant anti-unionism, created an internal situation that both helped and hindered its musicians for the future. By the mid-twentieth century, the Boston Symphony would be the subject of a major battle, to be won by James C. Petrillo, one of union history's most colorful leaders.

By 1917, only instrumental and vocal soloists could be legally admitted as musicians to the United States. At this time, the AFM continued to discourage the employment of foreign musicians in its orchestras, maintaining that they undercut American wage standards. The AFM did not permit union membership unless an individual declared intention of becoming an American citizen and obtained papers of intent. The AFM finally succeeded in convincing federal legislators that U.S.

a

P A Y R O L L

MINNEAPOLIS SYMPHONY ORCHESTRA

For the Week Ending Monday, October 25, 1920.

$Scale = {}^\$40.^{00}$

#	Name		#	Name		1994.
1	Basso, A. B.	$40. *Violin*	37	Kovarik, F. J.		$42.50 *Viola*
2	Bauer, J. K.	70. *Violin*	38	Kuchynka, Frank		85. *Pr. Bass*
3	Baum, G. C.	55. *Violin*	39	Le Barbier, Henri		100. *1st Trpt*
4	Boessenroth, Bohemian	40. *Trpl, Violin, Percussion*	40	Letvak, Philip		40. *Violin*
5	Booth, L.	40. *Bass, Tuba*	41	Liegl, Ernest		50. *Flute*
6	Busse, H. H.	40. *Violin*	42	Lindenhahn, Richard		100. *1st Horn*
7	Conradi, Otto	40. *Violin*	43	Maddy, H. D.		40. *Violin*
8	Costa, Benedetto	* 44. *Violin*	44	Mathieu, H. F.		60. *Horn*
9	Cunnington, H.	85. *1st Bassoon*	45	Minsel, Rudk.		70. *Horn*
10	Cunnington, S.	50. *Contra Bassoon*	46	Murray, Edward		45. *Violin*
11	Damm, A.	40. *2d Violin*	47	Nelson, Joseph		55. *Flute, Piccolo*
12	Doucet, Louis	75. *English Horn*	48	Nyberg, Gosta (Carl)		40. *Bass, Percussion*
13	Dupuis, Adore	85. *Oboe*	49	Obermann, Frank		50. *Violin*
14	Duvoir, Alexander	100. *1st Oboe*	50	Perkins, Harry		40. *Violin*
15	Erck, Christian	50. *Cello*	51	Pleier, Ludwig		75. *Cello*
16	Erck, E. J.	50. *Violin, Horn*	52	Pomero, Giovanni		45. *Viola, Violin*
17	Faetkenheuer, Wm.	75. *Tympany*	53	Rich, Leon		65. *Cello*
18	Fields, Dale	50. *Bassoon*	54	Roentgen, Engelbert		100. *Pr. Cello*
19	Gatscha, John	45. *Violin*	55	Rudolf, Carl		40. *Cello, Percussion*
20	Gebhart, Otto	70. *1st Trombone*	56	Ruhoff, H. A.		50. *Viola, Piano*
21	Gebhart, V.	40. *2d Trombone*	57	Schugens, E. M.		45. *Bass (Trombone)*
22	Gluck, Alexander	60. *Violin*	58	Seddon, Tom		55. *Cello, Harp, Saxophone*
23	Goffin, M. D.	45. *Violin*	59	Shryock, Ray F.		45. *Violin*
24	Graves, C. C.	45. *Violin*	60	Silver, Eli		50. *Violin*
25	Grubner, James	65. *Horn*	61	Sperzel, John		75. *Tuba, Bass*
26	Halten, Olaf	40. *Bass*	62	Sperzel, Peter		50. *Clarinet*
27	Hoskins, A. M.	60. *Percussion*	63	Spoor, Samos		75. *Violin*
28	Hyna, Otto	55. *Bass*	64	Swalin, Benjamin		40. *Violin*
29	d'Isere, Guy	85. *Clarinet*	65	Thies, Fred		40. *Violin, Clar.*
30	Jordan, C. S.	50. *Violin*	66	Uterhart, Carl		75. *Violin*
31	Keller, Wm.	45. *Violin*	67	Wagner, F.		55. *Bass, Tuba*
32	Klimitz, Richard	55. *Bass*	68	West, W. W.		42.50 *Viola, Cello*
33	Knutsen, K.	40. *Cello*	69	Williams, H. J.		100. *Harp*
34	Koch, Oscar	50. *Cello*	70	Woempner, Henry		75. *Flute, Violin*
35	Koehler, Albert	65. *Trumpet*	71	Woodard, G. H.		100. *Violin*
36	Komarovsky, Constantin	50. *Cello*	72	Ziebel, Sigmund		45. *Violin*
		1994.				4154.
			73	Ransom, Geo.		50. *Cello*
						4204.

* One Dollar deducted from salary account tardiness at rehearsal.

Archives of the Minnesota Orchestra, Performing Arts Archives, University of Minnesota Libraries.

musicians were also laborers and deserving of protection under the law. In 1932, Congress revised the Alien Contract Labor Law by narrowing the definition of an alien musical artist. President Herbert Hoover signed the amendment, making it impossible for foreign musicians to enter the United States under artist exemptions.

Enter the Little Caesar

I was no good as a trumpet player. I got desperate. I hadda look for a job. I went into the union business.

James C. Petrillo

On Chicago's West Side in 1892, the year after the Chicago Symphony Orchestra's founding, James Caesar Petrillo was born to an Italian immigrant family. He quit school in the fourth grade, thus ending his formal education—not unusual during that era. As a youth, Petrillo delivered newspapers and played trumpet in his own band, already showing notable talents as an organizer.

At the age of twenty-two, Petrillo was elected to an office of the American Musicians Union, a rival union to Chicago's Local 10 of the AFM. Voted out of office three years later, he joined Chicago Local 10 and quickly rose to the presidency of the powerful local by the age of thirty. He held the office for forty years, becoming the absolute king of 293,000 members of the American Federation of Musicians in 693 locals throughout North America.

In the 1920s, the Chicago Musicians Local 10 was one of the largest in the country, supervising the employment of 11,310 union members. Petrillo developed Local 10 into one of the most powerful union organizations in the nation, often by methods that reflected Chicago's gangster atmosphere of that era. The bulletproof glass in the president's building of Local 10's West Washington Street headquarters and the bodyguards positioned on each of its landings gave tangible evidence of Petrillo's confrontational style. Petrillo himself was chauffeured in a bulletproof limousine, and in 1933, rumors circulated that he had been kidnapped by the mob for a ransom of $50,000—and that Local 10 had paid.

Known as "Little Caesar," Petrillo favored a negotiation style that included pounding the table and screaming to get the results he demanded. Jon Burlingame reported in his book *For the Record,* a history of America's recording musicians, that "more than one musician reported seeing Petrillo settle disputes by pulling out a concealed gun and placing it carefully on the table before him." With threats and other questionable tactics, Petrillo endlessly fought for better job conditions for his large and diverse union membership. He established the "standby" system: if a nonunion musician was hired to play in a theater, for instance, a local union musician had to be paid to "stand by."

Prohibition, Radio, and Talking Pictures: Changing Technology

> It is the opinion of the Federation leadership, based upon exhaustive study, that mechanical music . . . will fail eventually to give satisfaction in any theater as a substitute for the appearance of artists in person.
>
> *AFM president Joseph Weber, 1929*

The Great Depression overlapped with the dark days of Prohibition, which lasted from 1920 to 1933. Musicians and everyone else associated with the hospitality and entertainment industries lost jobs in taverns, hotels, cafés, and restaurants. During the thirteen years of Prohibition, the AFM worked diligently with other labor groups to repeal the Volstead Act. The Twenty-first Amendment, repealing Prohibition, restored some jobs to U.S. musicians, but relief came too late for many others. By 1933, many displaced musicians found it impossible to get work, and their options were scarce. Another development would prove to have an even more profound effect.

Vaudeville and live theater orchestras had employed many fine musicians in the first decades of the twentieth century. Working as a theater or pit musician in the 1920s had been a plum job, requiring little travel and providing a dependable income. In 1927, that culture changed dramatically with the appearance of the first "talkie" movie, *The Jazz Singer.* In a few years, theaters throughout America became equipped for sound, replacing 22,000 theater musicians with the new technology. Some musicians migrated to Hollywood, where they remained in studios for the duration of their careers, recording film scores that were musically and technically challenging. Only a few large movie houses continued to employ musicians for live performance.

In addition, two major radio networks were founded in the late 1920s, providing some employment opportunities. Two orchestras in the Midwest, the Detroit Symphony and the Minneapolis Symphony, had become the first in the nation to broadcast their sounds to a radio audience, Detroit in February 1922, and Minneapolis, under guest conductor Bruno Walter, in March 1923. Within a few years, these individual broadcasts had multiplied in many cities. Musicians initially performed on the radio for free in the early part of the decade; they believed that the publicity they received was adequate compensation. The union, however, did not agree. The AFM began to establish local and national scales for radio work.

At the same time, the recording industry expanded significantly. In a long and unsuccessful battle with the networks to ensure employment of radio staff musicians, the AFM had taken a stand to represent them. The union believed that the new recording technology would not become a serious threat. Unfortunately for the musicians, the radio listening public did not care or may not even have noticed whether the music was performed by live or recorded artists. Publicity campaigns on behalf of live music appeared to be fighting a losing battle against the exciting new technologies of radio, recordings, and talking motion pictures, which were taking a toll on the demand for live music.

The union won a battle for New York City theater orchestra musicians in 1927, but not without mob violence and one of the largest strikes in AFM history, a four-day standoff involving two thousand musicians. This conflict brought forward Clarence Darrow and David Lilienthal, two of the twentieth century's most famous lawyers, who defended the AFM.

New York Local 802 strike against the movie theaters raised awareness of the threat to live music and the need for more aggressive national policy from the AFM. President Weber proposed that the radio networks hire more staff musicians and limit the use of recorded music in their broadcasts, and he backed up his demands with the threat of a strike. Over a period of negotiations, the networks agreed to increase their budgets to half a million dollars annually to hire more musicians for their studio orchestras.

The AFM failed to force the film industry to take responsibility for the substantial replacement of musicians by technology. This failure continues to resonate in the twenty-first century. As George Seltzer pointed out in his 1989 book *Music Matters: The Performer and the American Federation of Musicians*, "Embedded in this unremarkable campaign is the tale of what happens when working-class consumption of popular culture overrides the interests or concerns of popular culture workers, in this case, theater musicians . . . and most fundamentally, this is a story about technology and workers' control, and how utterly ill-equipped the union was to deal with the transformation of the work of art in the age of mechanical reproduction."

A positive result of the new technology for musicians and for the world of symphonic music was the unique institution of the National Broadcasting Company Symphony Orchestra, which could not have existed without the medium of radio. The performances heard by millions of captivated listeners around the world established radio as the most powerful instrument developed up to that time for cultural extension. The NBC Symphony Orchestra was established in 1937 by General David Sarnoff, wholly owned by the National Broadcasting Company, and created expressly for one of the most renowned conductors in the world, Arturo Toscanini. This elite orchestra included some of the world's finest instrumentalists, a stunning "who's who" of great musicians whose live performances had a profound impact on the generation of listeners who heard their radio broadcasts through 1954. The NBC Symphony Orchestra reached one of the widest audiences in the history of classical music. Its concerts were broadcast weekly from Rockefeller Center's huge and renowned Studio 8-H over the NBC radio network (and were later featured ten times on NBC television). The musicians' schedules included performances on radio dramas, quiz shows, and children's programs, all presented by the NBC network, and the orchestra made many recordings under Toscanini.

The Philadelphia Orchestra also embraced the new technology. Under the leadership of Leopold Stokowski, the Philadelphians performed the first commercially sponsored coast-to-coast symphonic broadcasts on the NBC network in 1929. Carried by fifty radio stations, they were relayed by shortwave across the world. Far ahead of his time, Stokowski experimented with lighting and electrical instruments during live performances, which gained him and his orchestra a great deal of attention. He believed in the potential of radio and film to capture more listeners and to promote orchestral music. The 1940 Walt Disney film *Fantasia* was to make the creative conductor and his orchestra household names, popularizing symphonic music for millions and introducing them to the groundbreaking new technology of stereophonic sound.

In Chicago, AFM Local 10 president James C. Petrillo's concerns over the recording industry's threat to the musicians' livelihood had begun in the late 1920s. In 1937 Petrillo instituted a recording ban within the local's authority, claiming that making records was taking work away from union musicians. He eventually succeeded in making the recording companies pay all artists for each record sold. This was the first of several major battles Petrillo fought with the recording industry, and a harbinger of conflicts to come.

The WPA Subsidizes the Arts: A Historic First

The Works Progress Administration (WPA) was created by President Roosevelt in 1935 partly in response to lobbying by unions across America, including the AFM, for a public works program that would give a boost to the thousands of unemployed artists and artisans affected by the Great Depression. Better known for its engineering and public works construction programs, the WPA also included the Arts Program, a first venture into government subsidy of the arts. Artists produced paintings, drawings, sculptures, and thousands of murals on and in public buildings. Writers produced everything from guidebooks to plays, which actors performed under WPA grants. Many kinds of musical groups were subsidized to give thousands of performances across the country. During the late 1930s and early 1940s, radio listeners heard live performances by symphony orchestras, jazz musicians, and chamber groups, as well as solo recitals by young musicians, all thanks to the WPA.

Russell Brodine, a bassist in the Saint Louis Symphony Orchestra, described the WPA experience in his memoir, *Fiddle and Fight*: "In 1937

I joined the WPA Symphony, which played free concerts for schools and for institutions such as the one named, in wrought-iron over the entrance gate, 'Home of the Incurables.' How brutal can you get? The orchestra in which I played brought music to many people who otherwise would never have heard it. We were paid the standard WPA salary, about $21 a week. Someone in Washington learned we were not putting in full workdays like other WPA workers. From then on we were required to be in the rehearsal hall eight hours a day whether or not we were playing. Rehearsing and concertizing requires intense concentration. It is impossible to rehearse for eight consecutive hours, so we whiled away the time playing cards."

The WPA laid an important foundation for the future of symphony orchestras. It helped keep the arts in America alive during the bleakness of the Depression. By September 1939, the WPA had employed eight thousand musicians.

Meanwhile, the AFM was losing membership, declining from more than 146,000 in 1929 to only about 100,000 in 1934. By the end of the decade, the combined effects of radio broadcasts, recorded music, sound motion pictures, Prohibition, and the Depression had eroded the number of union members, until a new national regime by Petrillo took over in 1940.

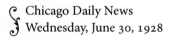

Chicago Daily News
Wednesday, June 30, 1928

Unsigned editorial

The Symphony Orchestra's Plight

Ten months ago The Daily News by appealing to friends of the Chicago Symphony orchestra raised a fund of $30,000 which helped to give another season of useful life to that fine organization. The money was expended to supplement the sums provided for the orchestra's support by the Chicago Orchestral association. Specifically it was expended to meet certain wage demands made by the Chicago Federation of Musicians on behalf of the members of the orchestra. The purpose of The Daily News in raising the fund, as it announced at the time, was to obtain for the orchestral association an ample period in which to adjust its affairs in a way to bring about a permanent settlement of its differences with the musicians in its employ.

Nothing, however, seems to have been done since then to prevent a recurrence of the controversy over the orchestra's minimum wage scale. No guaranty has been provided, no additional endowment has been obtained by the orchestral association, so far as the public is aware, and no additional use of the orchestra to furnish increased revenue has been arranged for. Consequently the association asserts once more that it cannot meet the musicians' demand for a minimum weekly wage of $90. So it appears to have decreed the dissolution of the orchestra, one of the best in the world and for many years an intellectual and artistic necessity to Chicago's host of music lovers.

It would be idle to attempt to apportion responsibility for the revival of the wage controversy between the orchestral association and the musicians' union. It seems clear, however, that the association's effort to retain the minimum wage scale of two years ago is unreasonable.

The controlling members of the association are singularly self-centered while they hold the fate of the orchestra in their hands. It is not their orchestra to dispose of as they please. They occupy a position of trust, administering funds and other property which came into their keeping in a way to make the orchestra supported by the proceeds of that property a semipublic institution. If the association had a proper realization of its position before the people of this community it would present to them a full, frank and readily understandable statement of its financial affairs. Clothed in its abounding virtue it is neither readily approachable nor readily comprehensible. The great orchestra which the association guards, one is inclined to fear, cannot survive if nourished exclusively on aloofness.

The statement of the orchestral association that its failure to rent Orchestra hall justifies its refusal to give its musicians the wages they ask is no suitable response to the union's demand. Manifestly it is unfair to make the members of the orchestra suffer for a failure in management.

The orchestral association faces serious problems with which its management seems unable to cope. There is no doubt that many friends of

continued on next page

continued from previous page

the orchestra are ready and anxious to support intelligent and effective leadership such as is required in the existing emergency.

If the present directing heads of the association fail to solve the problem that faces them it may be assumed that a reorganized body will provide properly for the future of the orchestra through effective administration and, if necessary, through open solicitation of an increased endowment. It would be a great pity, however, if there should be even a temporary disbanding of the splendid corps of highly trained musicians so carefully formed into a well-nigh perfect organization under the baton of Mr. Stock. That eminent director recently has made it known that the music schools of Chicago fear they would lose more than half their normal number of students if the symphony orchestra should disappear as an inspiring force in the city's artistic life. Other heavy losses, perhaps less immediately manifest, would be sustained by the community as a result of the orchestra's disintegration.

Two

Petrillo Battles the Recording Industry, 1940–1958

There is no other union like this one. The members of others work at their trades. Our poll reflected what the Musicians' Union itself admitted: fully 75% of its 250,000 members make their living in occupations outside music . . . , so, some 1190 delegates come from locals across America to make the rules by which the working musicians—concentrated mainly in Los Angeles and New York—make their living.

Reader's Digest, *December 1956*
("The Union That Fights Its Workers")

"What's the difference between [Jascha] Heifetz playing the fiddle and the fiddler in the tavern? None! They're both musicians and they both belong to me!"

James C. Petrillo, quoted in
the New York Times, *August 14, 1940*

WORKING HIS WAY UP the hierarchy of the American Federation of Musicians, James C. Petrillo was elected its president in 1940, at the age of forty-eight. While representing 158,000 musicians nationwide, he also retained the presidency of Chicago's powerful Local 10. Petrillo was determined to unionize the musicians not yet under his control and to continue to fight on behalf of live music, and against recordings and broadcasts on a national level.

In 1942 Petrillo forbade his Chicago musicians to make recordings for use in broadcasting and would not allow eager young union musicians or anyone else to replace them. Congress responded to this action by passing the Lea Act in 1946, also known as the "anti-Petrillo act." The Lea Act made it a criminal offense for unions to "use coercion . . . to win observance of its rules by radio stations."

The AFM under Petrillo now gained the dubious distinction of becoming the first union ever investigated by Congress, as well as the first union to have legislation passed specifically to control its actions. In 1947, however, the Lea Act was declared unconstitutional.

On another front of his campaign for union control, Petrillo took on conductors, solo instrumentalists, and their accompanists, who since the AFM's founding in 1896 had been exempt from union participation (although some conductors did hold membership).

When the American Guild of Musical Artists (AGMA) was organized as a labor union in 1936, soloists and conductors were encouraged to join. As soon as he became president of the AFM, Petrillo demanded that they resign from AGMA. He argued against AGMA, fearing that dual unionism would contribute to an erosion of union bargaining power. (Many years later, this would become an AFM battle cry against symphony orchestra and recording musicians when they formed their own networking organization.) Petrillo caused a national uproar in August 1940, when he demanded that all solo instrumentalists and symphony conductors join the AFM. The controversy led to strong criticism of both the AFM and AGMA, and Petrillo was reviled by an indignant press. "Everybody calls me the tsar, the chieftain and this and that," he said. "What can I do?"

AGMA attempted an unsuccessful lawsuit. In the end, the court decided in Petrillo's favor, and the rush to join the AFM began, although the union granted honorary memberships to many famous soloists of the era. As soon as soloists and conductors were forced to join (and, in the case of foreign musicians, to obtain permission from the union to appear in the United States), Petrillo's next step was to forbid them to perform with or to conduct the nonunion Boston Symphony Orchestra.

Boston Symphony Finally Unionized

All American orchestras had been unionized by 1900, with the exception of the Boston Symphony. Since its inception in 1881, the BSO had remained nonunion, and although the players generally received higher annual incomes than those of comparable orchestras, they worked longer seasons (which included several weeks of "Pops" concerts) and were subject to virtually unlimited rehearsal calls. As nonunion players, they were unable to perform anywhere else, and their tenuous job security with the Boston Symphony depended upon the whims of conductors, backed by the BSO's management and its founding benefactor, Henry L. Higginson. Any attempts by the musicians to unionize would have been at great risk to their employment.

Higginson had himself hired the original orchestra and conductor on a contract basis, with the promise that he would pay any deficits incurred. He resisted labor organization and threatened to disband the orchestra if its musicians joined the union. Higginson insisted on dealing individually with players, including personally renewing and signing their annual contracts. He took full advantage of his primary weapon: most of the musicians were Europeans who would not be able to work anywhere else in the United States if they quit or were fired from the BSO.

In 1920, one year after Henry Higginson's death, BSO musicians made a serious effort to improve their wages and working conditions. In a public confrontation, Concertmaster Frederic Fradkin refused to obey the conductor's signal to rise from his chair and lead the orchestra in acknowledgment of the audience's applause. The trustees fired Fradkin, and a majority of the orchestra immediately resigned in protest. Conductor Pierre Monteux finished the season with a bare minimum of players; on one occasion, only twenty-two musicians were onstage. "It is characteristic that the management of the Boston Symphony was not vindictive and invited all of the 'strikers' back . . . Fradkin, however, not only left the orchestra when the 'strike' failed, but practically disappeared from the concert world" (Dickson, pp. 52, 54).

Even though a large percentage of the BSO joined the AFM, and many musicians picketed and attempted to form a small rival orchestra, the BSO directors successfully avoided unionizing the orchestra. In less than a year the BSO was rebuilt with new, nonunion members. The new music director, Serge Koussevitsky, was impressed with the American talent he heard; and in spite of the AFM blacklist of Boston Symphony members, by the late 1930s most of the orchestra was native-born and -trained. "In those days the trustees of the orchestra were fiercely opposed to anything smacking of 'organized labor.' Ernest B. Dane, an oil millionaire, was chairman of the trustees and he would rather have seen the orchestra collapse than join a union. Dane personally made up the deficit of about one hundred thousand dollars a year. Actually for a few years he was almost our sole benefactor, adamantly refusing to recognize the union and just as doggedly willing to pay for his obstinacy" (Dickson, p. 54).

Undaunted, Petrillo proceeded with a plan to further isolate the orchestra. After winning the fight to make soloists and conductors join the AFM, and thereby making it impossible for them to perform with the BSO, Petrillo set out to force RCA-Victor Records to cease its exclusive recording of the BSO, a threat to the orchestra's prestige and reputation. "They're through," Petrillo announced. "We've taken them off the radio and off the records."

The attendant publicity caused other labor unions to take notice of the controversy, including the stagehands union, which refused to allow the BSO to appear in unionized halls on tours. "It was not generally known at the time, but Koussevitzky himself finally instigated the proceedings which led to our joining the musicians' union. One day he telephoned his friend Carl Dreyfus, Boston newspaper publisher, and said, 'Carl, I vould like it to meet this Petrillo.' Dreyfus, by no means a friend of labor in general or of Petrillo in particular, told Koussey he would see what he could do. And after judicious inquiry plus a few telephone calls he got through to Petrillo, who was more than eager to meet Koussevitzky. A meeting was arranged, and on the appointed day Petrillo drove up to the Koussevitzky estate in the Berkshires in a bullet-proof limousine, flanked by three bodyguards. The meeting was held in the Koussevitzky living room, and in attendance were Petrillo, his bodyguards, Koussevitzky, Carl Dreyfus, and one of the orchestra's trustees. During the course of the meeting the B.S.O. gentlemen were astounded at Petrillo's knowledge of the orchestra's affairs, financial and artistic, and all were impressed with his intelligence, candor, and reasonableness. Petrillo was ready to promise no interference in the internal affairs of the B.S.O., provided they would join his union" (Dickson, p. 54).

Under overwhelming pressure, the BSO management finally signed an agreement with the AFM in December 1942, bringing all orchestra members and conductors into the Musicians Union. The caveat to this agreement was that the AFM restriction on importation of players from one local to another was lifted for some locals, including Boston's (only later to be reinstated). For the time being, the Boston Symphony could hire players from anywhere in the United States or Canada. "About three weeks after we were finally in the union, he (Koussevitzky) stopped the orchestra at a rehearsal and said, 'Gentlemen, I do not like your sound. Since you join the union you play like employers!'

"Before joining the union Boston Symphony musicians were enslaved to their jobs. The conductor could, without notice, call for extra rehearsals at any time of the day or night, with the rehearsals lasting indefinitely. If nothing else, the union has 'tamed' the tyrannical, whimsical, terrible-tempered conductor, who enjoyed his outbursts at the expense of the player. The musicians' union has given to musicians everywhere a sense of dignity and a measure of self-respect and has in no way lowered artistic standards. Musicians as a group have too much innate pride in themselves ever to compromise their standards. The International Conference of Symphony and Opera Musicians (ICSOM) is a comparatively recent effort of symphony and opera players to band together, within the confines of the musicians' union, for the purpose of discussing and solving their own peculiar problems. It is hoped that this organization will play a significant role in the future of music in America" (Dickson, pp. 55, 56).

Now Petrillo was ready to target the recording and motion picture industries. Unable to stop recordings from being made, he was determined to establish a system of royalty payments from recordings. In 1942 he imposed a ban on all recordings by union musicians. It was the first full year of American involvement in World War II, and the ban was to last twenty-seven months.

The timing could not have been worse, for the musicians and for public morale alike, and the federal government even suggested the ban was hindering the war effort. After a call from President Roosevelt and appearances before Congress, Petrillo agreed to negotiate a settlement with the recording industry. A final settlement was reached in 1948, after a second ban of more than eleven months.

The result was an innovative strategy to pay royalties from record sales to the AFM, which in turn would use the funds, which became known as the Music Performance Trust Fund, to supply free, live music to the public. According to the Chicago Federation of Musicians centennial booklet, published in October 2001, "One of the very best things that Petrillo was responsible for is the tradition of live, public performances of music, free and available to the general public. He noted that his musicians needed jobs and people needed to hear great music. Thus began the Grant Park Orchestra and the Music Performance Trust Fund concerts. Today these concerts are still being conducted, not only in Grant Park but also in parks all over Chicago, playing everything from jazz to pop to polkas to rock 'n' roll."

Brad C. Eggen, president of Twin Cities AFM Local 30/73, has also praised Petrillo's efforts: "Approximately one-quarter of a million dollars of live music performance occurs in the Twin Cities area alone as a result of MPTF efforts, largely the product of Petrillo's war against the recording industry. In defense of Petrillo's often poorly perceived initiatives in the 1940s, they are credited with the development of the MPTF—a collective organization of musicians and the recording industry, funded by a percentage of income from recordings, dedicated to and providing hundreds of thousands of dollars of live music performance annually."

Not all musicians celebrated the agreement. Those who recorded watched their earnings being funneled into the trust fund, and suspicions grew that Petrillo was using it as a personal bank account. Their frustrations would come to a head in the late 1950s, with a battle in Los Angeles that would end Petrillo's national empire.

Recording Musicians versus Petrillo

"We can continue to let Petrillo and company rub our noses in the dirt, or we can appeal to the courts and to Congress to protect our rights and break this immoral dictatorship."

Los Angeles Local 47 president Cecil Read,
quoted in Reader's Digest, *December 1956*
("The Union That Fights Its Workers")

In the early 1950s, recording musicians were seeking satisfaction for the same issues involving contract ratification and committee representation that symphony musicians were to demand later in the decade. Up to this time neither symphony nor recording musicians had any pension, royalty, or other kinds of benefits. Meanwhile, the Music Performance Trust Fund was growing by millions of dollars every year, receiving payments from record companies, movie and jingle producers, and filmed television shows. In 1951, Petrillo negotiated an agreement with the four major television networks for use of union musicians in recording television scores. It required payment of 5 percent of the overall budget by every producer, to be paid to the trust fund.

Most Hollywood producers found this payment to be an unrealistic financial burden and began to record overseas, resulting in immense loss of work for Los Angeles studio musicians. Some tried to reason with Petrillo. Desi Arnaz, of *I Love Lucy*, met with Petrillo to try to change his mind. Five musicians flew to New York from Los Angeles with Arnaz, but Petrillo would not allow them into the meeting. One of them, trumpet player Vince DiBari, said that "upon leaving Petrillo's office, Desi called [Petrillo] every name under the sun in Spanish." Others also protested and tried to come up with solutions. Edgar Bergen turned to tape-recorded music, and Ozzie Nelson pleaded with Petrillo to allow a simple flat fee instead of the fixed percentage. "I'll use twenty musicians," Nelson offered. "They'll have to be sacrificed," was Petrillo's answer.

Two unilateral actions taken by Petrillo in 1955 constituted the last straw for the recording musicians. The first was that a $25 payment due each player for television soundtracks was diverted to the MPTF, causing a loss of $2.5 million in nine months for the Los Angeles musicians. The second was that the 10 percent wage increase that had been negotiated for the musicians in the Phonograph Record Agreement was diverted directly to the trust fund. It had been the first increase for musicians in eight years.

Petrillo did not conceal his actions; on the contrary, he felt he had a right to carry them out. In fact, Article 1, Section 1 of the AFM bylaws gave the president leeway to make policy and change rules as he saw fit, earning him titles such as "Little Caesar" and "Musical Hitler" in the press.

The recording musicians finally reached their boiling point, and for the first time a musicians' local raised its voice against Petrillo for redress of its grievances. The rank-and-file revolt began in February 1956, when 2,800 members of Los Angeles Local 47 met to oust its president from office and replace him with Cecil Read, a trumpet player and the local's president.

Read denounced Petrillo at the meeting. As head of Local 47, Read had personally tried to reason with Petrillo, who responded, Read said later, by "pounding on the table, yelling and blustering about what a great man he was, how much he had done, how much the musicians owed him, et cetera. At the end of a lengthy tirade about how he had fought for the Trust Fund principle, he stated, 'I would kill before I would let anyone touch that fund, and I'm not a killing man.'" Read and twelve of his colleagues were expelled from the union, but the majority of Local 47 members continued to support them. Among the expelled professionals were Jack Dumont, who played saxophone for Benny Goodman; Marshal Cram, trombonist with the Harry James Band; and Uan Rasey, first trumpet with the Saint Louis Symphony and also first trumpet at Twentieth Century Fox film studios. During 1957 the group filed four lawsuits against the AFM for more than $15 million. In 1958, during a twenty-week strike of the studio orchestra recording musicians, they broke with the AFM to form a rival union, the Musicians Guild of America. Petrillo's fear of dual unionism became a reality.

The Musicians Guild of America (MGA), led by Read of Los Angeles Local 47, in an election sanctioned by the National Labor Relations Board in 1958, was granted the right to negotiate with the major studios. In spite of the divisiveness and ill will their departure from the AFM created, the musicians had achieved a formidable victory. The result made labor history and forced the recognition, respect, and salary that the musicians had desired and earned.

Even more remarkable was the end of James Petrillo's tenure as president of the AFM. In May 1958, Petrillo resigned because of his failure to negotiate successfully with the recording musicians and film producers. The formation of the Musicians Guild of America by the recording musicians finalized his defeat. "Film Musicians Kick Out AFM, Support New Guild; Petrillo Group Meets Stunning Defeat in Vote," was the headline in the July 12, 1958, edition of the *Los Angeles Times*. Although he no longer ruled as national union "tsar," he remained president of Chicago

Local 10. From that base, he chose not to change his tactics with the musicians of the Chicago Symphony Orchestra, continually thwarting their demands for improved conditions, until his leadership there would meet the same fate.

From Chicago Sun-Times, *December 10, 1962 (Courtesy Walfrid Kujala).*

Three

Struggle and Activism, 1950–1962

The Christian Science church held services on Wednesday between our morning and afternoon rehearsals. They had lots of flowers onstage and I was setting up my instruments before the afternoon rehearsal and was leaving the stage when Reiner appeared near the stage exit. Not knowing anything else to say I asked, "Nice of them to have flowers for us, isn't it, Dr. Reiner?" He replied, "Dot is for your funeral."

As told to the author by retired CSO contrabassoonist
Richard (Dick) Lottridge

THE LABOR MOVEMENT that swept America in the late nineteenth and early twentieth centuries had left symphony musicians behind. By the end of World War II, most orchestra players belonged to the American Federation of Musicians, but the union did not secure for them the pay raises and improved working conditions enjoyed during that period by their counterparts in other professional unions.

The majority of the AFM's membership during and after the war worked in big bands, popular or commercial settings, recording studios, theaters, and vaudeville. Many union musicians worked as day jobbers for casual employers, accepting the standard wage scale for various types of work for which they were hired without direct union bargaining. These nonsymphonic musicians provided the major source of funding for the AFM, as well as the votes for union officers and initiatives. Union leaders were primarily concerned with the majority of their membership and had little knowledge of or interest in the symphonic musician.

Board presidents and administrators of American symphony orchestras made contract and wage agreements with the local union officials behind closed doors. They would subsequently announce the outcome by saying, "This is your raise, boys," and expect that the gentlemen (and meager numbers of women) of the orchestra would comply. Dissent or complaints could cost the musician's job. Such bargaining affected only a small part of the membership of larger union locals—fewer than one hundred in a roster of thousands.

Local union officers were unfamiliar with the working conditions that comprised professional orchestra life. They often listened with considerable sympathy to the pleas of financial hardship the boards and managers put forth. Orchestra musicians saw a gradual erosion of their professional standing.

Symphonic musicians became increasingly aware that the locals could not solve the specific problems of day-to-day orchestra life, and they wanted to form their own representative committees. They believed in the basic union rights of representation and ratification of their master agreement (the agreement entered into by and between the orchestral association, the employer, and the local union that represents the group of musicians belonging to a specific orchestra).

Players committees were a particular sore point at this time, not only with local unions, but also with most orchestra managements. Made up of a half-dozen elected musicians each, these committees sought to effect change but had little power. Their effectiveness varied with each orchestra; they were generally only token representatives, sometimes permitted to observe, but never to participate in, negotiations between local union representatives and orchestra management. Principal players were able to negotiate individual contracts above the union scale established in the agreement, but all nonprincipal players had no choice but to accept what they were offered by the management and union.

A long-standing approach called "local autonomy," which excluded symphony players from decisions being made by union representatives on their behalf, granted the AFM local union officers the authority to negotiate local symphony players' contracts. In 2000, the president of Twin Cities Local 30/73, Brad C. Eggen, said: "From major local to major local, you would likely find that the bulk of the resources were applied to initiatives on behalf of casual musicians. You may also find, unfortunately, that the work of the AFM for several decades was based on precedent, and 'initiative' was not a commonly used term." (In the twenty-first century, "casual" musicians remain the voting majority within the AFM membership, although because of the increased length of their orchestras' seasons and their full-time contracts, symphonic musicians provide the major portion of the AFM work dues and per capita dues funding.)

Even as the postwar economy boomed, symphony musicians' salaries and working conditions remained static, with minimal improvements, agreed to by local union officers without consultation with members. Longing for decent compensation, job protection, union representation, and other improved contract terms, symphony musicians found little or no support from local AFM chapters.

The musicians were further demoralized by the defection of some of their colleagues for other professions, whether related or unrelated to music, that would offer better pay and more stability—anything to earn a decent living. In 1958, for example, the Cleveland Orchestra paid its players a base salary of just $130 per week and could guarantee them only thirty-eight weeks of employment per year. Kurt Loebel, violinist with the Cleveland Orchestra from 1947 to 1997, recalled, "It was a part-time job, so that people had to do other things to earn a living. Cleveland Orchestra concertmaster Dan Majeske sold Fuller brushes from house to house."

Many musicians taught, privately or in schools, to supplement their meager incomes. Others searched for work in other fields, and some took part-time jobs selling almost anything—automobiles, appliances, insurance, real estate, liquor, clothing, hosiery, and, later, snowblowers. Other vocations included short-order cook, jeweler, hotel night clerk, librarian, house painter, and elevator operator. In the "off" season, some musicians found orchestra positions in summer venues like the Santa Fe Opera, Grant Park (Chicago) Concerts, Boston Pops, or studio work in Hollywood. But those were the lucky ones, and a small minority at that.

Orchestra musicians had the same obligations as any other professionals—putting food on the table, raising families, and somehow maintaining the high level of performance that was expected of them the moment they returned to the orchestra in the fall. Such maintenance came hard for hands that had painted houses and flipped burgers for four months.

Furthermore, the musicians did not know whether the conductor would renew their contracts from one season to the next. Fear, paranoia, and frustration were the hallmarks of the day. Violin pedagogue Josef Gingold recalled, in a 1991 interview for the *New Yorker*: "Among the players, fear joined with a sense of privilege. It was a feudal kingdom with the conductor as king, the first-desk players as dukes, and everybody else as serfs."

The autocracy of the conductor terrorized musicians, and they never rehearsed or performed without fear of losing their jobs. One well-known conductor rationalized this widespread attitude by commenting that musicians "are like birds and do not wish to stay in any one place for very long." Music directors were free to fire players at will. In 1952, one year before piccolo player Emil Ekt would have qualified for an annual token pension of $900, he was fired, after twenty-nine years with the Chicago Symphony Orchestra.

A "pension review" committee determined the qualification of each Chicago musician to receive a pension. The Chicago Symphony Orchestra Pension Plan provided in Article II, Section I, that "while the Association intends its pension funds to be administered in accordance with this Plan, it reserves the right, at the discretion of the Board of Trustees, to grant only such pensions as the Board shall approve and to modify or discontinue any pension." This policy and the firing of Emil Ekt were further catalysts for change among symphony musicians, in Chicago and elsewhere.

In November 1962, the termination of another colleague resulted in this headline in the *Chicago Daily News*: "Firing Points Up Symphony Woes." The accompanying article explained: "For 37 years, Schima Kaufman played violin in the Philadelphia Orchestra, and at the age of 60 his contract was not renewed for the next season. Music Director Eugene Ormandy recommended dropping Kaufman on grounds that his performance did not measure up to the symphony's standards. The orchestra voted 86 to 6 against the discharge of Kaufman. Mandatory retirement is at the age of 65, at which time he would be qualified for a monthly pension plan. The Association's lawyer states that 'any policy, in the long range, that results in a curtailment of management's right to retire men who have reached inefficiency, is bound to have a serious effect on the performance of the orchestra. The conductor must have the right and power to decide.'"

Often, the conductors actively discouraged the growing activism. In his 2001 memoir *Fiddle and Fight*, former Saint Louis Symphony double bassist and labor activist Russell Brodine wrote: "One day at a rehearsal the conductor [unnamed] got into the act and talked to the orchestra about how needless it was to form a committee or to be confrontational about such things as pay and working conditions. 'My friends, we are all musicians, we are artists. We are not here for ze profit, we are here for ze art.' One of the musicians reminded the conductor that at $1,900 a season they certainly were not there for the profit, but that since he was getting more than $30,000 per season, the conductor ought to be supportive of his musicians' needs." In 1953, when the annual salary of Cleveland Orchestra musicians was $3,240, Music Director George Szell was receiving $48,000 a year. (Today, in 2005, the Cleveland Orchestra music director, Franz Welser-Möst, receives an annual salary of $1.2 million, while the minimum salary for musicians by the end of the current two-year contract will be $2,010 per week, or approximately $104,500 annually.)

Former Cleveland Orchestra violinist Kurt Loebel recalls that Szell controlled everything at Severance Hall—from toilet paper to program book. "He read the program notes before conducting the concert and would call in the program annotator on the spot and give him a hard time about some detail he disapproved of," Loebel says. "Szell was the first one at the hall in the morning and would look over the parking lot to see who was coming in and with whom, at what time, and what car he or she was driving. He once called in a violinist and told him to get a better instrument. The player said he couldn't afford it. Whereupon Szell said, 'I see you got a new car!' and fired the musician."

Josef Gingold, concertmaster under Szell from 1947 to 1960, related many colorful stories about his life in the Cleveland Orchestra, including how Szell would criticize his weight and tell him what and how often he should eat. Szell required all the principal players to come to his house on Sunday mornings to be coached in solo passages, note by note. When one of the musicians did not provide a phone number, Szell sent him a telegram. Not even famous soloists could escape his outspokenness;

when a well-known violinist asked the conductor to start the piece again, "from scratch," Szell replied, "You never said a truer word in your life."

In spite of Szell's intensity, Gingold had the greatest respect for the conductor's musicianship. "His sense for detail," Gingold said, "particularly in the works of the classics, was so acute that it often left one limp after a two-hour rehearsal trying to meet his demands. After every one of these sessions I came away having been enriched with a store of musical knowledge." He also had a personal relationship with Szell and was one of the few who saw the other side of the conductor, including his cooking and linguistic skills, sense of humor, and unusual generosity. Szell anonymously came to the aid of players with serious health or personal problems, and if the good deed was discovered, he would complain, "Ever since you found out that I'm somewhat human, you've tried to take advantage of me!"

"It happened during one of my private lessons with Professor Gingold at IU in 1961. Once in a while Uncle Joe (no reference to Joseph Stalin, who was given that benevolent name by President Harry Truman), as I called him, would have little gab fests about one thing and another during a lesson. On this occasion he brought out a piece of cardboard with a ribbon and a medal attached to it, à la an Olympic medal, upon which was written the words 'To our hero Joe Gingold from his colleagues in the Chicago Symphony . . . HOW COULD YOU HAVE STOOD IT SO LONG!!' This was sent to him by some of the CSO members after George Szell had spent two weeks as guest conductor with them" (as remembered by Carl Nashan).

Henry Fogel, Chicago Symphony Orchestra president from 1986 to 2003, discussed power sharing and the tradition of the iron-fisted conductor in his essay "Are Three Legs Appropriate? Or Even Sufficient?" that appeared in the journal *Harmony* in April 2000:

> The insularity of boards and the authority demanded by conductors up to the middle of the 20th century have been sources of adversarial relationships. More and more, we've (management of Chicago Symphony Orchestra) discovered that strong institutional management and leadership is not about power. It is about sharing empowerment and about consensus shaping. But this

means that one doesn't always "win." George Szell would appear to have been the model for the mid-century music director. He unquestionably built a great orchestra in Cleveland, one that remains as his legacy today, some 30 years after his death, and he did so in part with the force of his own powerful personality, but in part by building a constructive partnership with his board and management. While most conductors, particularly through the 1950s, did exercise complete control over their musicians, they eventually figured out how to develop some type of give-and-take relationship with board and management. And that simply solidified the three-legged stool concept—a concept which had little role for the musicians.

Fogel went on to say: "I would submit that, until the 1960s, most orchestra leaders (management or board) would not have included the musicians as 'stakeholders.' Prior to the development of ICSOM, and the strengthening of the role of the orchestra's own musicians (instead of union officials) in determining the direction and outcome of the negotiations, musicians were really seen as the hired help. There are many stories that illustrate the ways in which musicians were thought of and treated, and such stories are the background for some of the hostility that remains in today's labor-management relations."

The musicians of one orchestra in a southern state still smart when they tell the story of one of their board members stopping a musician from walking into the main public entrance of their concert hall on a performance night, violin in hand. "You aren't supposed to come in here," said the board member. "This is for the public. You have a stage door in back."

Like many other musicians from the Szell era (1946–1970), violinist Kurt Loebel emphasizes that "hand-in-hand with the musical accomplishments, there had to be the professional gains," for which he and many other symphony orchestra members across the United States were working. Loebel was elected chair of the committee representing the musicians of the Cleveland Orchestra. His reasons for committee involvement reflected the feelings of many of the musicians in the 1950s and '60s: "It was a part-time job. I was young and had to support a family.

All the major orchestras faced similar problems, but we were the first to seriously rock the boat. The union, management, and older musicians provided a lot of opposition. If we were to have any kind of future we had to fight and use the only weapon available—strikes." Szell was not pleased with the musicians' proposals and in 1960 threatened resignation when he felt the musicians' demands were "unreasonable."

Postwar relationships between union locals and symphony musicians continued to deteriorate. Unable to participate in negotiations or have a voice in the decisions made between the union and management, musicians' frustrations and hostilities grew. Even without the power to function effectively, committees continued to pressure their local unions and discuss their common problems far into the night with colleagues at home and throughout the country. Yet, in spite of personal and professional tensions, musicians performed at the highest of standards, as the many exemplary postwar symphony orchestra recordings demonstrate.

The Saint Louis Survey

> While we were on tour, we worked far into one night formulating the questionnaire. We made a graph, it was as simple as that. We got it copied and collected names of individuals in as many orchestras as we could. In some cases we sent it to a symphony hall addressed to "Orchestra Committee." We collated it with a cover letter on the bus between towns and sent it out.
>
> *Russell Brodine*

The Saint Louis Symphony Orchestra players committee began to think that there might be greater strength in numbers. In smoky buses on the dusty roads of Texas in the midst of a 1958 tour of the South, they came up with the idea of sending out a questionnaire to members of other major orchestras regarding length of season, minimum weekly salaries, unemployment compensation, hospitalization plans, pension plans, vacation, touring issues, and dismissal review procedures. Musicians from twenty orchestras responded, including America's largest-budgeted and most prestigious: the Metropolitan Opera Orchestra, New York Philharmonic, Philadelphia Orchestra, Boston Symphony Orchestra, Cleveland

1958 first known musician survey pre-ICSOM (Courtesy Wayne Barrington).

Orchestra, Chicago Symphony Orchestra, Minneapolis Symphony, and Los Angeles Philharmonic.

The findings were stark. Not one orchestra offered full-time employment. At forty-six weeks, Boston's season came closest, by far, to full-time, thanks to its flourishing Pops Orchestra and the Tanglewood summer festival. Musicians in only five of the responding orchestras had the right to ratify their own contracts. Only seven orchestras offered a basic pension plan. No more than three offered hospitalization coverage, and only one, the New York Philharmonic, provided paid vacation time.

The Saint Louis musicians circulated the results among orchestras nationwide, no small feat in the pre-Internet era. They hoped that, armed with this information, players everywhere could more boldly and authoritatively lobby their locals to work for better contracts. They may not have realized at the time what a difficult road lay ahead for some of their colleagues in other orchestras. "We didn't realize the impact long term," Brodine reported.

The Saint Louis survey began to be noticed throughout the profession. Those orchestras with committees demanded the right of contract ratification, and the few that did not started to organize. Orchestra musicians communicated by mail and late-night, postconcert telephone conversations.

"The idea was that we would have AFM support, getting the orchestras together, airing problems of mutual interest," said Joseph Golan, committee chair, principal second violin, and member of the Chicago Symphony Orchestra from 1953 to 2002. "We tried to work within the Union. We tried to go the proper way." But strained relations between the symphony musicians and their locals led to another way. Even after a nationwide call in 1960 by symphony orchestra players for a symphony component of the union's annual conventions and a symphony department within the AFM, the musicians union rejected both proposals.

Musicians in the Chicago Symphony, one of the few orchestras without a representative players committee, became increasingly frustrated. Petrillo, the powerful president of Local 10, showed no signs of giving up his long-held office or his insensitivity to symphony concerns.

For years, even the ritual of being paid had been demoralizing for CSO musicians, who were required to stand in line to collect their pay. According to Joe Golan, "One of the managers held his derby out. You had to drop a little something in his hat in the way of a tip on your way to the head of the line. Paychecks were not always handed directly to players; often they were conveniently dropped at their feet. This was one of many not-so-subtle methods of harassment, particularly directed towards committee members," says Golan.

In addition, the musicians of that era rehearsed and performed under a tyrant from the old school, Fritz Reiner, Chicago Symphony conductor from 1953 to 1962. His famously economical conducting style was known to the players as the "confidential beat," so confidential that a bass player once peered jokingly through a set of binoculars. He was fired. Many of the players nervously anticipated "their turn in the barrel," as they described Reiner's propensity for publicly humiliating them. Rudy Nashan recalls that Reiner "loved to make you play alone—over and over—but not tell you exactly how he wanted it played. He was merely waiting for a clam, for nervousness to appear." According to musicians who witnessed this exchange, all vividly remember the following story:

> Principal Oboe Ray Still's turn in the barrel came shortly after he joined the orchestra. After Still had flawlessly played the first-movement oboe solo in the Beethoven Symphony No. 6, Reiner stopped the orchestra, shook his head without explanation, and demanded that the oboist "Play it again!" The musician played it as he had before, without error. Reiner again stopped the orchestra. "Haven't you ever played this piece before?" he asked. Unfazed, Still replied, "Of course I have, Dr. Reiner, I played it in Baltimore." Peering over his half-moon glasses, Reiner replied with disdain, "Yes, with de Orioles, no doubt."

Nashan recalls: "Once, in a *Bolero* rehearsal, the trombonist, Frank Crisafulli, had a slight problem and requested an opportunity to try his solo phrase again. No Go! from Reiner. Instead, Reiner asked another trombonist, who happened to be a first-year member of the CSO, to play it. He had the same problem. Reiner was furious. At the rehearsal break, Crisafulli spoke again to Reiner. No Go. Instead, Reiner conducted the performances with the trombone solo cut out! That's what I call intimidation."

The oppressive workplace atmosphere, combined with formidable opposition from President Petrillo, catalyzed the CSO musicians to form a committee and soon thereafter to organize the first meeting of symphony players. In spite of the considerable risk involved, they could no longer be suppressed.

In the spring of 1959, Local 10 musicians union representatives unexpectedly showed up at a CSO rehearsal to announce that the orchestra was reducing the six-week season at its summer venue, the Ravinia Festival (the musicians liked to repeat Sir Thomas Beecham's ironic assertion that Ravinia was the only train station in the world with its own symphony orchestra—because the Chicago Symphony concerts there were constantly interrupted by the noise of the nearby trains), from four concerts a week to three, and that unless the orchestra players accepted an immediate 15 percent pay cut, the entire summer season would be canceled. As they were desperate for a summer season, the players agreed to the cut. "However," former hornist Wayne Barrington explained, "there were enough strong feelings that we elected an informal orchestra committee." (Even so, the union and management did not recognize and formally allow a committee for several years.)

That was not all the bad news. Management also announced that Reiner had canceled the prestigious eleven-week U.S. State Department–sponsored tour of the Soviet Union and Western Europe that was to have taken place in the fall of that year. Members of the committee remember that Reiner explained his reasoning to the orchestra by saying, "It rains in Moscow that time of year, so we're not going." The CSO players were shocked and furious at this news. They had never toured outside the United States and were demoralized to miss this opportunity. The contemptuous joke among the musicians was that they were the best provincial orchestra in the world. Rather than engaging a substitute conductor to salvage the tour, CSO management pulled out entirely. Leonard Bernstein and the New York Philharmonic went instead.

It would later be known that Reiner was suffering from congestive heart failure and was quite ill at the time. Had the musicians been informed of his poor health, according to violinist Joe Golan, perhaps they would have been more sympathetic to his cancellation of the tour. But at the time, they did not know the whole story, and the more they thought about it, the angrier they felt. One day in the locker room, some members grabbed an old suit of tails, laid a baton across it, and proceeded to take turns stomping on the Reiner effigy. Reiner heard about this demonstration and demanded an apology from the musicians. According to Sam Denov, one of the committee members and the CSO timpanist, "When the personnel manager informed the orchestra of this demand, I was so outraged, it prompted me to make the first spontaneous speech I had ever given in my life. I said that if there was to be an apology, it should be from Reiner to the musicians, not the other way around. The orchestra burst into spontaneous applause. The meeting soon adjourned, and Reiner never got the apology."

An apocryphal story circulated that Reiner had warned that after his

℘ The Chicago Symphony had no orchestra committee until 1959. According to Principal Oboe Ray Still, "It was not my incentive alone to form the committee—I happened only to be the first chairman. . . . The immediate cause of our determination to form a committee was the action of the Orchestral Association to reduce the scale of the Ravinia season from $150 to $125 a week. . . . James Caesar Petrillo, who was then the chief of the union Local, had warned the players of the orchestra against forming a players committee. He threatened to tear up their union cards so that they could never work in the U.S. again . . . he had this ridiculous power. . . . The custom was for him to meet with the president of the Orchestral Association (a real dictator named Dr. Eric Oldberg), and they would make up a 'sweetheart's agreement' without any consultation with the orchestra. A telegram would appear on the bulletin board stating the new scale, and the 'above scale' players would know that they would get their little bonuses. I was quite sure of my value to the orchestra and of my playing, and I know that Dr. Reiner had great confidence in me, so I was not afraid of being fired by Oldberg or Petrillo. Sharrow felt the same so he joined the committee soon after. There were many threats and we were only a little more than half the orchestra. . . . After a few weeks we had enough courage to confront Petrillo at the union and actually surrounded his desk, almost eighty strong. He reluctantly said, 'If yez had a committee ya understand it won't mean nuttin'.' I remember that I said, 'Does this mean that we can form a committee?' He then repeated, 'It won't mean nuttin',' but within a year or so we had helped negotiate a new contract in Mayor Daley's office (after Dr. Oldberg had cancelled the season because of a threatened strike—and the public outcry was enormous!). Dr. Oldberg quit his job, he was so enraged. He had run the show like a dictator for a long time."

Ray Still, retired principal oboe, Chicago Symphony Orchestra

death he would dig himself out of his grave and haunt the musicians. Their response: "Let him dig. We'll bury him upside down."

According to Joe Golan, referring to the formation of the CSO's first informal players committee, "Those events [the State Department tour

cancellation and the reduction of the summer season] certainly precipitated our coming together. We didn't really *all* come together," he says.
"There was a big schism. There were a few of us that got it started, and
there were many people who were afraid to make any commitment. At
that time, the local union and the [CSO] administration were in bed
together."

Musicians who hesitated to join the reform effort may well have felt intimidated by the combined forces of union and management. They knew
the stories of their older colleagues who had been threatened with loss of
union membership in 1940 when they had pleaded with Petrillo for the
right to form a committee. The national newsletter, *Senza Sordino,* later
described their efforts this way: "By unanimous decree of the Orchestra
membership, a committee was created, similar to those long in existence
in other orchestras. Its primary purpose was to try to force the union
to recognize the special problems of the symphony orchestra, and to try
to achieve decent contracts and democratic participation in the future. It
was generally agreed that the sole reason a committee was necessary was
the total apathy and social irresponsibility of Local 10 leadership, coupled
with its proven inability to truly represent the rank and file."

The new CSO committee faced a formidable foe in Petrillo. Ani-
mosity between Chicago Symphony Orchestra members and the "Little
Caesar" had been high for decades. "He didn't like symphony music. He
thought we were all aristocrats," recalled Rudy Nashan.

The CSO administration also monitored the fledgling committee, and
even meeting together in small groups proved risky. Several of the committee members remember one particular occasion: "We were meeting
in this big dressing room where the chorus used to meet," said Denov. "It
was a real dark room and in the corner was this little piano. We started
filtering into the room after the rehearsal and somebody turned on the
lights. One of us noticed someone hiding under the piano. It turned out
to be the CSO's manager, crouching in the shadows."

Following the Ravinia cutbacks and foreign tour cancellation of 1959,
the Chicago players committee sought the counsel of an attorney. During one of their meetings, a CSO manager evicted the committee from
Orchestra Hall on the grounds that the presence of a lawyer was for-
bidden, as was any players meeting with more than three participants.

Management also forbade the posting in Orchestra Hall of any commit-tee announcements. They put the company bulletin board under lock and key to prohibit meeting notices from being posted. So the musicians found a creative way to avoid trespassing on the property and make a point at the same time. They wrote notices of meetings on bits of paper attached to helium balloons and floated them backstage. Management could not prohibit air space in Orchestra Hall.

(Eight years later, the musicians of the San Antonio Symphony were denied permission to install a bulletin board in their new home at the beginning of the 1969 season. Discussions continued for fourteen weeks on this issue, with the result that a board large enough for one sheet of paper was installed within inches of the conductor's dressing room door. After the committee requested that more adequate space be pro-vided, the orchestra management allowed such a board, retaining the right to rescind the allotment of the space if it was used for "political purposes.")

In 1961, Rudy Nashan experienced consequences that confirmed some players' fears about participating in committee activism. After ten years of distinguished service with the orchestra—Chicago's trumpet section was world renowned—Nashan found himself suddenly demoted from second to fourth trumpet. "It was a perfect setup to discredit the mission of the players committee and destroy any camaraderie in the trumpet section," said Nashan. "We always car-pooled together, and for months before the demotion, my colleagues had known about this, but were too intimidated by management to say anything to me. No one said a word."

It wasn't until he went to the manager's office to renew his contract in May 1961 that Nashan learned, to his horror, that he was being moved back to fourth chair. He was told that his second trumpet po-sition had been filled by someone else and that he could take fourth chair or resign. He refused to sign under those conditions and imme-diately sought support.

First Nashan asked Reiner if he knew about this and if he had been dissatisfied with his playing. According to Nashan, Reiner told him he was very happy with his playing, but could do nothing about this demo-tion. (Although the conductor had the prerogative, he took no action in this case.) Nashan then went to Local 10 president Petrillo, who put him off, saying that he could not help him because he had been demoted for musical reasons.

Next Nashan went to the president of the orchestra's board of directors, who suggested he take third trumpet as a compromise. Nashan refused to be moved to third, because to do so would have displaced his third-chair colleague. He protested that he could not accept third chair because that would mean "you would do to him what you have just done to me." "You and your goddamn democratic principles," was the president's reply, according to Nashan.

In the end, Nashan had no choice but to accept fourth chair. As a gesture of support, his colleagues took up a collection and gave him $740 to make up for the salary he was losing as a result of the demotion. Two years later, after thirteen years of service with the orchestra, he made the wrenching decision to resign. But his work with the union would continue.

In another display of management tactics, five CSO musicians, some of whom were committee members, arrived at rehearsal one day in 1960 to find nonrenewal notices on their music stands. The five were percussionist Sam Denov, violinists Raymond Niwa and Sam Siegel, and violists Robert Coleman and Bill York. In a letter to the editor of *Senza Sordino* in October 2000, Coleman recalled that strange event and its aftermath: "I was one of the five people who were fired twice from the CSO. The first time, the management stated baldly to the press that we were being fired for our 'labor activity.' When our attorney and the reporters for the Chicago papers pointed out that the management was confessing to a violation of federal law, they hired us back. One year later they fired us again, this time giving 'musical reasons' as the cause. Since only the conductor could fire for 'musical reasons,' the reporters, recognizing the same five names, went to Fritz Reiner and asked him why he was firing us. He replied that this was the first he had heard about it! His exact words were, characteristically, 'Hmph. There are some people I would like to get rid of—but not them!' When the management heard that he had said this, they had to hire us back again."* In private correspon-

---

*Oboist Ray Still has confirmed the story. In private correspondence, he wrote: "The five players you speak about were fired by Oldberg for union activities that he did not like. He asked Reiner to do the firing. Sharrow [Leonard Sharrow, bassoonist] and I went to see Reiner and he told us (confidentially) that [firing

dence, Coleman said in 2001 that it was all "very amusing—and very frightening. We were supported every inch of the way by our excellent attorney, Lee Leibik, whose wisdom and aggressive spirit were two of the reasons that we ultimately triumphed."

The players appealed to Petrillo for help throughout this crisis, but he did not respond. Months went by. Golan recalls that when pressed, Petrillo claimed that "a propitious time had not yet come to meet with Oldberg." This repeated line struck the players as an attempt to stall them past the six-month deadline for filing charges of unfair labor practices with the National Labor Relations Board.

Barred from meeting at Orchestra Hall, the musicians gathered in private homes to talk. Denov pleaded with his colleagues for support: "If the members can't protect these people, we will never have a committee that means a thing. No one will be safe." The musicians were clearly united in their opposition to these firings and were preparing to go out on an Unfair Labor Practice strike. When CSO management heard of these plans, the dismissal notices were rescinded.

In the challenging times of this organizing effort, the leaders knew the risks, but they also felt they had no choice. "The only security we had," recalls Nashan, "was each of us to each other, even if it was only five or six guys." Golan adds, "People let us fight their battles with our blood." Before long, they would have the support and unity of the orchestra behind them. They knew there was no other option, and they prepared for battle with orchestra management and with Petrillo, who was still the president of the powerful Chicago local union. Wayne Barrington recounted: "News of problems within the orchestra was reaching the papers. Mayor Daley was making note of it, and Petrillo was on the front pages talking about 'those rebels.' The orchestra association didn't much like that kind of notoriety. Seymour Raven, business manager at the time, figured he was really going to settle matters. He issued a 'fat fiat' that we couldn't hold meetings in Orchestra Hall!" The committee leaders began publishing a newsletter to announce orchestra meetings and to inform their colleagues of other orchestras' struggles to gain rights.

those particular] five [was] not *his* idea. He had asked for three others to be fired for incompetence, and Oldberg hid behind Reiner on this. It turned out OK because the five hired a lawyer and he got them reinstated."

Musicians nationwide were also closely watching a storm brewing in Cleveland.

Endless Battles in Cleveland

Probably no inside symphony orchestra fight or orchestra-vs.-union fight across the country has, as yet, been so sustained or become quite so intense as Cleveland's. The dispute here also is believed to be the first taken to court.

Cleveland Daily News, *March 5, 1963*

Founded in 1919, the Cleveland Orchestra was similar to other established major orchestras when it came to labor practices. Conductor was king, and contracts were offered on a year-to-year, take-it-or-leave-it basis. "When I joined in 1957," recalls retired Cleveland Orchestra violinist Kurt Loebel, "there were no fringe benefits of any kind. The management would post a notice on the bulletin board telling you to see management to sign your contract. The scale and other details were discussed with the president of the union and their lawyer, whom we didn't trust. If anyone wanted a raise he would have to see [music director] George Szell, who up to his dying days had control over every detail connected with the business and artistic part of our job.

"He had no children of his own, the musicians were his progeny. He watched from his office window as they arrived, noted the time, and noted who took their music home. Everything from stationery to record jacket design was under Szell's control. His personal contract prior to accepting his music directorship in 1946 had major demands: three coats of paint on the walls of the stage (color specified by him) and total control of artistic matters and specifics of our working conditions."

Beginning in 1954, and again in 1958 and '59, Cleveland Orchestra musicians were among the first in the nation to appeal to their local union for the right to ratify their own contracts. They wanted a voice in determining their pay and working conditions. They had already formed a committee and were seeking what they felt were their basic union rights. But the union would have none of it, denying the request for ratification on the basis that such an arrangement would not represent the majority of the local musicians union members.

Having found no support from their local, Cleveland Orchestra musicians appealed to the AFM. Petrillo, who still was AFM president, replied with his standard line, endorsing "local autonomy" and eschewing AFM intervention.

This state of affairs went unchallenged until the issuing of the 1960–1961 contract. The musicians asked for parity—equivalent salaries, pensions, and working conditions—with their colleagues in the Boston Symphony and Philadelphia Orchestra. The contract that they received met none of those standards. "Our contract called for a period of 31 regular weeks at a scale of $150 per week, with touring per diem of $13," says Loebel, who was an active players committee member. He adds that "as for working conditions, there were virtually no changes over previous contracts. There was no mention of a pension plan, hospitalization, severance pay, vacations, days off for religious observance, life insurance, or recognition of the orchestra committee. There was no provision for outside arbitration in grievance or dismissal cases. The conductor's powers remained unchallenged as to hiring, firing, and seating."

The 1960–1961 contract read, in part: "The musician will observe all reasonable rules as to conduct and other such regulations which the conductor may make from time to time; he will accept at all times the opinions and wishes of the conductor concerning his services; when required by the conductor he will perform obligate or solo parts standing and in front of the orchestra without additional pay; the musician at all concerts will appear in the dress officially designated by the conductor. In case of dismissal, if the musician is in his third consecutive season of employment, he must receive a year's notice." The summer season was not included in the contract. The Cleveland players were furious, and word of their outrage spread to their colleagues around the country.

They sought support from the Landrum–Griffin Act, passed in 1959, which guaranteed union members throughout the land the right to express any view, argument, or opinion regarding the conduct of their unions' affairs. In March 1961, Cleveland Orchestra musicians took their union, Local 4, to federal court in an attempt to gain ratification rights. A month later, however, the court held that Landrum–Griffin did not provide the relief the musicians sought.

To make matters worse, the musicians' own union came back at them with a vengeance. In September, the executive board of Local 4 entered

1961 summons from AFM Local 4 to Cleveland Orchestra musician Kurt Loebel (Courtesy Kurt Loebel).

a series of formal charges against sixteen members of the Cleveland Orchestra, all of whom had served on orchestra committees. The charges accused them of, among other things, "promoting disunity within the union . . . engaging in activities inconsistent with union principles . . . and placing obstacles in the way of the successful maintenance of the Local by acts and published threats." The charges carried the threat of a $3,000 fine per musician, as well as expulsion from the union. In reply to these charges, the musicians' lawyer filed a countersuit to restrain the local union officers from trying the musicians and sought the following provisions:

- The right of ratification;
- The right to participate directly in negotiations;

- A court ruling to set aside and declare null and void the present three-year contract under which they were working;
- Payment of $20,000 each to the sixteen orchestra members; and
- An injunction permanently restraining Local 4 from bringing them to trial.

In the March 5, 1963, *Cleveland Daily News,* an article about the musicians' struggle cited several other major orchestras and conflicts with their unions, including Philadelphia and Chicago. The Boston Symphony was mentioned for its good relationships—once again the exception to the rule, because the Boston local of the musicians union had not been involved until 1942, and it had allowed the musicians' highly developed committee organization to remain. Music Director George Szell was quoted in the same article: "While we're at work, we should forget all of our differences."

Although performances were the first priority, the musicians could no longer put aside their mounting frustrations. The resulting agreement with Local 4 granted the orchestra a strike vote, requiring a 60 percent majority to rescind. This gave the musicians some voice in orchestra affairs, but it was not a mandate for the right to ratify its contracts. The orchestra was divided between the young and aggressive and the older musicians, some of whom were afraid to express any dissent. But the Cleveland players committee was determined to forge ahead in spite of the risks and lack of unity. Although the lawsuits brought between the Cleveland musicians and Local 4 were eventually dismissed, their battle for ratification would continue for years.

Petrillo Challenged and Defeated

"Don't you know who you're talking to, kid?"

Chicago Mayor Richard Daley, screaming at Chicago Symphony Players Committee Chair Joe Golan during Daley's mediation of contract talks with the union and CSO administration (from Golan correspondence, 1998)

Mounting nationwide dissent led the AFM to convene a special Symphony Symposium in New York in the summer of 1961. It was the first conference in AFM history to deal exclusively with the concerns of symphony musicians, especially the crucial situation in Cleveland. But the union made clear that this gathering was merely for the informal airing of grievances. No decisions were made and nothing meaningful was accomplished. The AFM convened two more such symposia before the end of 1963, but they served only to widen the gulf between the symphony players and the musicians' union they felt was letting them down.

Opposition to Petrillo extended beyond symphony musicians and their supporters. In 1961, a diverse group of Local 10 musicians formed an organization called Chicago Musicians for Union Democracy, or CMUD, which comprised diverse groups of musicians throughout Local 10. All were fed up with the autocracy of their local, but only the symphony players had the advantage of being together day after day. Through the symphony players committee they could bring collective pressure to bear against the union. Like the Cleveland players, they were inspired by the passing of the Landrum–Griffin Act, which in addition to guaranteeing the right of union members to express any view, argument, or opinion regarding the conduct of union affairs, mandated a union election of officers before 1963. "There were about six of us 'personae non gratae' who went around the block to Toffenetti's Restaurant, where we held secret meetings in a back room," hornist Wayne Barrington recalled. A group of symphony and freelance musicians began discussing plans to contest the upcoming election, the first such effort since 1917. Inexperienced in the ways of formal union procedure, they hired a parliamentarian to coach them. Sixty CSO musicians held a preliminary session to inform themselves of union bylaws and to review Robert's Rules of Order. "It was revolutionary. We were determined to inform ourselves," remembered Joe Golan.

The first opportunity to challenge the incumbent regime came at a Local 10 meeting in October 1961. With hundreds of members in attendance, including the local's entire executive board, its officers faced a determined, informed opposition. All sixty CSO musicians came prepared to monitor the meeting for adherence to Robert's Rules of Order.

After the agenda was distributed, Petrillo made a change in the order of business. This change did not appear in the printed agenda, but was proposed from the podium by Petrillo. Originally, Petrillo's request of $500 per week, or $25,000 annual pension for himself, was to be voted on at the beginning of the meeting; Petrillo had moved it to the end. The players suspected that he was attempting to delay this discussion until his biggest detractors, the symphony musicians, had to leave for a scheduled rehearsal. All were prepared to challenge him. But he recognized only one of them.

"Ya got a bone to pick, kid?" Petrillo shouted. Rudy Nashan knew how to respond. He rose from his seat and, under the pressure of the moment, dropped the papers he carried in his hand. They scattered on the floor at his feet. He gathered the papers, and his presence of mind, and moved not to change the order of the agenda. The motion was carried by a large majority. For the first time in forty-five years, a Petrillo motion was defeated.

Petrillo's next ploy was to filibuster. "The speech was the history of Jimmy Petrillo," said one of the musicians, Sam Denov. "It took two or three hours. He knew his days were numbered and we were ganging up on him. He had been president for forty years. He wanted to get rid of the symphony guys and he wanted a pension. Petrillo, as president of this local, never made more than $500 a week. How did a guy who made $500 a week become a millionaire? The easy answer is that he was being paid off by everybody under the sun. The MPTF [Music Performance Trust Fund] was set up as a slush fund for his reelection to international office [AFM president]." This was not the first challenge to Petrillo; four years before, Local 47 musician Cecil Read had denounced Petrillo during the revolt by recording musicians for using the $14 million Trust Fund as his "personal political slush fund to perpetuate himself in office" (Burlingame, p. 15).

Petrillo's speech dragged on until another CSO member invoked Robert's Rules of Order. Joe Golan recalled what happened next: "Sam Siegel, one of our violinists, stood up and said, 'Mr. President, I rise to a point of order. You've been talking for two and a half hours now, and you haven't gotten past 1937!' Petrillo ended his speech ten minutes after that, and the meeting was over."

It was a milestone; Petrillo had been publicly confronted by some of his "symphony boys." This resounding victory led within a year to the complete ouster of Petrillo and his forces from control of Local 10. Although successfully invoking a "point of order" may seem like a small victory, in such an oppressive atmosphere, even this was important in that it further fueled the members of Chicago Musicians for Union

From the Constitution and By-laws of the Chicago Federation of
Musicians, Local 10, AFM, 1960

By-laws Section I
Duties of the President

(a) The President shall enforce a due observance of the Constitution and By-Laws and countersign all orders drawn on the Financial Secretary-Treasurer . . .

(b) He shall have a vote in case of a tie.

(c) He shall be judge of order, subject to appeal without debate.

(d) He shall preside at all the meetings of the Local and the Board of Directors when possible and for his services he shall be paid the sum of Five Hundred Dollars ($500.00) per week . . . He shall have supervision of all matters pertaining to the welfare of the Local . . . It shall be his duty and prerogative to exercise supervision over the affairs of the Local, to make decisions where, in his opinion, an emergency exists; and to give effect to such decisions he is authorized and empowered to promulgate and issue executive orders, which shall be conclusive and binding upon all members; the power so to do is hereby made absolute in the President when, in his opinion, such orders are necessary to conserve and safeguard the interests of the Local; and the said power shall in like manner extend to and include cases where existing laws are inadequate or provide no method of dealing with the situation . . . he shall have the power to order members before the Board of Directors, call strikes, and draw funds in payment of all expenses occasioned by the exercise of his duties . . .

(g) He shall appoint all committees and as many assistants to the President as may be deemed necessary. The assistants to the President shall be under the complete supervision of the President, the salaries to be paid the assistants to be determined by the President, with concurrence of the Board of Directors.

Democracy. CMUD enlisted the services of a lawyer who also was working with the CSO committee on their contract negotiations. The orchestra management prohibited the attorney (Lee Leibik) from entering Orchestra Hall, so Leibik invited the musicians to his office, which became the "eye of the storm."

One month later, in November 1961, the first issue of the *CSO Members' Committee Newsletter* was published. It became the basis for a communications network not only among the Chicago Symphony musicians but also among many other U.S. and Canadian orchestras.

In 1962, the CSO players committee expanded the 1958 Saint Louis questionnaire for another go-round. This second national survey collected data from twenty-six orchestras on such issues as committee formation, vacation time, minimum notice of schedule change, radio and television appearances, recordings, participation in contract negotiations, duration and specifics of master agreements, and cost-of-living information.

Joseph Golan, the chair of the CSO players committee, met frequently with James Petrillo to resolve contractual issues within the Chicago local. Petrillo finally agreed to three requests: that Local 10 officially recognize the CSO players committee, that the committee be allowed to participate in contract negotiations, and that the players be granted the right to ratify their own contracts.

Although this was a critical victory for the musicians, ongoing negotiations regarding the orchestra's new contract were at a complete impasse. Players wanted to increase their thirty-week season to fifty-two weeks. Their salary request of $12,000 a year represented an increase of almost $3,000. According to a newspaper account, CSO president Eric Oldberg called these and other requests "ridiculous and irresponsible." For his part, committee chair Golan stated to the press during the dispute that the CSO was a "part-time orchestra" run under a system of "paternal despotism." He said that the players' second jobs as clerks, handymen, cab drivers, and factory workers made them rusty on their instruments. "We view the 52-week contract in two ways," said Golan. "First, as a fair wage for men who have studied, worked, and rehearsed most of their lives trying to create good music; second, as members of an orchestra, we must be allowed to work together throughout the year so that we may improve as an orchestra."

Petrillo and Oldberg called on an even more powerful establishment figure than themselves, none other than Chicago mayor Richard J. Daley, to mediate the contract dispute. "Their strategy was to get me in the mayor's office and all three of the 'good old boys' would gang up on me in order that they might break down my resistance," said Golan. "For eighteen hours without food or water, they took turns trying to intimidate me in hopes of settling the agreement in favor of management. At one point, red-faced and blustering, Daley screamed at me, 'Don't you know who you're talking to, kid?'" Golan did not give in. Faced with the very real possibility of a strike by the players, the administration and union acceded to a few demands. These included an improved basic pay scale, a longer season, provisions for grievance and dismissal procedures, pension and health benefits, and recognition of the Chicago Symphony Orchestra players committee. The contract was ratified in September 1962.

Despite the official approval of contract ratification, Petrillo continued to thwart the CSO players. In November 1962 he decreed that CSO members would not be allowed to take any engagements outside their regular CSO concerts.

In addition to this freeze, Petrillo also announced that the players committee would be barred from negotiations of the contract covering their summer concerts at Ravinia. The players lost no time in filing unfair labor practice charges against Local 10. "It's the committee and the orchestra itself rising in its defense," Golan told a reporter from the *Chicago Daily News* (November 17, 1962). "The semi-hysterical outbursts and retaliatory tactics of Petrillo have now publicly exposed facts long known to members of Local 10." He went on to say that "the leadership has lost contact with the rank and file members and its undemocratic practices are much more closely attuned to management than the musicians it is supposed to represent. Petrillo's threats of loss of employment and reprisals constitute clear and patent unfair labor practices."

The election of Local 10 officers occurred a few weeks later. All union offices were contested, and of the twenty-eight CMUD candidates, five were from the Chicago Symphony Orchestra. The others represented every aspect of the music profession in the Chicago area. The monumental effort to regain union rights from Petrillo's dictatorial control was nearly a year in the making, with a telephone campaign that reached nearly all 11,000 members and a large, successfully funded publicity drive. The publicity over Petrillo's conflicts with the CSO did not help his reelection campaign.

The *Chicago Sun-Times* reported on December 6: "The outcome took

From Chicago Sun-Times, *December 6, 1962 (Courtesy Walfrid Kujala).*

everyone by surprise, including members of the CMUD steering committee, who admitted they had not expected to win so much. Their movement started only a year ago during the local's annual business meeting and eventually grew into one of the most effective in a series of rebel movements that have recently shaken veteran leadership in Chicago labor. The upset will change markedly the relationship of the union with the Chicago Orchestral Association. Two symphony men are now on the Local 10 board and Petrillo, who sometimes held down the symphony men when they wanted to blast management, is gone."

To everyone's shock, CMUD's slate of twenty-eight candidates had soundly defeated Petrillo and his regime. It was the end of an era and a stunning rejection of one of the most powerful leaders in American labor history.

The new president of Local 10 was fifty-seven-year-old Barney Richards, a freelance musician who had never held union office. CMUD's mission was to replace what it felt was Local 10's paternalistic and autocratic leadership with a more representative and participatory approach, to work toward racial integration of the local, and to win the right for symphony musicians to participate in their own contract negotiations. The newly elected vice president, Rudy Nashan, sought advice on improving the union from an officer of the Pastry Chefs and Cooks Union. After comparing the two unions' rule books, the Pastry Chefs officer opined that "the musicians of Local 10 had little more than a penal society with all the rules and regulations set *against* its members."

Four

The Birth of ICSOM: A Labor Revolution

It is unlike any other labor/union relationship that I know of;
the musicians' movement was a labor relations revolution among
professionals.

> *Labor lawyer I. Philip Sipser (1919–2001), known to
> ICSOM members as "the Heifetz of negotiators"*

HE CHICAGO MUSICIANS, organizing from within, had developed a fine-tuned network that became the basis for a national communications system that facilitated the exchange of much information of mutual importance to symphony orchestra musicians all over North America. The survey that the CSO players' committee distributed to twenty-six orchestras in 1962 became the basis for their next big move. Once they had received all the surveys and compiled the results, the committee members convened a landmark meeting in Chicago on May 12 and 13, 1962, amid cries of "dual unionism" from the AFM. For the first time in their collective history, musicians from North America's leading orchestras gathered to plan for their future. Twelve orchestras— Boston, Indianapolis, Philadelphia, Chicago, Los Angeles, Pittsburgh, Cincinnati, Cleveland, New York, Saint Louis, Toronto, and the Metropolitan Opera—sent thirty representatives. The delegates elected Joseph Golan and Wayne Barrington, both members of the Chicago Symphony Orchestra, chair and secretary, respectively. The musicians shared many goals. First, they wanted to address salaries, working conditions, and contract problems cited in both the Saint Louis and Chicago surveys. Additional aims included the launching of a national symphony newsletter, establishment of an industry-wide pension fund, institution of fair audition and probation practices, and the inclusion of attorneys in contract negotiations. The two days of meetings at Roosevelt University in Chicago were a tremendous success.

In early September 1962, the musicians who had attended the historic Chicago conference in May came together in Cleveland with a widening network of orchestra players for the formal ratification of the creation of ICSOM, the International Conference of Symphony and Opera Musicians.

The organization's founding members were the principal orchestras of Baltimore, Boston, Chicago, Cincinnati, Cleveland, Detroit, Indianapolis, Metropolitan Opera, Minneapolis, New York, Philadelphia, Pittsburgh, Rochester, Saint Louis, and Toronto.

The Cleveland meeting set the mission statement of the new organization, which would provide the first effective forum for symphony musicians to talk and work together for the benefit of all. Boston Symphony Orchestra Assistant Concertmaster George Zazofsky, the first president-elect and a dedicated leader in the ICSOM effort, told the *Boston Globe* several years later, "It was a further objective to direct continuous cooperative efforts within the framework of the American Federation of Musicians of the United States and Canada, AFL-CIO."

It was a time of great pride for the musicians involved. Zazofsky's daughter, Erika, forty years later came to appreciate the full extent of what he and his colleagues accomplished. At the time, in the early 1960s, she remembers, she was unaware of its impact on the symphony orchestra profession and of her own role in it. Perched on her father's bed with a Smith-Corona manual typewriter, Erika typed as her father dictated the letters he wrote to various musicians throughout the country. "He was not highly educated, so he asked me to help with the syntax and sentence structure after he formulated the ideas he was trying to convey. It was quite ordinary for me to help him in this way, and I thought nothing of it until years later, when I realized what I had passively participated in. My father and the others, who stuck their necks out, were the true radicals of their day. They did not realize it then, but when I look back at what they accomplished, and the status of orchestral musicians today, they were truly free thinkers."

Once founded, ICSOM gained strength and reputation. All was not smooth sailing as the organization began navigating the difficult decade

1966 Senza Sordino *articles concerning ICSOM.*

of the 1960s. Even among its membership, some of the musicians feared ICSOM's potential to secede from the AFM. Some older players had other concerns. Many had been intimidated for so long by conductors, management, and the union that it was difficult for them to imagine that they might be able to control their musical and professional destinies. Most had endured the Depression, and many had fled Europe before, during, and after the Second World War. To them, ICSOM was a revolutionary idea, and no one knew where it would lead. They worried—not without good reason—about the possible consequences. Membership in ICSOM did not cost anyone a job, although committee activism that led to its formation was a very real risk. Nor did it break off from the union or hatch any Communist plots, as had been suspected; rather, it became a force for positive change.

The year 1963 saw the publication of the organization's first newsletter. Its name, suggested by Chicago Symphony flutist Joan Bennett, was *Senza Sordino*, Italian for "without mute." Chicago Symphony violist Robert Coleman, *Senza*'s first editor, wrote in January 1963: "It is with both trepidation and pride that we introduce this first issue of *Senza Sordino*. It has been put together against the pressure of both time and limited funds and no doubt bears the scars of its difficult (one is tempted to say 'Caesarean') birth. The point of view of this publication is to be that of orchestra musicians, as distinguished from orchestra managements and musicians' unions. The rash of controversies and bitter contract disputes which has plagued musicians coast to coast makes this newsletter almost a necessity. It can be fairly said, we believe, that the same conditions and motives which have given rise to the mushrooming of orchestra committees also resulted in this newsletter."

Indeed, the birth of ICSOM brought with it new and stronger committees in its member orchestras. These groups went from a passive role to taking historic action. Among the resolutions passed unanimously in that first gathering in Cleveland in September of 1962, although it was not adopted until 1969, was one asking that the AFM establish a symphony, opera, and ballet department for the purpose of assisting orchestras, locals, and the AFM in resolving problems particular to those organizations.

Another key imperative continued to be contract ratification, which only a few orchestras had achieved by this time. Symphony musicians wanted the same rights as their colleagues in the recording industry and trade union members in other kinds of work, including the right to ratify their own contracts at the local level. At the inaugural ICSOM meeting, it was resolved to take this request to the AFM. The courageous resolution bears restatement: "That the international executive board of the AFM promulgate as the official policy of the AFM the principle that the right of contract negotiation at the local level is a necessary foundation for responsible democratic trade unionism, and that the IEB [International Executive Board] exert every power it possesses to insure that this principle, long observed by almost all trade unions outside the AFM, henceforth be observed by all locals within the AFM." One by one, musician locals, under pressure from ICSOM, granted symphony musicians the authority to ratify their own contracts. By 1965, all of the major orchestras in the United States and Canada—except Cleveland, where troubles would continue for years to come—had ratification clauses in their master agreements.

While the formation of ICSOM could hardly have come as a surprise to the AFM, the union reacted with fear and defensiveness. As George Seltzer wrote in his 1989 history of the AFM, *Music Matters*, "ICSOM was not welcomed by the AFM hierarchy. There were accusations of dual-unionism." "Dual unionism" was a mislabeling that only fanned existing fires. In this context, dual unionism would imply that ICSOM sought to leave the AFM to form its own union. Fed up with the status

> ## 𝄞 *ICSOM Purpose Statement Formulated in 1962*
>
> The International Conference of Symphony and Opera Musicians is an association of professionals whose concerns and efforts are dedicated to the promotion of a better and more rewarding livelihood for the skilled performer and to the enrichment of the cultural life of our society. It is further an objective to direct continuous cooperative efforts within the framework of the American Federation of Musicians of the United States and Canada.

quo and alienated from their locals, some ICSOM members at the time would have liked to secede from the AFM. But the vast majority saw ICSOM as a constructive part of the workings of the national federation and wanted to try to work within its structure. "The idea was to put something back into the AFM that simply wasn't there," recalled Wayne Barrington.

The AFM had reason to fear ICSOM. In 1958, Los Angeles studio musicians, dissatisfied with the AFM, had broken off and formed their own union, the Musicians Guild of America. Clearly, the AFM worried that ICSOM was headed in the same direction. An orchestral secession would have a great monetary effect on all AFM locals, because of the loss of revenue in the form of monthly work dues they received from each orchestra musician.

McCarthyism Hysteria

"I will not cooperate with this committee. My answer will be the same if you keep me here a month."

Pianist and teacher Edith Rapport, invoking the First and Fifth Amendments repeatedly during House Un-American Activities Subcommittee hearings, Los Angeles, 1956

McCarthyism hysteria cast its long shadow over ICSOM. Chairman George Zazofsky and vice-chair Sam Denov drew the attention of Walter Trohan, a syndicated conservative columnist for the *Chicago Tribune*.

Trohan speculated that "ICSOM members followed the pattern which has worked successfully in Communist-infiltrated or controlled groups, although none of the officers or committee members of the group have Red records."

In Trohan's view, ICSOM was attempting to "take over" America's orchestras, and its leaders had "Russian sounding names." One wonders how Trohan would have felt about the 2005 appointment of Secretary of Homeland Security Michael Chertoff.

Erika Zazofsky recalled her father's fears of McCarthyism even into the early 1960s. She remembers that he worried about phone tapping and was reluctant to sign his name to traceable documents, even checks. She believes her parents felt threatened and that they were confident their suspicions were not simply paranoia. "Also, during that time, because my family's background was Russian and they spoke Russian and French, and because Dad was so active as chairman of the orchestra, we had many Russian soloists—esteemed violinists David Oistrakh and Leonid Kogan—to our house after their performances with the Boston Symphony Orchestra. My mother was famous for her borscht and other Russian dishes, and they'd sit around after concerts and eat and drink vodka. I have several photos that my father took of those times, and he would point out to me faces that I couldn't recognize. He'd say, 'This is their interpreter, but everybody knows he's KGB.' Even having these people around the house was cause for concern to a youngster, but somehow their musicianship transcended the fear of 'connection with a commie' in the post-McCarthy climate."

At the end of the Second World War, the United States' alliance with the Soviet Union started to erode and the "Red Scare" began. U.S. Senator Joseph McCarthy of Wisconsin captured national attention in February 1950 by alleging that the State Department was riddled with card-carrying members of the Communist Party. His activities gave rise to the term "McCarthyism," referring to the use of sensational and highly publicized personal attacks, usually based on unsubstantiated charges and innuendos, as a means of discrediting people thought to be subversive. Chaired by Senator McCarthy, the House Un-American Activities Committee (HUAC) began its campaign to purge the country of any suspected "Communist influences." It investigated Communist infiltration among labor unions, screenwriters, directors, and actors, finding Hollywood a particularly attractive target because of its high profile in American culture. The most notable member was forty-four-year-old Richard M. Nixon.

HUAC had begun its hearings of the Screen Writers Guild in 1947, eventually succeeding in blacklisting successful screenwriters and disrupting—in many cases ruining—the professional and personal lives of hundreds more in the film industry. The so-called friendly witnesses included Ronald Reagan, Robert Taylor, Gary Cooper, Jack Warner, Louis B. Mayer and Robert Montgomery. The most famous testimony involved the so-called Hollywood Ten, highly respected in their fields and including seven screenwriters, two directors, and a producer. All had agreed among themselves to exercise the Fifth Amendment, which was their right, in order to protest what they felt was an encroachment on their First Amendment rights to freedom of expression. They had prepared statements in their own defense but were not allowed to read them, and the televised hearings deteriorated into shouting matches, punctuated by the pounding gavel of committee chairman and House Republican J. Parnell Thomas. The courts and the committee did not agree, and all ten were held in contempt. Most served up to one year in jail.

Many Americans were deeply troubled by HUAC's actions. Television and radio coverage riveted the nation's attention during the 1954 Army–McCarthy hearings, where the committee's ruthless, unsubstantiated allegations were chillingly on display. Although McCarthy was discredited and censured by the Senate in December of that year after he failed to prove claims of Communist penetration of the U.S. Army, HUAC continued its relentless investigations into labor unions.

In April 1956, a HUAC subcommittee held a week of hearings in Los Angeles for the purpose of investigating Los Angeles Musicians Union Local 47 for infiltration by the Communist Party. During one week, some thirty-five to forty members of Local 47 were summoned for questioning. The tactics used were the same as were used against the Screen Writers Guild. HUAC wanted names. At least sixty alleged Communist Party members were added to the committee's list by "friendly" witnesses, including members of the symphony orchestras of Indianapolis, Saint Louis, Cleveland, Philadelphia, and Los Angeles. Symphony work was still a part-time career in the 1950s, and some musicians traveled to Los Angeles for studio work during the summer. "Unfriendly" witnesses, who were already under suspicion, had three options: (1) They could claim they were not and never had been members of the Communist Party; (2) they could admit or claim membership and then be forced to name other members; or (3) they could refuse to answer any questions and take the Fifth Amendment, just as the screenwriters had done in 1947.

The committee discovered several friendly witnesses. Three hundred people in the Los Angeles hearing room heard thirty-seven-year-old trumpet player and studio musician William Waddilove name twenty musicians as Communists or Communist sympathizers. Don Christlieb, a film studio bassoonist, named twenty more of his colleagues in the same fashion. He stated: "In 1941 many people were window-shopping for some kind of Socialist ideology. . . . I walked in and made a purchase. I bought merchandise which was unreturnable and too hot to handle. I hope I can return a small piece of it today." At the end of Christlieb's testimony, a committee member "asked that he be given a warm vote of thanks by the committee" (*Los Angeles Times*, April 20, 1956).

Albert Glasser, film composer, and his wife, Katherine Glasser, named more than two dozen Hollywood personalities, including musicians, who they said attended Communist meetings in their home during a six-month period in 1943. Glasser described how he and his wife had joined a Communist front group in 1943, quitting a few months later: "They told us we were smart kids and that we should help organize the musicians congress that was to be held later that year on the UCLA campus." He testified that he and his wife were skeptical about joining the party and signed their membership cards with their left hands to disguise their handwriting. "I'm darn glad this committee has called me in so I can clear my name and reputation," he said. Glasser thought American liberals were "needlessly frightened" of the Un-American Activities Committee" (*Citizen-News*, April 19, 1956).

Not everyone called by the committee was sympathetic or helpful to its cause. Open defiance and hostility were expressed by some, reminiscent of the Screen Writers Guild hearings. Edith Rapport, a pianist and teacher at the Los Angeles Conservatory, invoked the First and Fifth Amendments repeatedly. Five others invoked the Fifth Amendment as well. Cheers ensued after Thomas Walfrid Nelson said to the subcommittee, "I hope my appearance here will hasten the day when this committee will no longer be able to exist" (*Los Angeles Times,* April 21, 1956). Three "unfriendly" studio musicians who refused to testify were fired by Universal Studios and faced possible contempt-of-Congress charges based on their "irregular testimony," according to Republican Representative Gordon Scherer of Ohio (*Mirror-News,* April 20, 1956).

In 1956, the AFM and President Petrillo issued the following statement to the national membership in response to many inquiries it received concerning the HUAC hearings: "Although the West Coast hearings were completed the latter part of April, the HUAC Sub-Committee has not yet published its report. [HUAC follow-up requested from AFM; it was not available.] It appears that a certain 'hard core' of Hollywood and Los Angeles musicians failed in an effort 'to organize a worldwide protest to President Eisenhower' to stop the hearings." The British Musicians union informed the AFM that it had been contacted to assist in the protest, but that it was adopting a "hands-off policy." AFM president Petrillo responded: "If they are not Communists, they have nothing to worry about. If they are proved Communists they have good reason to worry because in addition to the position in which they have placed themselves with their own government, they will lose their membership in the AFM" (AFM review of the hearings as presented through the press, April 1956). Attached to Petrillo's statement was a collection of press reports of the Los Angeles hearings during the week of April 16–23, 1956.

> "This seems to us about the most shameful in the growing list of indignities occasioned by the McCarren Act and the paranoid policies of the State Department. It is bad enough that six men [apologies to Ms. Ruth Budd] have been done a grave personal injustice; it is worse that no practical remedy is available. . . . Incidents such as that of the Toronto six make it increasingly embarrassing for Americans to speak sneeringly of other countries' 'iron curtains.'" (*Nation,* June 14, 1952; see also Lewis, *Fiddling with Life*)

In an era of increasingly pervasive paranoia during the 1950s, McCarthyism knew no borders. A small group of symphony musicians in

Canada had experienced its consequences firsthand in 1952. In the spring
of that year, the Toronto Symphony Orchestra (TSO) was preparing for
a concert in Detroit, when the U.S. Immigration Service notified TSO
management of a problem. Six of the Canadian musicians in the orchestra were rejected for the standard visa applications, and it was ruled that
"their presence would be detrimental to the best interests of the country"
(Lewis, p. 16). The McCarren-Walter Act of 1952 enabled border officials to limit alien entry to the United States on the basis of an applicant's
political belief or *suspected* political belief, without supporting evidence.

At a board meeting following the visa rejections, the orchestra manager, Jack Elton, announced that six suspect musicians would be dismissed and new members would be hired. "For artistic reasons there
could be no substitutes for such an important concert, leading, as it
might, to other American engagements" (Lewis, p. 16). The Toronto
Symphony Orchestra master agreement under which the musicians
lived was no different from that of their American colleagues at the time.
Musicians were hired on a yearly basis, and although there did not seem
to be any musical reasons for their dismissals, the Toronto Musicians'
Association (Toronto Local 149) portrayed this as "a straight contractual matter. The Federation has always been keen on keeping contracts,
but there is nothing wrong in the orchestra's not rehiring musicians"
(Lewis, p. 17). Toronto Union president Walter J. Murdoch was friendly
with AFM International president James Petrillo and took seriously the
union's bylaw that urged the union to "purge its membership of all subversive elements" (Lewis, p. 24).

Steven Staryk (who would eventually become Chicago Symphony
concertmaster in 1963) was one of the six fired Canadian musicians. In
Thane Lewis's *Fiddling with Life: The Unusual Journey of Steven Staryk,*
Staryk describes how the lack of union support meant that the six were
on their own and could not afford to push their case too hard for fear
of being blacklisted in the United States as well. Ruth Budd, bass, was
another one of the "Symphony Six." Budd recalled nothing in her background that would alert the McCarthy crowd, but their brainwashing
worked. "I was tainted to the point that I overheard colleagues in the
dressing room saying, 'Oh, she must be a communist, she reads a lot'"
(*International Musician,* August 2003).

The musicians' appeal to the International Executive Board of the AFM was rejected, and they received no support from the Toronto Symphony's conductor, Sir Ernest MacMillan. (Musicians in a European orchestra faced a similar situation, with a different response from their management and conductor. In preparation for an American tour in the 1950s, some of the musicians of the Concertgebouw Orchestra of Amsterdam were denied visas. The tour was canceled.)

Realizing there was no support forthcoming from his union, Staryk tried to enlist help by contacting as many people as possible, writing petitions, attending meetings, and trying to bring the public's attention to the situation. But there was little response, even from the Royal Conservatory of Music, with which all of the six musicians had been connected. Ultimately, the American consulate in Toronto handed down its decision: Staryk was "barred for life" from entry into the United States (Lewis, p. 22). The hearings that led to this decision were a miniversion of the HUAC hearings, in which names, information, or anything else the twenty-year-old might have to offer were demanded. "I was the youngest of the six and I think he was hoping to get the list of all those 'reds under the beds' out of me. He couldn't understand that I had never been a member of any organization except the AFM and the public library, the two institutions I belonged to that required me to carry a card!" It was not until Staryk accepted the position of concertmaster with the Chicago Symphony Orchestra in 1963 that he entered the United States on a temporary visa, having been denied entry twelve years before by both the United States and Canada. He was unsure even then of the political climate and had to wait two years to be cleared by the orchestra before his long ordeal finally ended.

Postscript to the Era

On May 5, 2003, the U.S. Senate opened long-sealed transcripts of the closed-door hearings conducted by Senator McCarthy in 1953–54. FBI file 100-HQ-370562 describes the subject as "self-employed as a composer of music" and as reportedly linked to Communist front groups. Within six months Aaron Copland was classified as a Communist. Using informants, the government spent the next two decades monitoring his whereabouts, analyzing his comments, and taking note of his friends and associates. The file discloses that the FBI wanted to prosecute Copland for perjury and fraud for denying he was a Communist, and Director J. Edgar Hoover enlisted the CIA's help in monitoring the composer's travels. Suspicions about his politics caused his music to be removed from President Eisenhower's inaugural concert in 1953. He was called to testify on May 26, 1953, before a secret Senate investigations subcommittee. Others asked to testify at the secret hearings were writer Dashiell Hammett, poet Langston Hughes, and U.S. Army Colonel Chester T. Brown. During the two-hour hearing, Copland repeatedly denied affiliating knowingly with Communists. He said he signed many petitions in support of liberal causes, but that his involvement was superficial. "I spend my days writing symphonies, concertos, ballets and I am not a political thinker," Copland said at the hearing. In his memoirs he wrote: "I became a victim of a political situation. I tried to carry on as usual. But I lost a great deal of time and energy (not to mention lawyers' fees) preparing myself against fictitious charges." A December 1955 FBI memo stated there was "insufficient evidence to warrant prosecution" (*New York Times*, May 6, 2003; *Los Angeles Times*, May 20, 2003).

Five

Visionary Leaders and Progress
of the 1960s

The symphony field is the only field in which the lawyer does not represent the entire union, only some of its members. This situation is completely unique in labor history, and that's a critically important difference. The symphony members did not have the strength of the union behind them. Here was a group of rank-and-file who organized themselves, kept the movement alive, retained counsel, fought a three-front battle against the AFM, locals, and management . . . and lived to tell about it.

Labor lawyer I. Philip Sipser

*I*N MOST LOCAL NEGOTIATIONS, the players had felt they were not adequately represented by their union lawyer. With the exception of the Boston Symphony Orchestra, all orchestras were fighting for three basic union rights:

- Recognition of the players committee;
- Members' participation in negotiations; and
- Right of ratification of the master contract.

The American Federation of Musicians under James C. Petrillo had refused to grant these basic union rights to musicians and maintained control by giving local autonomy to individual union chapters. So long as they violated no federation bylaw, local leaders were not obliged to consult members when signing an agreement on their behalf.

Through ICSOM's efforts, symphony orchestra musicians won the right to hire legal counsel, an important issue in labor negotiations. That right did not come easily.

Before ICSOM asserted its collective power, AFM locals and orchestra managements had negotiated contracts without participation of musicians or their legal representatives; in some cases, orchestra boards even included union officers, creating an impossible conflict of interest. In spite of union objections, some orchestra musicians did hire their own lawyer.

In Chicago, where CSO musicians were barred from announcing or holding meetings in Orchestra Hall, attorney Lee Leibik became involved both with the orchestra players committee and with the burgeoning CMUD, the Chicago Musicians for Union Democracy. Unable to find another suitable place, Leibik offered his office for meetings with the musicians. According to those who worked with him, Leibik was extremely generous with his time and advice and proved an invaluable resource for the musicians. The CSO management never allowed him to sit in on negotiations.

Other orchestras had similar troubles, and most were floundering with unresponsive union representation. The first improvements in relationships between players and the union began at the local level, when—occasionally—the musicians were allowed to use outside legal representation.

George Zazofsky, Boston Symphony assistant concertmaster and the first formal ICSOM chair, urged his colleagues in 1962 to "consider retaining an outstanding attorney preferably stationed in New York to help coordinate our efforts and increase our overall effectiveness." It took several years for ICSOM to find a suitable lawyer. I. Philip Sipser, a blue-collar union lawyer representing iron, dock, and brewery workers, had

---

"If the word philharmonic means 'brotherhood,' the word symphony means 'in union.' If you don't have that, you don't have anything."

—George Zazofsky

never represented artists or professionals until he successfully mediated a contract negotiation for the New York Philharmonic. Zazofsky asked him if he would serve ICSOM for a trial period of six months. Sipser agreed, and at the end of the six months was officially hired in 1967 as ICSOM's first legal counsel. His appointment began an era of major consequence to many ICSOM orchestras.

Sipser had been fascinated with labor law from his early days of study in Brooklyn, New York. In the 1950s and '60s, he worked intensively on behalf of brewery workers, formulating a unique pension plan and negotiating the reduction of their work week from forty to thirty-five hours. The groundbreaking pension plan foreshadowed his later work with symphony orchestras. When his friend and colleague Leonard Boudin asked him to mediate a deadlocked labor disagreement for the New York Philharmonic, Sipser was surprised and intrigued by the request. Having no experience with cultural unions or as a mediator, he agreed to try for no fee.

After Sipser's successful experience as mediator with the Philharmonic, one of the orchestra's violinists, Ralph Mendelson, and Max Arons, the president of Local 802, presented him with a pen set inscribed "To the Heifetz of negotiators." His work with musicians became the source of his greatest challenges, his most dramatic achievements, and the most personal gratification. Sipser described the musicians union relationship with the symphony players as "unlike any other labor/union relationship that I know of." He called the musicians movement "a labor relations revolution among professionals." He also spoke fondly of the musicians he met over the years and identified closely with them.

In 1971 Sipser welcomed to his firm a new member who would immediately be swept into the musicians labor movement and ICSOM representation. Leonard Leibowitz started in March of that year as an associate attorney and became partner in 1973. In August 1985, Leibowitz left to start his own firm and became sole ICSOM counsel in the same year.

Like Sipser, Leibowitz had had no previous experience with cultural groups. Until he joined Sipser's firm, he had worked with Teamsters, auto workers, and hotel and restaurant workers. Leibowitz recalled: "As soon as I started with Sipser, my assignments included ICSOM, and I immediately joined him in Tanglewood, Massachusetts, for that summer's Boston Symphony negotiations. By the end of that summer he sent me to Dallas to do that symphony's negotiations by myself. Also that summer, he took me to Seattle for my first ICSOM conference, and I have been to every one since then."

Leibowitz remembers how hectic the schedule became when he and Sipser began getting involved with ICSOM orchestras' negotiations. "Elsewhere our acceptability [by the local unions] became such that in one year in the mid-to-late 1970s, I was actually doing thirteen orchestra negotiations in thirteen different cities at the same time! Ah yes, those were the days. I would find myself pounding on the table, shouting 'Pittsburgh doesn't deserve such a great orchestra, if this is all you can pay,' and the guy on the other side of the table would look at me and say, 'You may be right about that, but this is Detroit!'"

A significant transformation in the negotiating process was taking place. Gradually the two distinguished ICSOM lawyers and many other private lawyers were beginning to be allowed into negotiations along with the players' committees. According to Leibowitz, New York Local 802 president Max Arons said of Sipser and Leibowitz at an AFM convention, "I don't know why you local officers are complaining about them representing your orchestra. If they get a good settlement, I stand in front of the TV cameras and take credit for it. If it's not good, I blame them." Good relationships began to develop in the 1970s between the lawyers and the union local presidents, a major positive development after so many years of ill will.

In Cleveland, there was continuing conflict. The situation there exemplified the extreme hostility between the union and the symphony musicians; improvement came only over a decade of struggle. The lawsuits brought between the Cleveland Orchestra musicians and Cleveland Musicians Union Local 4 in 1961 had been eventually dismissed. The resulting agreement granted the orchestra a strike vote, requiring a 60 percent majority to rescind. This had given the orchestra musicians some voice in their own affairs, but it was not a mandate for ratification.

Kurt Loebel, violinist and committee chair, described the situation: "Unfortunately, the orchestra was divided between the aggressive, younger (I was in my thirties at the time) and the older musicians, some of whom were afraid to rock the boat." Before ICSOM had engaged Sipser's services, the Cleveland Orchestra musicians in 1967 hired lawyer Bernard Berkman, who had established a liberal reputation with other nonprofit organizations in the area. Local 4 was not ready to accept such a presumptuous tactic by the musicians. As had happened in Chicago with attorney Lee Leibik, Berkman was refused entry into negotiations and was not allowed to enter Severance Hall (home of the Cleveland Orchestra) or the union building when important meetings took place. In response, the committee refused to talk to management or to the union unless their lawyer was present. The musicians eventually decided to send their demands by mail.

The union continued to disregard the musicians' demands to allow the committee to be assisted in negotiations by legal counsel of their choice and proceeded to negotiate without committee participation. In the negotiation, Local 4 arbitrarily voted to change the 1961 bylaw regarding a strike vote, reducing the required 60 percent of the membership to a simple majority, without prior submittal to membership or even informing the musicians. On the basis of the new simple majority ruling, the union and management signed the contract.

In spite of the turmoil, they came up with a surprisingly tempting offer. For the first time in its history, the musicians of the Cleveland Orchestra obtained fringe benefits, including a minimal pension, paid vacation, health plan, grievance procedure, and some improvements in working conditions. However, on October 6, 1967, orchestra members filed suit in Common Pleas Court challenging the validity of the new contract. They asked to void the agreement, nullify the union's bylaw change, and set aside the vote. Due to disunity within the orchestra and subtle pressures put on some players, the number of litigants was reduced to forty-seven. It was not until two years later, in July 1969, that an out-of-court settlement was reached. The word *ratification* still did not appear in print, but the equivalent was finally achieved after years of bitter struggle.

The right to strike that had been unavailable to symphony musicians before the founding of ICSOM had become a powerful tool that the musicians now held in reserve. Festering frustrations, mistrust, and bad relationships between the unions and orchestra managements resulted in three strikes in 1966: the Philadelphia Orchestra, Indianapolis Symphony, and Los Angeles Philharmonic. Dr. Edward Arian, retired bassist with the Philadelphia Orchestra, wrote a comprehensive account of his orchestra's labor struggles in his book *Bach, Beethoven, and Bureaucracy.* A combination of factors had produced a steady deterioration of labor relations from 1963 to 1966, such that, according to Dr. Arian, "by the time negotiations were scheduled to begin for a new contract in 1966, the hardening of attitudes and accumulated hostility on both sides precluded anything but a bitter strike." It was the Philadelphia Orchestra's fourth strike since 1954.

The first strike in the history of the Cleveland Orchestra occurred in 1970. ICSOM's lawyer, Sipser, attempted to represent the musicians at the bargaining table, but Local 4's president, Anthony Granata, refused his participation, "because he represents ICSOM, and that is a dual union if I ever saw one." Local 4 instead asked Lester Asher, lawyer for the Chicago Federation of Musicians, to join in negotiations. After attempting to find a resolution, Asher was frank in his assessment of the conflict in Cleveland, telling the press that the Cleveland management "does not want a first-class symphony orchestra for Cleveland . . . On the basis of my hours of meetings I am left with the conviction that they have only contempt for the majority of the musicians they employ and little interest in the cultural interest of Cleveland."

By 1970, ICSOM had been in existence for eight years; but even its strength in numbers and moral support among the members had not alleviated the turmoil for their Cleveland colleagues. Following a decade of some of the worst union relations in orchestra labor history, the musicians voted 79 to 17 to strike. Issues under dispute ranged from salary, pension, and better working conditions to demands for a voice in choosing their own conductor. Some press reports said that the death of Music Director George Szell was the catalyst for the strike. For the Cleveland musicians after twenty-four years of his autocratic rule, it was the beginning of democracy.

The *Wall Street Journal* headline "Militant Musicians" reported the strike in Cleveland and pointed out that during the past four seasons seven U.S. orchestras had struck. The concerns raised by management

> ♪ The Cleveland Orchestra management sent the following warning to the Orchestra Committee on July 17, 1971: "You will have observed some musicians together deciding to grow beards, shave them off, and grow them again.... This clearly detracts from the professional standing of the individual musician and mars the dignity of the orchestra as a whole." Subsequently filing a formal grievance against the hirsute musicians, the management requested that the committee "supervise and police" their colleagues. The committee responded: "Dress is solely a reference to the uniform of the performing musician on stage . . . and we insist that you join us in drawing the line at such private matters as long hair and beards, and that the grievance will be dismissed by mutual agreement."

as quoted in the article typified management positions of the era: "Many orchestra administrators and a sizable number of critics and fans worry that the musicians' demands may lead to a long term decline in the quality of symphony orchestras. Traditionally, they point out, the American symphony has functioned under the nearly absolute authority of the conductor—and they fear that the undermining of this authority could lead to artistic disaster. 'The art of producing marvelous music is very different if it all comes out of a lawyer's contract,' says Amyas Ames, chairman of the New York Philharmonic Society." The article also quoted Michael Maxwell, general manager of the Cleveland Orchestra, who said of the demands by musicians, "The danger is that demands will swing to a degree of being completely unreasonable and will begin the immediate decline of the symphony orchestra as an institution." Maxwell continued to argue that the deficit, the end of the Ford Foundation funds, and the lack of a recording contract made it impossible to meet the musicians' demands.

Kurt Loebel was chairperson of the eight-member orchestra committee during the strike of 1970. In a formal statement released by the committee, he insisted Cleveland Orchestra musicians wanted only to keep up with the cost of living, achieve a dignified pension (which was less than two hundred dollars a month after forty-three years), job protection, and a voice in the selection of the music director. In 1974,

Leibowitz and Sipser returned to negotiate the Cleveland strike together. In 1978 and until recently, Leibowitz has done all negotiations without Sipser. Leibowitz describes how it evolved: "In Cleveland, Mike Scigliano [of Local 4], Granata's successor, and I had a great relationship, which spilled over to the orchestra and the committee, and Mike became their biggest fan." It was a long way from the years of acrimony.

Retired in 1997 after fifty years as Cleveland Orchestra violinist, Loebel recalls the tumultuous events of those years: "I was chairman of the committee when we had a bitter six-week strike. We lost that one because of disunity, eventually resulting in the organized betrayal behind our backs by a group of our colleagues, and the union's changing the voting rules overnight. The management had been totally inflexible and looked upon us as their workers. However, as a result of the 1970 strike, we finally succeeded in bringing in Lenny Leibowitz in subsequent negotiations (I. Philip Sipser had previously been rejected by management), who dealt with management in a less polite fashion and also knew how to deal with a succession of union officials who were semiliterate, under control of the management, and really not fighting in our interest." Loebel says that "little by little, between 1970 and 1997, the situation improved and the relationship between musicians, management, and the union (finally a union president who could think, read, and write), was a good one. I consider the present contract (1997) the best we ever had; but the many young and excellent players are totally unaware how all these goodies were achieved."

The Strike Fund

> I am glad to know that there is a system of labor where the laborer can strike if he wants to! I wish to God that such a system prevailed all over the world.
>
> *Abraham Lincoln, March 5, 1860*

The ability to strike and have a strike fund available, one of the long-sought goals since ICSOM's founding, was a crucial achievement of the 1960s. The establishment of the AFM Symphony and Opera Strike Fund was finally achieved in 1970 by a loan of $250,000 from the Federation. It provided fifty dollars per week in benefits for members of orchestras on strike through a thirty-five-dollar annual assessment per member. Later this fee was taken over by the locals. In 2001 the strike fund was worth more than $2 million and had disbursed more than $4.9 million to forty-four separate strike or lockout situations, according to the 2000–2001 ICSOM directory. ICSOM chairman George Zazofsky initially proposed the establishment of such a fund in 1967, and his successor as chair, Sam Denov, pursued the matter. Sipser negotiated the details with AFM president Herman Kenin. During the negotiations, the parties agreed that an effective strike fund was in fact a strong weapon at the bargaining table and would enable the musicians to more effectively fight for their future. Its existence assured the musicians of a small bit of security in case of work stoppage during a strike.

Union Affiliation

Be it resolved: That this convention of the AFM authorize and instruct the International President at the earliest possible date, to convene and preside over a conference of symphony orchestra representatives, which have been elected by the musicians of their respective orchestras, for the purpose of drafting legislation which will

1) establish a Symphonic Department within the Federation
2) grant the employees the right to organize an orchestra committee, to elect their own officers and to conduct their own affairs, subject to the proposed amended Bylaws of the Federation
3) grant the right to ratify, by secret ballot, the terms and conditions of their respective collective bargaining agreements

Symposium of Symphony Orchestra Delegates,
May 12, 1962

Although this resolution demonstrates that orchestra members of the AFM wanted to stay within or have some kind of relationship with the AFM even before ICSOM was officially established, not all musicians shared this majority view. So much dissension, bitterness, and hostility had formed between the locals and the musicians, it is no surprise that there was some talk within the newly formed ICSOM of leaving the union altogether. Furthermore, ICSOM's attempts to gain recognition from the AFM or even have meaningful discussions, as proposed in the pre-ICSOM symposium, had fallen on deaf ears. This added to members' frustrations with the union's leadership.

As the new legal counsel for ICSOM in 1967, Sipser faced several immediate challenges. His trade union background shaped his perspective of the issues. In spite of a healthy amount of disagreement and controversy among some of the representatives, Sipser felt it would be a disaster for a musician to seek work as a nonunion member. As he later explained, "The AFM called the affiliation 'the Sipser agreement,' because they did not want to acknowledge its [ICSOM's] existence until the very last minute. The idea of ICSOM becoming a division of the AFM came from my representation of the brewery division of the Teamsters. We had negotiated an affiliation agreement with the Teamsters, and I did the same thing here." In 1969 the AFM agreed to establish a Symphony Department, formally affiliating ICSOM with the organization.

The Contributory Pension Ends

The 1970 Minnesota Orchestra negotiations established a benchmark in the U.S. symphony orchestra world for pension contributions and distributions. The pensions (for all the ICSOM orchestras) were "terribly designed," according to Sipser. The Minnesota Orchestra revised the concept of the management of pension funds. The final agreement included a completely restructured pension plan by eliminating the employee contributions, which up until that time had been as high as 3 percent.

At the annual ICSOM conference in September 1970, Sipser had spoken to the delegates about pensions and fringe benefits, explaining how some pension funds were administered with less than maximum benefits to pensioners. He showed how to modernize ultraconservative actuarial assumptions and funding methods, resulting in substantially increased pension benefits without any increased cost to the management and without employee contributions. He further suggested the possibility of

Until the change brought about by the 1970 Minnesota Orchestra contract agreement, many U.S. symphony orchestras relied for their pension funds upon employee (orchestra members) contributions, supplemented by occasional special benefit concerts, for which the musicians
provided their services. Orchestral players received no Social Security in
the 1940s—participation in federal Social Security was voluntary for nonprofit employers; thus, they had no assurance of old-age security available
to employees in other industries. The Philadelphia Orchestra did not start
a successful pension plan until 1943, upon the initiative of the musicians.
The Orchestral Association contributed one hundred dollars per year per
member, and the musicians matched this. However, 80 percent of the
total income of the fund came from the musicians, who donated their services for recordings and performing in pension and children's concerts.
The Minneapolis Symphony pension fund concerts were established in
1940. It was not until 1962 that a contributory pension fund was formally
established for retirees, which was discontinued in 1970, as explained in
this chapter.

Many well-known entertainers and famous concert artists contributed their talents to the cause over the years. In Minneapolis, many popular performers such as Jack Benny, Danny Kaye, Oscar Levant, Morton
Gould, Henry Mancini, Peter Schickele, and Mitch Miller donated their
performance fees to the musicians retirement fund, while leaving the audiences and the musicians with warm memories. The comedian Jack Benny,
who liked to say that he would gladly have given up all he had achieved
through comedy to play the violin like Jascha Heifetz or Nathan Milstein,
performed credibly as violin soloist with many orchestras throughout the
country; he alone raised more than $4 million on behalf of pension and
general orchestra funds during his lifetime.

a refund of all employee contributions while retaining the same benefit
formula, asking management, "How do you want to pay it back, in one
lump sum, or over the length of the three-year contract?"

In Minneapolis, negotiating committee chair Carl Holub recalled
the unforgettable experience: "Phil [Sipser] called me in the middle of
the night. 'It's in the pension! We can solve it, it's in the pension!!!!' he

screamed. Peering over his half-glasses across the table during negotiations the next day, he said to the association actuary, 'You're a thief
of the worst kind, robbing from the old.'" During the 1970 Minnesota
Orchestra negotiations and subsequent one-week lockout, the union
lawyer for Minneapolis Local 73 reacted to Sipser's pension proposal:
"If you're successful, I'll give you the local!" Later Sipser was astounded
by this incredible comment, remarking, "As if the union local was his to
give away!!"

In most instances the sole pension fund was one in which only the
musicians were making the contributions. Sipser argued that any pension expert would agree with his proposal to eliminate employee contributions. The Minnesota Orchestra management brought in a lawyer
of their choice, Harry Blackmun (who was later appointed to the U.S.
Supreme Court). As a pension expert, Blackmun agreed that Sipser's
proposal would not adversely affect the pension. The Minnesota Orchestra's contributory pension plan was terminated in 1970, becoming
the first noncontributory pension plan in the industry, funded entirely
by the Orchestral Association. It was a major accomplishment and the
beginning of substantial increases in overall pension payments. Other
orchestras used Sipser's plan as a model in subsequent negotiations. As
a result of the change in the payment structure, one estimate holds that
$2 million to $3 million of pension contributions were returned to symphony orchestra players over the course of the 1970s. In Boston alone,
for example, there was a return in three years of more than $500,000.

The New WPA for the Arts

In the years following World War II, European governments lavished
precious reconstruction resources on cultural organizations, notably orchestras. In Germany, for example, the Berlin Philharmonic was one of
the first institutions up and running, even though the Philharmonie,
its concert hall home, had been destroyed in 1944. In May 1945, only
one month after the fall of Berlin, the orchestra resumed performing
in makeshift halls all over the divided city—including the cathedral,
Beethovenhalle, Admiralpalast, and Titaniapalast.

Rebuilding the war-shattered cities of Western Europe included al-locating money for cultural institutions such as orchestras and opera houses. By 1960, every small town in Germany had a state-funded or-chestra. In France, the federal government promised regional and civic authorities reimbursement toward musical revitalization. Public fund-ing for the arts in Britain began in 1946, coinciding with the founding of the Royal Philharmonic Orchestra. In 1959, the House of Commons held its first-ever debate on arts provision, urging a substantial increase in government support and proclaiming the importance of maintaining the nation's cultural heritage.

In the United States, no federal attention to the arts had survived the WPA (Works Progress Administration) era of the 1930s. Advocates of government arts subsidy had attempted as early as 1950 to establish such support. Representative Frank Thompson of New Jersey introduced sev-eral bills and held hearings to discuss the state of the arts nationally, and the AFM and the American Symphony Orchestra League contributed to the discussion, providing information on the symphonic sector. In 1962 the League conducted a survey of its members regarding federal support of the arts. The results revealed lukewarm interest, especially from many of the major orchestra associations. Federal government subsidy was the sticking point. The League's survey showed that the smaller semi- and nonprofessional orchestras favored it, whereas the larger orchestras were not ready to accept federal subsidy. They preferred the existing system of support, by which the generosity of relatively few individuals and corpo-rations kept the orchestras afloat. But from January of 1961 to November 1963, President John F. Kennedy, largely owing to the urging and per-suasiveness of his wife, Jacqueline, ushered in an unprecedented era of awareness and support of the arts as national treasures, no small factor in preparing the way for the establishment of the National Endowment for the Arts in 1965.

The White House Opens Its Doors to the Arts

I see little of more importance to the future of our country and our civilization than full recognition of the place of the artist. I

look forward to an America which will reward achievement in
the arts as we reward achievement in business or statecraft. I look
forward to an America which will steadily raise the standards of
artistic accomplishment and which will steadily enlarge cultural
opportunities for all of our citizens.

President John F. Kennedy, in remarks at
Amherst College, October 26, 1963

The Kennedys created a golden era for performing artists, from the 158
scholars and creative artists invited to the presidential inauguration to
the focus on the White House itself as a showcase for America's leaders in the performing arts. "[This is] the most extraordinary collection
of talent, of human knowledge, that has ever been gathered together
at the White House—with the possible exception of when Thomas
Jefferson dined alone," President Kennedy said to the forty-nine No-
bel Prize winners, including composers, scientists, authors, and artists,
who were guests of honor at a White House dinner on January 19, 1962.
"Concerts for Young People by Young People," chamber music concerts,
poetry readings, and jazz were among the diverse performances that
the Kennedys hosted. The Metropolitan Opera Studio, Jerome Robbins
Ballet, American Ballet Theatre, Interlochen Arts Academy, American
Shakespeare Festival, New York City Center Light Opera Company,
and Robert Joffrey Ballet were among the arts organizations that performed at the White House. The press coined the term "Kennedy Command Performance," a concept that made a lasting impression on that
generation. The White House hosted concerts by cellist Pablo Casals
and violinist Isaac Stern, among many others, opening the doors of the
White House to the nation and stimulating an interest in the arts that up
to that time had been untapped.

One of the most memorable White House concerts was Pablo Casals's
performance on November 13, 1961. The eighty-four-year-old cellist had
lived in self-imposed exile from his native Spain and had not appeared
in this country since 1938, because of the United States' recognition of
the Franco dictatorship that he despised. Casals had established resi-

dency in Puerto Rico; President Kennedy invited him to play for a state dinner honoring Puerto Rico's governor, Luis Muñoz Marín. Broadcast nationally by NBC and ABC radio and recorded by Columbia Records for commercial distribution, the Casals concert drew international press attention. "It is evident that the present first family has a proper appreciation of the relation of art to life," wrote critic and musicologist Paul Henry Lang in the *New York Herald Tribune* the day after the concert. The program included music of Mendelssohn and Schumann and a suite of five pieces by François Couperin. Casals chose as an encore his arrangement of a Catalan folk song that depicted his people's longing for freedom. He tearfully told the audience that "'The Song of the Birds,' to me, is the song of the exile."

It was inspiring to witness so many great artists recognized and honored by our President and the First Lady. Jacqueline Kennedy took an active role in selecting the artists and often personally invited them to perform. She also relied heavily on the advice of White House press secretary Pierre Salinger, who had been a child prodigy on the violin and helped suggest artists who might appear. "My main concern," she said, "was to present the best in the arts, not necessarily what was popular at the time."

When the National Endowment for the Arts was established in 1965, Isaac Stern was asked to serve on its council—in part, he would later write, "as a result of conversations that I had initiated with President Kennedy, Mrs. Kennedy, and Pierre Salinger." Stern was an early advocate of government aid for America's arts, and he broke cultural barriers in China and the former Soviet Union by visiting students, performing, and holding master classes. The Academy Award–winning 1980 film *From Mao to Mozart: Isaac Stern in China* is a testament to the path he forged.

The White House's attention to the performing arts was not wasted on the faithful. A congressional report had warned that Soviet propaganda portrayed Americans as "gum-chewing, insensitive, materialistic barbarians." Congressman (later Senator) Jacob Javits of New York spoke of "an enormous propaganda weapon which the Russians are using against us, with the most telling effect, all over the world," urging his colleagues on Capitol Hill to recognize the need for governmental support of the arts (Lebrecht, p. 137).

The National Endowment for the Arts

America has a long way to go before our musicians, performers, and creative artists are accorded the dignity and honor to which their contributions to American life entitles them.

Secretary of Labor Arthur Goldberg, January 1962

In February 1962 President Kennedy had appointed August Heckscher as the first White House cultural coordinator. When Heckscher resigned in June 1963, he reported the great need for a national arts foundation to provide grants to states and arts institutions. President Kennedy planned to appoint a special commission on the arts in late 1963. His assassination in November of that year prevented such an appointment. Partly as a memorial to Kennedy, congressional interest in developing arts legislation increased, and by 1965 the National Council on the Arts and Humanities was established. Violinist Isaac Stern continued to urge federal support for the arts after President Kennedy's death. Through his friend and lawyer Abe Fortas (not yet appointed to the Supreme Court), Stern pursued the idea with President Lyndon Johnson. According to Stern, the president admitted he knew little about the arts, yet realizing its importance, he pledged his support. "Isaac, I don't know from beans about the arts, but you and Abe tell me this is a very important thing to do, and so I think it's important, and I will back it. And I promise you I will keep my cotton-pickin' hands off it," Johnson said (Stern, p. 269).

After four years of deliberation, the U.S. Congress established the National Endowment for the Arts in 1965. Funding began at $7 million, rising to $167 million in three decades. Orchestras did not become a major beneficiary of NEA allocations until several years after its founding. Because of a prevailing conservative attitude among orchestra boards, they avoided government involvement in their affairs. They feared possible tax effects and governmental intrusion on local policy making and fundraising, over which they maintained control. But it became clear that they could not continue to depend solely on contributions from board members, or even their communities. The economic challenges they faced and the pressures brought forward from the musicians through the formation of ICSOM created, in no small measure, a wake-up call to the symphony world.

The New York Philharmonic initiated a meeting of presidents and managers of seventy-seven professional orchestras in 1969. Their most important action was to appoint Amyas Ames, then president of the New York Philharmonic, as chair of a five-person steering committee to secure funding specifically for symphony orchestras through the NEA. They decided to request the federal government, for the first time in American history, to help symphony orchestras meet their deficits. As a result of this meeting and the work of the steering committee, the Partnership for the Arts was announced in 1970, chaired by Ames. It embraced not just the symphony orchestra field but all the arts, and it encouraged full funding for the NEA.

According to a 1966 Ford Foundation press release, the twenty-five symphony orchestras with the largest budgets reported total income from their endowment in 1965–66 as approximately 7.7 percent of their total budgets. Earned income had barely increased 4 percent since 1961, while annual expenditures had increased more than 6 percent, with a consistently widening gap between balanced books and rising costs.

In 1972, the arts were eligible to receive $30 million, and full federal funding would have been $200 million a year, or only $1 per person in the United States. "The time has come when everyone who cares for the arts should write to the members of the House Appropriations Committee to ask for *full funding* . . . for the National Endowment for the Arts," Ames was quoted as saying in the April 1971 edition of *Senza Sordino*. In the same newsletter, ICSOM chairman Ralph Mendelson urged all musicians to lobby, write, and call members of the House Appropriations Committee to request their support for Partnership for the Arts. In 1971–72 the total amount needed for all American orchestras turned out to be about $13 million. Ames made the comparison that the $13 million was "just about half the cost of one modern traffic circle."

NEA orchestra grants began with $33,575 in 1966. Three years later the amount had dropped to $21,250. The dramatic increase in 1970, due in large part to the efforts of Partnership for the Arts, allocated $931,600 that year. In 1971, $3,761,031 was awarded on the premise of raising additional sums on a matching basis. That year, a Manifesto for the Arts, cosigned by Jacob Javits (R-N.Y.) and John Brademas (D-Ind.), was entered into the Congressional Record.

ꕤ *Manifesto for the Arts*

(Read into the Record of the U.S. Senate by Senator Jacob Javits, Tuesday, October 19, 1971, and of the U.S. House of Representatives by Representative John Brademas, Thursday, December 2, 1971, and appearing in the Congressional Record of the first session of the Ninety-second Congress.)

The standard of living in this country cannot be measured by dollars alone—nor in miles of concrete highways and numbers of automobiles, nor by the gross national product. More important than these material or statistical factors are the values we cherish and the way we live. Deep in every community, in every family, is a hunger for what enriches life, and this force demands more services than it is getting from arts organizations—from museums, orchestras, opera, ballet and street theaters—wants more community activity in the arts, more teaching of it in the schools. We have not yet dramatized our interest in the arts as we do in sports, but they are estimated to be a $2 billion interest of the American people. Over 600 million people visit museums each year; over 12 million go to symphony concerts, and millions more attend opera, ballet, and other performances. Lincoln Center outsells Yankee Stadium by 3 to 1. The arts beat sports in the public interest of this country by 2 to 1.

In a country that is increasing its demands for public service and educational activity from the art organizations, government should share in paying for such services and beyond this, since art organizations cannot continue to raise ticket prices without excluding the public, government should help as it does with education. We should do for the arts and humanities in the 1970s what we did for the sciences in the 1940s and 1950s. The arts are an essential part of our common heritage and must be given a wholly new precedence that will bring them into wide use in our educational system and make possible new activity in our communities and in our homes. As a nation we must accord to the arts a place of honor.

Greater Government Support Mandatory

Fortunately, the principle of government support for the arts is now established in legislation for the National Endowment for the Arts, supported by the President and the Congress and funded at $29,750,000 million. This is almost double what we had before, and we are grateful for it. But it is only one and one-half per cent of the $2 billion that the American people spend each year on the arts and by the cruel logic of that fraction cannot succeed in materially helping. The simple truth is that the present legislation for the National Endowment for the Arts is not adequate for a nation of 200 million.

So we ask for new legislation embodying a new national program for the arts designed to help pay for the public service and educational work of the arts. To be effective we submit that federal aid for the arts must be equal to at least 10 per cent of what the American people spend on them, so this new legislation should provide no less than $200 million for the National Endowment for the Arts. $200 million is equal to only $1 per person in the United States (present legislation provides 15 cents) compared to $1.40 spent in Canada, $2.42 in West Germany, $2.00 in Sweden and $2.00 in Austria. It is only one per cent of what we spend on roads each year, the cost of about 15 miles of superhighway, but it is needed to sustain the arts.

We strongly endorse the National Endowment for the Arts as the practical and sound approach for federal support. The legislation should provide that federal support go through the National Endowment to qualified art activities on the condition that they have broadly based support, are of good quality, well managed, and perform an educational or public service for the community. The amount of support should give consideration to the overall costs of the arts rather than to special activities, because it is the overall costs of the well managed art group that determines its ability to serve the community, and it is these total costs

continued on next page

continued from previous page

that are affected by inflation. Also, the legislation should provide funds to support the State Arts Councils and for new and experimental programs designated by the National Endowment for the Arts.

The time has come to drive for the goal that really matters. All those who care for the arts, for the humanities, for education should make a direct request to their Congressmen, to the Senators and to the President for new legislation. What we ask is not the subsidy so common in Europe, for under this proposed legislation federal aid for the arts would average only 10 per cent—to be meaningful it must be at least that—leaving 90 per cent to be paid for from ticket sales and other earnings and from the support of individuals, corporations and local governments.

What we ask is modest, when measured in terms of other federal projects. Above all, what we ask for is a wholly new precedence for the arts and humanities—for that which gives our living richness and meaning.

NEA funding gradually increased after 1971 and reached a peak of $10,175,000 in 1990, at which time it decreased and remained at an average of $8 million until a major reorganization in the 1990s. The amounts distributed to symphony orchestras for the first thirty years of the NEA's existence were as follows:

1966	$33,575	1977	$8,620,950	1988	$9,228,500
1967	$10,000	1978	$8,605,180	1989	$9,255,000
1968	$25,000	1979	$9,181,180	1990	$10,175,000
1969	$21,250	1980	$9,200,550	1991	$8,838,000
1970	$931,600	1981	$9,946,187	1992	$9,336,000
1971	$3,761,031	1982	$8,875,335	1993	$7,911,600
1972	$5,307,259	1983	$7,619,000	1994	$7,567,300
1973	$4,760,085	1984	$9,454,000	1995	$7,771,800
1974	$7,173,444	1985	$9,315,500	1996	$3,835,000
1975	$7,279,669	1986	$8,943,700		
1976	$8,645,979	1987	$9,118,700		

In 1997 the NEA was reorganized after congressional budget cuts. Separate allocations for programs such as orchestras ceased to exist. "Our funding now is organized by function," says Court Burns, NEA music specialist. "Creativity, Organizational Capacity, Arts Learning, Access, and Heritage/Preservation—organizations may apply in any of those categories. Tracking the funding of orchestras after 1997 is now more difficult, [but] it is more than likely that the total is slightly higher [than before 1997]."

1997	$3,881,553
1998	$3,574,500
1999	$3,650,500
2000	$3,089,500
2001	$2,529,500

Even taking into consideration the NEA's reorganization, and even without accounting for inflation, the NEA's $2,529,500 allocated for orchestras in 2001 was lower than it had been thirty years earlier.

In 1974, ICSOM musicians took an active role in politics by writing letters to many senators and representatives, urging them to introduce a bill making a provision on the income tax form for every citizen to check off an automatic, deductible contribution to the arts. A Harris Poll taken in 1974 found that 64 percent of the adult public would be willing to pay an additional five dollars in taxes if the money were directed toward arts and culture.

I. Philip Sipser, ICSOM counsel emeritus, wrote to the *New York Times* on February 8, 2001: "The fact is that members of ICSOM did engage in fund-raising by writing letters to every Congressman and Senator, urging them to introduce a bill making a provision on the income tax form for every citizen to check off an automatic deductible contribution to the arts. In fact, Representative Fred Richmond (D-NY) filed such a legislation 25 years ago. It was the belief of the members of ICSOM that fund-raising was too important to leave to management only."

In a later interview, Sipser elaborated on this point: "Unlike most workers in labor/union relationships, workers in the arts are intensely interested in their work product, its criticism and public reception. Classically, the trade union stance is, 'We do our work, and it's your job to find the money.' This effort at involvement in fund-raising is an example of greater musician participation. The musicians merely want their opinions taken into serious consideration; they want input, not determination."

Congressman Richmond, a former chairman of the board of Carnegie Hall, New York City, had a long-standing concern for the arts. The 1975 ICSOM conference was the first professional artistic organization to which he made an appeal for support of the bill. In July of that year he filed the legislation, HR 8274: "To provide an opportunity to individuals to make financial contributions, in connection with the payment of their Federal income tax, for the advancement of the arts and humanities." Two years later, in October 1977, the bill had seventy-nine cosponsors in the House, but it did not yet have the full support of the National Endowment for the Arts and the American Symphony Orchestra League. Ultimately, the legislation failed.

The Ford Foundation Symphony Program

> The financial condition of most American orchestras contrasts sharply with their rich artistic quality. As a result, orchestra players are underpaid and too many must work at other, often nonmusical, jobs for most of their income. This, in turn, tends to discourage talented young people from undertaking professional symphonic careers. The fact that orchestras—the oldest and best-supported of our noncommercial institutions in the performing arts—are in great need dramatizes the plight of other artistic institutions. This program, therefore, highlights the massive requirements of all of the arts in our society.
>
> *Sigmund Koch, director, Humanities and Arts,*
> *Ford Foundation. Ford Foundation press release,*
> *July 9, 1966*

Until the establishment of the NEA in 1965, U.S. governmental support of the arts had not existed (with the exception of the WPA projects of the Franklin D. Roosevelt administrations). Before the NEA, the Ford

Foundation program was the most comprehensive philanthropic activity in the arts in either the private or the public sector.

Established as a nonprofit organization in 1936 by Henry and Edsel Ford, the foundation extended a helping hand to worthy causes in need of support. Before it became a national organization in 1950, the Ford Foundation had made grants in the 1930s and '40s to organizations of all types, almost entirely to charitable and educational institutions in Michigan, home of the Ford Motor Company.

Since 1951 the Ford Foundation had received numerous applications from symphony orchestras for some sort of aid. In 1957, the foundation established a program in humanities and the arts and began studying the place of the symphony orchestra in American culture. In the absence of any government program, the foundation carried out an unofficial national inquiry into the situation of artists in various fields, which led to the conclusion that there was an economic crisis in the arts.

A precedent-setting request from the Detroit Symphony in 1964 for a major contribution to its endowment campaign prompted a great deal of deliberation at the foundation and resulted in a decision that the foundation would further explore the entire national symphonic field. By the mid-1960s, the musical world had begun to acknowledge that orchestras of high artistic quality were not limited to the so-called Big Five (the principal orchestras of New York, Boston, Philadelphia, Chicago, and Cleveland). The founding of ICSOM in 1962, and musicians' increasing demands for year-round employment, including basic benefits, compounded the challenges that all orchestral associations faced. In addition to serving as artistic leaders in their communities, orchestras provided necessary resources to ballet and opera companies, choral groups, and such educational activities as school concerts, private lessons, coaching, and youth orchestras. How could they provide these services at a time when they did not have sizable, stable endowments?

W. McNeil Lowry was the guiding light of the Ford Foundation's Symphony Program, established in 1966, as a result of the 1964–65 study. He had been named director of the Foundation's Humanities and Arts Program in 1957 and in 1964 became Vice President for Humanities and the Arts. Under Lowry's guidance, a grant of $105,000 in 1957 had enabled the New York City Opera to present a season of American operas, and another of $210,000 that same year to symphony orchestras across the country went toward the commissioning of eighteen new symphonic compositions. Not only was Lowry a dynamic force in establishing the Symphony Program, he also helped make the Ford Foundation America's largest nongovernmental arts patron and the first foundation to support dance. Determined on success, Lowry provided a visionary, hands-on approach with far-reaching consequences. He later recalled that "the Symphony program did years of staff work between that time of the grants in 1966. That Program was in front of the Board three times, and only in the last time in the form of actual grants, because it took a hell of a lot of shaping, and we kept the Board with us all the way through."

The Ford Foundation created its Symphony Program with the following three objectives:

To improve artistic quality by making it possible to devote more of the musicians' energies to orchestral performance;

To strengthen orchestras and enable them to increase audiences, extend their seasons, and diversify their services; and

To raise the income and prestige of the music profession, thus making it more attractive to talented young people.

In its news release of July 6, 1966, the foundation recognized "the devotion and self-sacrifice of players, who have received less than a dignified wage for their talents. The present movement to upgrade the economic status of the orchestra musicians is important, not only for the players concerned, but for the health and quality of artistic activity throughout the U.S."

After interviewing hundreds of representatives from twenty-five major, thirty-three metropolitan, and nine "near-metropolitan" U.S. orchestras, the Ford Foundation recommended sixty-one orchestras for grants, asking many of them to submit ten-year plans. Foundation trustees voted to establish an unprecedented $80.2 million matching-grant endowment plan, to be distributed in varying amounts to the sixty-one orchestras, which ranged in size from the Toledo Orchestra all the way up to the major orchestras of the nation's largest cities. The foundation emphasized that the scale of its grants had nothing to do with any rank-

Symphony Orchestra Program

Endowment Matching Requirement	Matching Achieved at 6/30/71	Share of Endowment Trust	Grants Without Matching Requirement	Endowment Matching Requirement	Matching Achieved at 6/30/71	Share of Endowment Trust	Grants Without Matching Requirement
$4,000,000				**$600,000**			
Boston	$4,133,721	$2,000,000	$500,000	Birmingham	$ 682,858	$ 600,000	$200,000
Chicago	4,025,429	2,000,000	500,000	Oklahoma City	599,982	600,000	150,000
Cleveland	6,540,427	2,000,000	500,000	Phoenix	666,656	600,000	250,000
Los Angeles	4,000,000	2,000,000	500,000	**$500,000**			
Minnesota	7,924,814	2,000,000	500,000	Columbus	597,804	500,000	100,000
Philadelphia	4,132,421	2,000,000	500,000	Florida	523,832	500,000	100,000
$3,000,000				Kalamazoo	758,850	500,000	100,000
Cincinnati	3,000,000	2,000,000	500,000	Louisville	556,898	500,000	200,000
National (D.C.)	3,114,054	2,000,000	500,000	Nashville	506,658	500,000	200,000
Pittsburgh	3,000,000	2,000,000	500,000	New Haven	606,728	500,000	100,000
San Francisco	4,124,855	2,000,000	500,000	New Jersey	517,370	500,000	150,000
$2,000,000				Richmond	500,508	500,000	150,000
Dallas	2,036,808	2,000,000	500,000	Sacramento	538,039	500,000	200,000
Detroit	1,960,916	1,000,000(a)	500,000	San Diego	531,816	500,000	100,000
Houston	2,022,582	2,000,000	500,000	Toledo	510,091	500,000	150,000
Indiana	2,347,885	2,000,000	500,000	Tulsa	561,037	500,000	100,000
New York	2,001,252	1,000,000(a)	500,000	Wichita	608,620	500,000	150,000
St. Louis	2,000,475	2,000,000	500,000	**$400,000**			
$1,000,000				Memphis	404,822	400,000	100,000
American (N.Y.)	0(b)	1,000,000	500,000	Omaha	486,012	400,000	100,000
Atlanta	1,017,763	1,000,000	750,000	**$350,000**			
Baltimore	1,008,489	1,000,000	750,000	Festival (N.Y.)	0(c)	350,000	75,000
Buffalo	1,009,373	1,000,000	750,000	Little Orchestra (N.Y.)	81,309(b)	350,000	75,000
Denver	1,002,657	1,000,000	750,000	Rhode Island	354,708	350,000	150,000
Hartford	1,003,664	1,000,000	350,000	Shreveport	397,520	350,000	75,000
Kansas City	132,092(b)	1,000,000	750,000	**$250,000**			
Milwaukee	1,239,232	1,000,000	250,000	Brooklyn	77,866(b)	250,000	75,000
New Orleans	1,073,667	1,000,000	750,000	Fort Wayne	250,000	250,000	75,000
Oakland	1,000,808	1,000,000	350,000	Hudson Valley	250,778	250,000	75,000
Oregon	1,074,655	1,000,000	250,000	Jacksonville	264,343	250,000	75,000
Rochester	1,009,641	1,000,000	750,000	Puerto Rico	no trust participation		375,000
San Antonio	1,068,418	1,000,000	750,000	Total: 76,750,000	84,405,376	58,750,000	21,450,000
Seattle	1,109,354	1,000,000	750,000				
Utah	1,053,832	1,000,000	500,000				
$750,000							
Honolulu	781,741	750,000	350,000				
North Carolina	843,171	750,000	250,000				
Syracuse	776,075	750,000	250,000				

(a) Supplements previous Foundation grant.
(b) Dropped from participation in the endowment trust fund as of 6/30/71.
(c) Discontinued operations in 1969 and dropped from participation in the endowment trust fund.

1966 ten-year, $80.2 million Ford Foundation Symphony Program (Reprinted with permission from the Ford Foundation letter of February 1, 1973).

ing, artistic or otherwise, of the grantee orchestras. (See the above table for grant amounts.) The point was to raise the tide for all boats. To receive the endowment grants, each orchestra had five years to double or match the amount offered in the grant. Three-quarters of the overall program funds went to this two-to-one matching grant. All but a handful of the orchestras succeeded in reaching that goal. The endowment program used up three-quarters of the program's funds. The rest was doled out to twenty-five orchestras in yearly individual grants. These expendable funds were earmarked as "developmental." They could be directly applied to operations and did not require matching.

Lowry was quoted in the May 1966 issue of *Monthly Labor Review* as saying: "The Ford Foundation grants, growing local subsidies, and the establishment of the principle of federal support attest to the gradual emergence of the American symphony orchestra from its own economic 'Dark Ages.' Negotiations this year may provide additional benefits to a significant number of symphony orchestra musicians outside the Big Five, thus continuing to transform players from seasonal laborers, often migrants in the musical vineyards, to year-round professionals."

In a Ford Foundation oral history interview, Lowry was asked to respond to critics who charged that the $80 million Symphony Program in effect would only raise the union contract rates. His reply was direct and unequivocal: "The criticism was ill-founded. The demands of the union musicians and the inflation of the costs of performers in all branches of the performing arts, but particularly in orchestras, [were] there. The average wage of symphony orchestra musicians in the year in which we made the grant equaled the average wage of secondary school teachers only in seven cities of the United States, and most orchestra players were moonlighting to beat hell. Finally, the press release itself and all statements by the Ford Foundation listed seven objectives of the [Program] and said that major orchestras were moving closer and closer toward the longest possible season . . . 42, 44, 46, finally 52, . . . weeks a year. Therefore the Program would help not only in the number of services given to orchestra musicians, but it would help also in the exposure of symphonic music to the public, and in different kinds of performances, for young people, and so on. It specifically stated that the money given by the Ford Foundation was not designed to intervene in union strikes or union demands because, except for $29 million of it that was spread over five years of expendable funds for those 61 orchestras, the rest had to go for an endowment. They all had matching terms, most of them in our favor; and everybody could figure what would happen if the unions tried to gobble up that money, because they couldn't touch it" (Lowry, p. 533).

By the 1965–66 season, most orchestra musicians had gained the right to ratify their master agreements. That year, no fewer than sixteen major orchestras were renegotiating their contracts. The players committees arrived at the negotiating tables armed with the master agreements of at least ten comparable orchestras, enabling them to compare salaries and working conditions at a glance. Yet, through the ICSOM network, musicians had heard rumors of the pending Ford Foundation grants. They wanted full disclosure and did not want to continue discussions until they were accurately informed of the dollar amounts that would become available from the new endowment program.

In a letter to the Ford Foundation, Helen Thompson, executive vice president of the American Symphony Orchestra League, expressed concerns over a growing crisis. In 1966, at least sixteen of the major orchestras were renegotiating their contracts. Many musicians of the League's member orchestras felt they lacked information about the dollar amounts that the foundation's endowment program would award and how the awards would affect their orchestra's financial structure. The League took no position on this matter, according to Mrs. Thompson, except to offer assistance to facilitate or assist the foundation and to inform it of "a situation that is becoming more crucial day by day" (letter, April 15, 1966). At the same time, the orchestra managers, in many cases, had not finalized plans with the foundation and could not make any commitments to the musicians.

Edward F. D'Arms, associate director of the Ford Foundation's Symphony Program, pointed out that "if all the income from the endowment funds were applied exclusively to the annual salaries of the players in major orchestras, the average increase would amount to approximately $1,050, thus bringing their total salary to $7,600, which is hardly an inflated salary for one of the most gifted groups in our society. In 1965–65 the five top orchestras paid their players an average of $9,200, the remaining 20 major orchestras paid an average of $4,300, and 27 of the largest metropolitan orchestras paid an average of less than $1,200. Even disregarding the hardships which these salaries made inevitable for the present generation of symphony players, economic reward such as these would not succeed in attracting a younger generation to take their places" (*Senza Sordino*, December 1966).

The Ford Foundation Symphony Program moved full steam ahead. A year and a half after the creation of the program, music critic Donal Henahan reported that most orchestras were already spending the Ford Foundation grant money, although most were still struggling to raise the matching funds: "According to orchestra managers, musicians' pay has been going up steeply, sometimes directly as a result of the Ford offer. Seasons have been lengthened. Administrative staffs, operating budgets, costs in general have climbed. Musical standards, especially in smaller orchestras, have begun to rise" (*New York Times*, January 10, 1968).

"I cannot overstate the importance of these grants," recalled Richard

Cisek, president of the Minnesota Orchestral Association from 1978 to 1990. "It had a major, incalculable impact on orchestras. Because at the time of these grants, only Cleveland and Chicago had decent endowments. We [in Minnesota] asked for a five-to-one matching grant from Ford and were one of the first to achieve our goal. And, of course, remember that $2 million in 1966 dollars was close to $20 million thirty-five years later. We also hired two financial consultants to advise in the fund management."

July 5, 1966, Press Release
Minneapolis Symphony Letterhead

Minnesota Orchestral Association President's Comments On Ford Foundation Grant

Upon learning of the announcement of the Ford Foundation's Symphony Orchestra Program and the two and one-half million dollar share allocated to the Minneapolis Symphony Orchestra, Judson Bemis, president of the Minnesota Orchestral Association, stated:

> "The Ford Foundation announcement by reason both of its size and of its coverage has tremendous implications for symphonic music and symphony orchestras everywhere. With 61 orchestras across the nation sharing $80.2 million, it is inevitable that total orchestra resources, both in terms of dollars and artistic skills and abilities, will be substantially raised for years to come. This is an exciting day for those who love fine music everywhere.
>
> "Naturally, the Minnesota Orchestral Association is deeply grateful, proud and pleased to be among those receiving the largest grants. While even this large sum of money will not solve in itself our financial problems here as projected for the next decade, the Ford grant provides a tremendously important first step towards such a solution. The grant will call for two important responses from this community, one to meet not only the letter but the spirit of the challenge grant; the second to continue the annual guaranty fund at current levels."

ICSOM members saw at this historic time the opportunity to further their cause. The December 1966 issue of *Senza Sordino* exhorted players to get involved: "In order for the orchestral musician to gain the most advantage from these grants it is still necessary, as before, to show a united front to the management, and to ask for the reasonable economic position which everyone (and now the Ford Foundation, too) is willing to agree the musicians deserve." According to a Ford Foundation report published in 1973, the news was positive indeed. Of the sixty-one orchestras that received endowment shares, fifty-five succeeded in meeting or surpassing the matching requirements. Only four orchestras did not meet the requirement, and a fifth discontinued operations in 1969. Its shares were allocated among the fifty-five other orchestras. The total matching goal was $76,750,000; the orchestras that met the terms topped the goal by raising $84,405,376. According to National Arts Stabilization (NAS), an independent nonprofit arts management group founded in 1983 by the Ford, the Andrew Mellon, and the Rockefeller Foundations, at the end of the Symphony Program in 1976 the total infusion of funds exceeded $200 million, and orchestras met the program goals of raising and matching funds, although the balance sheets of the majority of participating orchestras did not show positive working capital. (By the end of the ten-year grant period there was no follow-up available from the Ford Foundation. The author was told it was not unusual for the foundation to move on to the next project immediately without an assessment.)

With this tremendous financial boost as a result of the grants, orchestra managers realized the importance of managing their money. They established fund-raising departments and hired financial experts. The Ford Foundation also encouraged the orchestras "to seek professional advice to devise comprehensive, long-range investment plans for making the most of their endowment funds" (Ford Foundation letter February 1, 1973; Special Report: "Symphonic Strains"). The Philadelphia Orchestra aggressively raised $4 million within four years in matching grants, and went on to raise a further $10 million. They also hired a professional consulting firm to manage the funds raised. Among other things, the firm urged that the association broaden its community representation by adding twelve new directors to its board, because the orchestra "belongs to the people of Philadelphia and . . . the new Directors should represent the community" (Arian, p. 58).

Next to the establishment of ICSOM, the Symphony Program was the best thing to happen to symphony musicians in the twentieth century. Clearly, the Ford Foundation sought to raise musicians' standard of living and to protect and develop their artistic product. And as W. McNeil Lowry observed in 1973, "That so many of the orchestras met the challenge and went beyond it represents a remarkable achievement."

The 1960s was a decade of immense national tragedies and triumphs. Response to these events was expressed in countless ways, including books, poetry, and visual and performing arts. The Ford Foundation recognized the arts, arts education, and symphony orchestras as the basis for a civilized society. The National Endowment for the Arts continued this philosophy until the 1980s, when the arts became a target of political conservatives, and NEA funding itself was questioned. The convening forces of an arts-conscious White House, the visionary people of the Ford Foundation and the National Endowment for the Arts, and ICSOM's acceptance by management and union sparked a public acknowledgment and support of the role of the arts in the United States, and in particular, of the symphony orchestra. Together they made history.

Six

Segregated Musicians Union Locals, 1941–1974

"We were investigated three times by Congress. Some senators would say to me, 'You are bragging about a great democratic union. Why do you have two locals in many cities and especially here in Washington, D.C.?' The AFM had by far more segregated locals than any international or national union. So you can see, the spotlight was on us. Merged locals must live together. All must work at it very hard, so as time goes on no one will say, 'Do you want to employ a black or a white man?' It will be, 'How many men do you want to contract for?'"

James Petrillo, in a speech to the
1971 AFM convention

 HE FIRST LOCAL for black musicians received its charter in Chicago in 1902. An 1896 U.S. Supreme Court decision had established the legality of separate but equal facilities on racial grounds, setting the precedent not only for schools and other societal institutions but also for the membership of the American Federation of Musicians. Of the original fifty black American musician union locals, the majority were in the South, although most large Northern cities also established segregated locals—Boston, New Haven and Bridgeport, Connecticut, Chicago, Saint Louis, Atlantic City, and Seattle among them. In 1941, when the AFM abolished subsidiary status and granted autonomy to the locals, the black locals elected their own representatives as delegates to the national AFM convention.

Under union segregation, the black musicians received some protection. The Federation ruled that its black members came under the
jurisdiction of the black local, no matter what type of engagement they
played. For example, if black musicians performed in a white club, the
black local had to enforce the wage and working conditions of the white
local, a rule meant to ensure equal pay. The Federation also ruled that if
a black musician were denied admission to a local, he or she could join
the nearest local that would accept the musician and should receive all
the privileges of membership of that local.

Racial segregation continued in the American Federation of Musicians for fifty-one years. The first merger of black and white locals took
place in 1953 in Los Angeles.

Serena Williams, current secretary and historian of Local 47 in Los
Angeles, periodically reprints an article about the amalgamation of Locals 47 and 767. In the pre–civil rights era of the early 1950s, the successful merger was extraordinary. Black and white musicians worked
determinedly together to accomplish this courageous step.

A graduate student and professional singer, Estelle Edson, doing research in the late 1950s for her academic thesis, "The Negro in Radio,"
not surprisingly found that there were few blacks working in the broadcast industry in any capacity. Marl Young became acquainted with Edson
while attending UCLA. "Because I was a musician, she felt that I would
have some insight as to the role of the black musician in the broadcast
industry. As far as I knew, there were no blacks working regularly in the
industry, especially on the networks—ABC, CBS and NBC. She asked
me if the fact that the Musicians Unions were segregated contributed
to the scarcity of blacks in the industry." According to Young, "with the
exception of New York and Detroit," the Musicians Union locals were
segregated throughout the United States, and all contracts in the Los
Angeles and Hollywood broadcast and motion picture studios were negotiated by the all-white union, Local 47. In the rare instance that a black
musician got a studio call, the corresponding black Local 767 adopted
the scales negotiated by Local 47.

Groups of black and white musicians had been meeting in private
homes to discuss the problems of the segregated unions. Ms. Edson suggested that they bring the matter to the officers of Local 767 to discuss the

issue publicly. Amalgamation efforts began in earnest by an interracial group of musicians, as Local 767 elected officers determined to bring their concerns to Local 47. Paramount among the problems of incoming Local 767 members were life memberships, seniority, and death benefit insurance. Enlisting the help of the Los Angeles NAACP, Local 47's Musicians for Amalgamation set about an arduous publicity campaign to get their message out to the members of both locals. Young wrote: "An October 1952 *Overture* article asked Local 47 members to accept the merger proposal presented to the Local 47 Board meeting of May 13, 1952. The article outlined the many advantages of having all of the musicians of the Los Angeles area gathered in one organization. Finally, in a hard hitting article titled 'MUSICIANS OF LOCAL 47, AMALGAMATION WITH LOCAL 767 WILL NOT COST YOU ONE CENT,' the committee pointed out that immediately upon amalgamation 600 Local 767 members would start paying dues and taxes (now called work dues) into the treasury of Local 47. This letter also dealt with the philosophical factors of wiping out segregation and living up to our stated (but not yet realized) American traditions. These musicians also published pamphlets, held unofficial discussion meetings with prominent speakers, and, in short, conducted a proud, professional campaign. Without this dedication on the part of our white brothers and sisters of Local 47, *THERE WOULD HAVE BEEN NO AMALGAMATION*, at least not at that time. On April 1, 1953, Local 47 started accepting Local 767 members as part of the membership of Local 47 and segregation was forever banished from the Musicians' Union structure in the Los Angeles area."

Rewarded with votes of approval from both, they approached the final step of working out details with the AFM's International Executive Board. On June 25, 1953, the two officially became one unified Los Angeles Musicians Local 47, with the recording secretary entering into the record that "all of the assets, real and personal and wheresoever situate, of Local 767, have been transferred to Local 47" (Young, "The Amalgamation of Locals 47 and 767").

The following year brought the Supreme Court ruling to end segregation in public schools, the beginning of a decade of struggle that produced the 1964 Civil Rights Act banning discrimination based on color, race, national origin, religion, or gender. At the 1957 AFM Convention,

Local 47 submitted Resolution number 34, calling for the AFM to take immediate steps to integrate all locals.

Not all black locals were eager for the immediate end to union segregation, however. Not only did many of them have more financial stability than their white counterparts, they also feared that a merger would reduce the numbers and effectiveness of their representatives in national union affairs. Sixty delegates signed a petition opposing forced integration "because of the financial aspect involved with some of the larger colored locals, who have spent many years of hard work to attain their present status in the Federation. . . . [A] merger should not be forced upon us, but accomplished by mutual agreement between parties concerned." Resolution number 34 was defeated.

In a 1957 *New York Times* interview, James C. Petrillo had voiced his concerns about forced integration. He made clear that he personally opposed segregation, but that he was even more strongly opposed to compelling locals to integrate: "The smaller locals would be swallowed up by the larger white locals." In 1964, two years after his defeat as president of Chicago Local 10, he was named head of the AFM's newly created Civil Rights Department. Although Petrillo had publicly stated his opposition to enforced integration, the AFL-CIO had passed a unanimous resolution that all locals must merge, and Petrillo was charged with enforcing that action within the AFM.

In the Chicago local, the newly elected leaders who had replaced Petrillo realized the tremendous challenges they faced. They took steps to merge Local 10, which was exclusively white, with Chicago's black union, Local 208. (Local 10 had 11,000 members, and Local 208 had 1,300.)

In order for the AFM to take control of the local after Petrillo's defeat, Local 10 was placed in trusteeship under the pretext that it was still segregated. Newly elected Local 10 Vice President Nashan explained Petrillo's advancement to the union's civil rights position: "When we took office in January of 1963, sixteen members of Local 208 came to us to apply for membership. We were put into receivership by the AFM for raiding another local's membership. We were automatically out of office, and a receiver was appointed, President Hal Davis of Pittsburgh's Local 60/471. He and I headed a merger group to work out a plan. James Mack, a flutist, headed the sixteen who had applied to Local 10 from Local 208.

When a plan was agreed upon, the new AFM president, Herman Kenin, appointed Petrillo president emeritus to implement the merger of all the remaining locals in some sixty cities that still had separate but equal locals for black and white musicians."

There was division among the black Local 208 as well. On March 21, 1963, one hundred members of Local 208 went to Musicians Hall to join Local 10. A committee, Chicago Musicians for Harmonious Integration, was formed to push for the merger. According to the *Chicago Defender* of March 23–30, 1963, "The move by Negro musicians in joining the previously all-white Local 10 of the Chicago Federation of Musicians left a 'sour' note with high ranking officials of the Local 208. Vice-president Charles Egar angrily stated that he and others 'are not in favor of the move.' Those in favor of the merger argued 'Besides paying lower quarterly dues rate—$4 instead of $6, the Negro musicians feel that they will now have more opportunities to land high-paying jobs.'" After several years of such quarreling, the two Chicago locals finally merged on January 11, 1966, thirteen years after the Los Angeles Local 47/767 merger. A decade of the amalgamation of musicians locals followed.

Across the country, black representation seemed to be swallowed by the mergers, just as the black locals had feared. Representation went from a high of seventy-three black delegates to the AFM when locals were segregated to a low of ten black delegates in 1974.

Despite civil rights legislation, pleas for integration by great political leaders, and the merger and integration of unions, segregation was entrenched in all aspects of U.S. society. The nation's symphony orchestras reflected this state of affairs. In 1958, the Urban League of New York charged racial discrimination by a wide range of established groups, from the New York Philharmonic and the Metropolitan Opera Orchestra to the three major television and radio networks.

Few opportunities existed for any person of color with talent and the desire to play in a symphony orchestra. Conductors and managers displayed little interest in encouraging or accepting such a person. Sanford Allen, the only black member of the New York Philharmonic, was hired in 1962, and in a *New York Times* article five years later, he decried "the unfortunate conditions that have kept Negroes from the field of classical music" (Seltzer, p. 117), including the lack of role models on stage, the segregation of local unions, and the closed audition process. At that time, the conductor still controlled all hiring and firing of musicians.

In 1957, the Cleveland Orchestra's music director, George Szell, always exceptional among conductors, fearlessly hired a black musician, Donald White, a cellist from Richmond, Indiana. The press noted the appointment. White immediately had problems joining the "right" segregated local in the city so that he could play in the orchestra. In Birmingham, Alabama, in 1961, while on tour in the South, Cleveland Orchestra musicians and their conductor refused to perform without White when they were told that a city ordinance required segregation onstage as well as in the audience. The orchestra manager informed the mayor of Birmingham that there would be no concert without Mr. White; the performance proceeded without further discussion.

In the early 1960s, a number of soloists, conductors, and orchestra musicians joined in the civil rights movement by refusing to perform for segregated audiences. Among them were pianists Gary Graffman and Leon Fleisher, violinist Jaime Laredo, and conductors Leonard Bernstein and Erich Leinsdorf. Some orchestras declined bookings where audiences were segregated. In October 1963, the Minnesota (then, the Minneapolis Symphony) Orchestral Association, in response to the orchestra committee's recommendation, adopted a policy of refusing to perform for segregated audiences. The issue required immediate attention, as the orchestra was about to embark on a tour of Southern states, at the height of the civil rights movement.

In his memoir *Fiddle and Fight*, former Saint Louis Symphony Orchestra bassist Russell Brodine wrote about integration issues and the Saint Louis orchestra's history of white male membership. "There were no African-American musicians in the Saint Louis Symphony and none of the great singers such as Roland Hayes and Paul Robeson soloed with the orchestra. Finally after World War II and the death of the most obstinate bigot on the Symphony Board, that bar was dropped. The merger of the two locals of St. Louis occurred and in 1968 several African-American musicians joined the Symphony" (p. 112).

The complex issue of the education, training, and hiring of musicians— including instrumentalists, singers, conductors, and composers—of minority groups has been the focus of many individuals and institutions during the past four decades. Although I cannot address the whole story and the many important concerns raised in this chapter, ICSOM members can take pride in the fact that their conference has played an active role in creating a work environment that extends equal treatment and fair employment practices to every professional musician, as well as an education environment that encourages musicians of all races to strive for a place in the symphony orchestra world.

As documented in *Forty Years of the International Conference of Symphony and Opera Musicians,* compiled by Tom Hall and published in 2002, ICSOM actively supported the annual AFM Congress of Strings and, until the discontinuation of the program, had provided scholarships named for two former ICSOM chairmen, George Zazofsky and Ralph Mendelson, as well as additional scholarships for minority group musicians. In addition, ICSOM has provided a great deal of support to the Music Assistance Fund Orchestral Fellowships (MAFOF) program over the years.

The Music Assistance Fund (MAF) began in 1965 as an independent charitable trust. Administered at first by the New York Philharmonic, and later by the American Symphony Orchestra League, MAF included an apprenticeship program that provided orchestral experience and union scale for talented minority musicians for a period of one year as they auditioned for orchestra jobs. ICSOM became actively involved in 1976 when the MAFOF apprenticeship program, "designed to provide talented minority-group musicians with professional experience that could lead to professional careers," was established (Hall, p. 58).

By the late 1960s, the beginnings of integration were evident among the orchestras of Minneapolis, Baltimore, Syracuse, Denver, Quebec, North Carolina, Richmond, Milwaukee, St. Louis, New York, Cleveland, and Pittsburgh, but concerned people in the orchestra field knew that they had a great deal of work to accomplish. By 1979 the statistics had climbed to forty-nine black musicians in twenty-eight major orchestras. Recently, the League and the Sphinx Competition, a program that provides support for African American and Latino music students, have joined forces to administer the work of the MAF. Through it all, ICSOM has continued to support this urgently needed program and in 2003 provided $500 scholarships to each of the nine semifinalists in the senior division of the Sphinx competition.

♪ *Mergers/Amalgamations of Segregated Musician Union Locals*

CITY/COMMUNITY	DATE	LOCAL NUMBERS
San Francisco	March/May 1960	6 and 669 merge to become 6
Denver	June/July 1960	20 and 623 merge to become 20
Sioux City	July 19602	54 and 743 become 254
Danville, Va., Greensboro, N.C., and Winston-Salem, N.C.	August 1960	112, 332, and 534 become 332
Kitchener and Waterloo, Ont.	April 1961	226 and 544 become 226
Sidney and Piqua, Ohio	March 1963	801 and 576 merged
Cairo, Ill., and Paducah, Ky.	November 1964	563 and 200 merged
Waupaca and Stevens Point, Wis.	December 1964	629 and 213 merged
Parkersburg, W.Va.	March 1965	185 and 259 merged
San Antonio	March 1965	658 and 23 merged
Dallas	June 1965	168 and 147 merged
Pensacola	June 1965	548 and 283 merged
Oklahoma City	November 1965	703 and 375 merged
Chicago	February 1966	10 and 208 merged
New Haven	March 1966	486 and 234 merged
Pittsburgh	March 1966	471 and 60 merged
Houston	March 1966	699 and 65 merged
Milwaukee	March 1966	587 and 8 merged
Springfield, Ill.	March 1966	675 and 19 merged
Washington, D.C.	September 1967	161 and 710 merged
Beacon and Poughkeepsie	December 1967	559 and 238 merged
Topeka, Kansas	December 1967	36 and 665 merged
Lexington, Ky.	December 1967	554 and 635 merged
Atlanta, Ga.	February 1968	462 and 148 merged
Louisville, Ky.	March 1968	11 and 637 merged
Mobile, Ala.	May 1968	407 and 613 merged

Montgomery, Ala.	May 1968	479 and 718 merged
Bridgeport, Conn.	August 1968	549 and 63 merged
Savannah, Ga.	August 1968	447 and 704 merged
Wilmington, Del.	December 1968	641 and 311 merged
Birmingham, Ala.	December 1968	733 and 256 merged
Youngstown, Ohio	January 1969	86 and 242 merged
Salamanca and Olean, N.Y.	February 1969	614 and 115 become 115-614
Buffalo	March 1969	43 and 533 become 92
New Orleans	January 1970	174 and 496 merged
Westfield and Springfield, Mass.	January 1970	91 and 171 merged
Toledo	February 1970	15 and 286 become 15-286
Naugatuck and Waterbury, Conn.	Spring 1970	445 and 186 become 186
Boston	May 1970	9 and 935 become 9-535
Kansas City	April 1970	34 and 627 become 34-627
Mohawk Valley, N.Y.	January 1, 1971	51 and 383 become 51
Dayton, Ohio	January 1, 1971	101 and 473 become 101-473
St. Louis	January 1, 1971	2 and 197 become 2-197

Although in September 1971 the AFM issued a statement that "there no longer are any local unions of the A. F. of M. segregated because of race," mergers continued for several more years. Among them were the locals in Framingham and Marlboro, Massachusetts, in 1972, Charlotte, North Carolina, and Rock Hill, South Carolina, in 1973, Providence, Rhode Island, and Attleboro, Massachusetts, in 1976, and Wallace and Coeur D'Alene, Idaho, in March of 1976.

(Source: AFM files)

Seven

Women's Issues

I do not like, and never will, the association of men and women in orchestras and other instrumental combinations . . . As a member of the orchestra once said to me, "If she is attractive I can't play with her and if she is not I won't."

Sir Thomas Beecham

$\mathcal{S}$IR HENRY WOOD, conductor of the London Queen's Hall Orchestra, and a near-contemporary of Sir Thomas, claimed to be the first conductor to admit women into a professional orchestra. In a 1913 letter to the *Times* of London, the famed British composer Ethel Smyth (named Dame Ethel in 1922), whose compositions included the suffragette anthem "The March of the Women," complimented Wood, while decrying the ingrained sexism that characterized the music world at the time:

Sir, Will you allow me to point out the significance of a new departure inaugurated, after years of striving, by Sir Henry Wood—namely, the inclusion of women in a first-class orchestra. To begin with, the mere fact of belonging to certain bands enables a player to ask a good fee for lessons, and as it is mainly by teaching that orchestral musicians earn a livelihood, it is easy to gauge the importance to women of admission within the pale—a privilege till now restricted, for some mysterious reason, to harpists. But another point seems, to me, more interesting.

Hitherto, after leaving the musical college, in which perhaps she led the band or played a wind instrument, a girl found herself

cut off from all connection with music, except through teaching.
The effect of this isolation on the music soul can be imagined. An
orchestral player will grumble at the grind of rehearsals and so on,
but meanwhile he is immersed in the stream, taking new ideas,
acquiring new technique, and equipping himself automatically
for the exercise of any special gift he may happen to possess. . . .
People often ask, where are the great women composers? I wonder
how many great male composers there would be if men had been
completely shut out from the workaday world of art, deprived of
the bracing, the concentration, the comradeship: the inestimable
training and stimulus of professional life.

It may be that time must elapse before we see the fruits of the
movement of which Sir Henry's splendid achievement is a symp-
tom; but judging by the portents in science, literature and other
branches of art, see them we shall someday.

I am, Sir, your obedient servant,
Ethel Smyth, Mus. Doc.

As Ethel Smyth pointed out, sexist attitudes existed in many professions. The consensus in Western society, that women did not incline toward making careers a high priority in their lives, sprang from the widespread belief that women possessed both physical and psychological limits
to their capabilities. From the early nineteenth century until the 1960s,
with symphony orchestra membership strictly controlled by invitation of
the conductor or manager, few women had the opportunity even to audition for a position in a major orchestra in the United States and Canada.

At the beginning of the twentieth century, America's new orchestras resembled those of Europe, composed predominantly of central-
European male musicians. With few exceptions, conductors chose female
musicians for their orchestras only if male musicians were not available to fill the positions. The conductor controlled the auditions, which
he usually held in private, only occasionally including the orchestra's personnel manager or a section leader. Having no obligation to offer equal
employment opportunities to anyone, the conductor maintained autocratic hiring practices. If the conductor did not have someone specific in
mind, the personnel manager might invite players he knew, or ask teach-

ers for recommendations. If a conductor *chose* to hire a woman, he had the right to do so in spite of grumbling and remarks among the men.

As Smyth pointed out to the London press in her letter, "for some mysterious reason" conductors sometimes found it acceptable to hire female harpists. In 1891, the Symphony Society of New York, which later merged with the New York Philharmonic, had a regular female harpist on its roster. In 1903, the Minneapolis Symphony hired harpist Loretta Dellone as its only female member. The Philadelphia Orchestra hired harpist Edna Phillips in 1930. (Many generations later in Europe, another harpist, Anna Lelkes, broke the men-only barrier in 1971, when she was hired by the Vienna Philharmonic—but not as a full member of the orchestra until 1998.)

Harpists aside, most women found it difficult, if not impossible, to join the ranks of major orchestras. On the other hand, the musicians unions welcomed them. As early as 1903, the American Federation of Labor required that the musicians union not discriminate against women. (Contrast this attitude to the situation of black musicians, discussed in the previous chapter, who remained in segregated musicians locals from 1902 until the first merger with the Los Angeles white local in 1953.) Gradually, American and Canadian musicians throughout North America came under the jurisdiction of the American Federation of Musicians, which accepted women into its ranks.

By 1917 all café, hotel, restaurant, movie theater, dance hall, and theater orchestras were unionized, providing employment for both male and female musicians. All major American symphony orchestras also were unionized at this time (with the exception of the Boston Symphony, which resisted until 1942). In the late 1920s and early 1930s, however, it was indeed unusual to see a woman in a major orchestra, let alone in a principal position; only a few were hired in that era. Conductor Otto Klemperer named twenty-year-old Ellen Stone principal horn of the Pittsburgh Symphony in 1937, and in the late 1930s another principal horn, Helen Enser, was hired by the New Orleans Symphony. In the 1930s, a small number of women were hired for section string positions by the orchestras of Baltimore, San Francisco, and Cleveland.

Twenty years after its founding with a female harpist on its roster, the Minneapolis Symphony Orchestra hired another woman. In 1923, violinist Jenny Cullen followed her teacher and mentor Henri Verbrugghen to the United States when he became the Minneapolis Symphony's music director, a position he held until 1931. A native of Glasgow, Cullen had served in Australia as concertmaster of the Sydney Symphony (established in 1915), where Verbrugghen, a Belgian, had conducted the orchestra and founded a music school in New South Wales.

The Minneapolis press gave Cullen rave reviews for her playing, characterizing her tone as "not in the least feminine, quite the opposite in

---

Women have always been accepted in, and perhaps even formed the backbone of, amateur and semiprofessional orchestras in the United States. Usually offering part-time work and paying "per-service," rather than on a seasonal basis, such orchestras play important roles in the lives of their communities. Rehearsals are usually held in the evenings or on weekends to accommodate the schedules of the musicians, male and female, who are employed in a wide range of full-time jobs and professions outside the music field. The numbers of women in such smaller-budget orchestras have always been higher than in the major orchestras, averaging between 42 percent and 46 percent, and the women have not encountered the kind of gender discrimination that kept them out of major symphony orchestras for so many decades.

In 1984, musicians of the regional orchestras—who define themselves as those with budgets lower than the so-called majors—found they needed to network among themselves to address their own problems and issues, just as the major orchestras had done in 1962 when ICSOM was formed. Established as a communication organization for regional orchestras, the Regional Orchestra Players' Association, or ROPA, came into being in 1984. Nathan Kahn, now a negotiator for the AFM Symphonic Services Division, has described in private correspondence how it came about:

"When I left the Tulsa Philharmonic for the Nashville Symphony in 1981, I found that the musicians of the Nashville Symphony were encountering many of the same problems that existed in Tulsa. That is, we were truly on our own in our attempts to negotiate and administrate our contracts. Our orchestras were growing and evolving. The formation of core orchestras in Tulsa, Nashville, and many other regional orchestras was presenting very unique and complicated problems for the musicians. Management fact." Jealousy and rumor abounded among her male colleagues, who suspected her of having an affair with the boss. Some of them feared that Verbrugghen would replace them with Cullen and the two other musicians the conductor had brought with him from Australia. The musicians union even raised the possibility of pulling all the union members from the orchestra in protest of the foreign musicians. Verbrugghen ignored the protests from all quarters and continued to offer Cullen solos that

often used core orchestras to divide and conquer the musicians. Although we sought advice and help on these and many concerns, our locals were ill-equipped to answer our many questions. ICSOM had very little if any experience in addressing concerns of per-service and core orchestra musicians. We had no orchestra network among ourselves, so communication among like orchestras was sporadic at best. I asked former ICSOM Chairperson Brad Buckley why ICSOM could not start a subgroup for regional orchestras, so that we could discuss our unique problems among ourselves. Brad replied that ICSOM's current membership requirements would render most regional orchestras ineligible for ICSOM membership. Brad said that what was needed was for the regional orchestras to form their own organization.

With that, I sent a letter to the orchestra committee chairs of thirty-plus Regional Orchestras (as defined at that time by the American Symphony Orchestra League) proposing the formation of a Regional Orchestra Players' Association. This letter got the attention of Lew Waldeck, newly appointed director of the AFM Symphony Department. Lew organized the first meeting of the Regional Orchestra Players' Association in Columbus, Ohio, in 1984. Thirteen regional orchestra representatives attended this meeting at their own expense and later became the charter members of ROPA. I was elected president, and following this conference, we started a newsletter, wrote ROPA bylaws, and in general, began to become more educated about how to conduct our business, through communication amongst the member orchestras, and with the AFM Symphony Department. ROPA celebrated its twentieth Conference in Memphis, in August 2003. In the same year, ROPA consists of sixty-three member orchestras, who have budgets ranging from $816,000 to approximately $12,000,000."

normally would have gone to the concertmaster. She remained within
the violin section, replacing no one. Cullen played in the Minneapolis
Symphony through Verbrugghen's tenure and those of his successors,
Eugene Ormandy and Dimitri Mitropoulos. She retired in 1949, an honored member of the community.

Leopold Stokowski was another famous conductor who was willing
to hire the best player, even if she also happened to be a woman (he
had already named Edna Phillips as principal harpist in 1930). In the
mid-1930s he appointed Elsa Hilger to a position in the cello section
of the Philadelphia Orchestra. Czech by birth, she and two sisters had
formed the Hilger Trio, moved to America in 1920, and played concerts throughout the country. In the 1930s they moved permanently to
a twenty-five-acre New Jersey estate.

Elsa became acquainted with Olga Samaroff, a well-known pianist
and musicologist, and the wife of Maestro Stokowski. Samaroff called
Hilger one day in 1935, urging her to come to Philadelphia as soon as
she could: the principal cello position in her husband's orchestra had
opened up. Hilger auditioned for the conductor in great secrecy—she
was, after all, not a harpist. She played solos for Stokowski for two hours,
and then she had to play for the Philadelphia musicians union, a typical
practice for some local unions in the days before audition procedures.

Stokowski was convinced. He hired Hilger for a position in the cello section, but did not name her to the principal position. "He probably thought
it was enough of a novelty to have me in at all," she remarked later. "I did
not realize at the time that Stokowski and I were making history. It was not
until my being chosen for the orchestra was written about in the newspapers that I realized the full extent of this move. I really did not think much
about it, it was just natural." Subsequently, the Philadelphia Orchestra's
next conductor, Eugene Ormandy, appointed Hilger to assistant principal
cello, and she played many solos throughout her career. Despite her many
performances and fine reviews by colleagues, conductors, soloists, and the
press, Hilger never acquired the first chair position. "I would have been
principal, but my pants weren't long enough," she said.

From 1941 to 1949 Helen Kotas was principal horn of the Chicago
Symphony. Ms. Kotas-Hirsch later described her experience as the first

female principal player in the Chicago Symphony: "I was treated marvelously by everyone. I had no problems with anyone. I had a wonderful relationship with conductor Bruno Walter, who often was guest conductor." She continued: "My audition consisted of sitting on stage with the conductor of the Chicago Symphony Orchestra, Frederick Stock (1905 to 1942), reading the sixth horn part to Richard Strauss's *Also sprach Zarathustra*. The personnel manager, Walter Hancock, was within earshot, overheard my playing, and shouted, 'Hire her!'"

In the spring of 1938, 150 female members of Musicians Local 802 of New York met together to discuss their mutual problems. Although not a great deal resulted from that New York meeting, it represented an opportunity to recognize that female musicians faced much greater difficulties than their male colleagues in being hired in all aspects of musical employment.

This changed in the early 1940s, when World War II took men from their professions faster than the vacancies could be filled. In their places, women flew airplanes, towed targets, worked capably in factories and defense-related positions—and filled men's chairs in major American orchestras.

In most cases, the hiring of women was seen as only a temporary wartime solution. At war's end, many of these women were expected to give up their jobs to returning soldiers. Not all of them did so, and their stories open a window on a generation of women who changed American society by securing a place for themselves in the workplace, the newsroom, and the battlefield—and on the concert stage. The press noted the presence of women on stage as a novelty, but a few enlightened conductors chose to hire a few highly qualified women for permanent positions.

An October 1944 article by Dorothy Riley in the *Minneapolis Sunday Tribune* noted the presence of four women in the Minneapolis Symphony. "Two of the players are symphony wives," Riley wrote, adding that "one of them wants to return to her role as housewife as soon as the war is over, and that the engagement with the symphony is definitely a wartime measure." Riley goes on to say that conductor "Eugene Ormandy has put his stamp of approval on women in the orchestra; he believes women have a definite place in a symphony orchestra."

Behind the scenes in the 1930s, Steffy Goldner Ormandy, a professional harpist, had told her friend Marie Euler Carlson how she had combined preparing for a solo engagement with the Minneapolis Symphony
Orchestra with her duties as the maestro's wife. "When she would say to
him," reported Mrs. Carlson, " 'Eugene, can ve not eat out tonight,' he would
look sad and say, 'umum—can't you just boil a pair of frankfurters'—but of
course she could not do it, she had to fry a little meat, make the asparagus
soup, and open a grapefruit, and of course that took time—so I guess it
was not too easy to be a cook, harpist, society lady, and wife of such a tem-
permental [sic]conductor" (memoirs of Mrs. Marie Euler Carlson, Minnesota Orchestra Archives). Mrs. Ormandy performed as soloist with the
Minneapolis Symphony Orchestra in the 1931–1932 season in the Mozart
Concerto for Flute and Harp—a break, apparently, from housekeeping,
socializing, and caring for her demanding husband.

In 1944 the Boston Symphony Orchestra held a fund-raising meeting
attended mostly by women. Music critic Alan Rich reported that the
orchestra's president announced that if not enough money was raised,
the orchestra would have to reduce the number of players and length of
its season and "lower its standards" by hiring female players. A collective
gasp emanated from the group. A year later, Ann C. De Guichard joined
the BSO as its first female bassoonist; there is no evidence that the BSO's
standards dipped noticeably as a result of the experience.

Eight years later, in October 1952, the same orchestra provoked this
headline in the *Boston Herald:*

Woman Crashes Boston Symphony

The *Herald's* music critic, Rudolph Elie, reacted stiffly to the naming of
Doriot Anthony Dwyer as principal flute by writing that "the breaking of
a tradition considerably older than the mere 72 years of the BSO seems
to me a very serious matter, and I am not a little dismayed by it."

Dwyer accepted all the attention with equanimity. Thirty years later,
in an interview in *Symphony* magazine, she recalled: "I was thrilled to be
in Boston, playing with this orchestra. And I felt freed really, because it
is a wonderful thing to play first flute, and it was something I had always

wanted to do." She recalled how she approached the auditions, knowing that a woman's opportunities were limited: "I always signed an application 'Miss,' so there would be no misunderstanding about my unusual name, Doriot. My teacher called conductor Charles Munch and recommended me to audition. 'We'll have ladies day,'" the conductor reportedly quipped to her teacher.

Undaunted, Dwyer played for two hours for Munch, for concertmaster Richard Burgin, and for Georges Laurent, the retiring principal flute. Munch was impressed but had not yet made a final decision. "Two weeks later he asked me back to re-audition, but I said I could not risk my job with the Los Angeles Philharmonic as second flute. They even offered to pay my way, but I said I would rather have one secure job than two possibilities." Munch then offered the job to a Swiss flutist, but the musicians union would not allow it, insisting there were equally qualified American candidates. Munch accepted their decision and requested Dwyer for the principal flute position. "The union supported me because of my capabilities—gender was not an issue for them, and I appreciated it very much. I was treated marvelously by everyone, and even was offered help and support. Of course, there was no women's dressing room, so the men offered me a very small room of my own." Dwyer remained in her position as principal for thirty-eight years, until 1990, when she retired.

"I'm Never Going to Hire Any More Women"

By 1948, 109 women had gained membership in the major orchestras of Baltimore, Chicago, Cincinnati, Cleveland, Detroit, Indianapolis, Los Angeles, Minneapolis, New York, Philadelphia, Pittsburgh, Rochester, Saint Louis, and San Francisco. Not all conductors were happy with the growing numbers of women being hired. According to a personnel manager who related the following story to the author, a certain conductor told a female violinist in 1954 that he would hear her audition for his major orchestra only if her husband auditioned well enough to secure his position. The "package deal" meant that the conductor would consider her husband before her, and if they *both* played well, then he might hire them—which he eventually did.

In the first half of twentieth-century America, it was common for neither men *nor* women to have dressing room facilities. As salaries, benefits and working conditions improved in the mid-1960s, new concert halls were built, and old buildings were renovated to properly accommodate both men and women. In the 1970s, when female musicians would frequently find no dressing facilities on tours throughout the country, a women's dressing room was finally built in Boston Symphony Hall.

The "dressing facilities" provided for the Chicago Symphony (mostly male) musicians in the 1950s were typical: a space in the basement of Orchestra Hall, next to the elevator that raised and lowered the piano and other stage equipment to and from the stage. Trumpeter Rudy Nashan recalls that "it was a dungeon, and there was only a men's room. The assistant harpist, the lone woman, used the backstage dressing rooms, or changed behind her instrument case. Our bathroom consisted of an entrance up three steps into a room; on the left was a wash bowl, followed by an inclined trough running the length of that wall into a pipe going down into the floor. The floor of our bathroom had several sewer covers, which gave forth an odiferous, if unmusical, odor! Fungi were our forte, and smoke permeated all nooks and crannies."

Another common example of "dressing room" conditions came to light when Kurt Loebel, violinist with the Cleveland Orchestra for fifty years, wrote a letter to the *Ann Arbor News* in response to an April 2002 article on the renovation of Hill Auditorium. Loebel recalled that he had performed with the orchestra in that hall twenty-one times under conductors George Szell, Lorin Maazel, Pierre Boulez, and Christoph von Dohnyani. "I wonder," Loebel asked the *News*, "whether anyone involved in the planning for the renovation has looked at the basement, where we [musicians] got dressed and had to find a place for our instrument cases, which held old, priceless instruments . . . [Y]ear to year [as] new modern buildings [were] going up on campus, the filth in the basement remained. Chunks of loose plaster, old rusty pipes, and inches of dust to step into when we changed our socks. Our trunks were so close together that we had to wait for the person next to you to get dressed before you could open your own trunk. I can't help mentioning this to you, since it is symptomatic in the arts world for the powers that be to be infected with an Edifice Complex, investing millions for buildings, but not for the needs of the people who create the Arts."

The principal conductor of the Minneapolis Symphony, Antal Doráti, hired two women in 1953. One of them was a violinist, Gloria Burkhart, who had won the "Miss Minnesota" competition, and the other a harpist, Joan Mainzer. A male harpist had preceded Mainzer, and she recalled that "Doráti hired four different harpists in five seasons, so changing his mind was par for the course."

In 1955, Eileen Lockwood wrote a *Minneapolis Tribune* article that typified the attitudes of the era. Carrying the headline "Symphony Has a Feminine Theme, Too," the article published eight photos, identifying the women, as was customary at the time, as "Miss" or "Mrs." Among Lockwood's observations: "The masculine strain, while dominant, has its feminine accompaniment in the Minneapolis Symphony Orchestra. . . . One of the two unmarried women in the symphony, Miss Mainzer played piano as a child. . . . It takes a little longer to discern Betty Anderson and Jane Tetzlaff among the sea of cellos. Like the four married symphony women, both have musician husbands."

In 1953, Doráti told a newly hired Minneapolis Symphony bassoonist, Martin Beckerman, "Don't count on your wife, because I'm never going to hire any more women." Beckerman's wife, Bernice "Bunny" Beckerman, had established a successful freelance career as violist. Ms. Beckerman later—in 1955—was allowed to audition for the Minneapolis Symphony and won a position. In 1961, her colleagues elected Bernice Beckerman the first woman chairperson of the members committee of the orchestra. In this leadership role, she once confronted the music director with a committee issue on behalf of the orchestra. He told her that "she was too emotional" and dismissed the issue.

Beckerman not only had the respect and confidence of the orchestra, she also had the responsibility as chairperson to pursue the matter. "The next time we met was with the Symphony Board Chairman attending," Ms. Beckerman said later. "After hearing from the string principals that the conductor's insistence on hearing *individual* (string players) performances of passages during rehearsal achieved nothing but intimidation, the chairman agreed it should not occur. The conductor had to respect him."

In her book, *Your Own Way in Music*, Nancy Uscher described the process by which the New York Philharmonic hired its first female member. According to Uscher, the year was 1960, and the phone rang in the home of the principal bass of the New York Philharmonic, Frederick Zimmermann. "Fred, we have no choice. This is the fifth time she's auditioned and she's STILL the best. We have to let her in this time. There is nothing else to be done now."

After pacing the floor for hours, Zimmermann was elated that his student, Orin O'Brien, had finally won the position. He had watched through four previous auditions as his male colleagues refused to admit the obvious. History was now being made as the New York Philharmonic accepted its first female musician.

Although the Saint Louis Symphony Orchestra had hired Dorothy Ziegler as principal trombone in 1945—and in 1972 would name trumpeter Susan Slaughter the first woman ever to become principal trumpet of a major symphony orchestra—the orchestra continued to reflect the sexist biases of its time. In 1962 a clause appeared in the *women's* contract of the Saint Louis Symphony to which neither the committee nor the union had agreed. The so-called pregnancy clause contained language such as "audience distraction" and "if the pregnancy is visually apparent or causes interference to render proper services, then this contract may be terminated." In his memoir, Saint Louis Symphony bassist Russell Brodine described his reaction and comments at an orchestra meeting: "I read that clause over three times; each time it sounded more disgusting. I pulled the contract out of my pocket and reminded my colleagues that this piece of paper was always with us—figuratively speaking—when we went to the supermarket, when we went to buy a car, and so on and on. 'But I'll be goddamned, if it's such a good contract that anyone should have to take it to bed with them,' I said." The clause disappeared after an orchestra meeting at which men and women alike objected to such discriminatory contractual language.

The possibilities for women to have full-time careers of any kind, including an orchestra career, were becoming realized. The development of the birth control pill revolutionized the lives of women and family life and enabled a woman to plan and control her life. As women's ranks increased in music professions, they assumed leadership positions within their orchestras and served as union stewards, members of negotiating committees, and delegates to ICSOM. At the same time, women's issues

and problems escalated in almost direct proportion to their finding orchestra jobs.

The quiet solution of the 1962 "pregnancy clause" issue in Saint Louis
apparently had no effect on another major American orchestra, which
issued a personal contract in 1978 with the following language:

> If a female becomes pregnant between the time she signs this
> contract and the opening of the season, this contract will be
> void. A musician who becomes pregnant during the season will
> be paid only for all services rendered up to the time she stops
> performing with the orchestra. Such musician will notify the
> employer of pregnancy, and misrepresentation of condition
> relieves the employer of any liability.

That same year, Congress passed the Pregnancy Discrimination Act to
protect women from discrimination in the workplace. By that time, 1978,
this federal legislation had a significant impact on the symphony orchestra world. The 1979–1980 statistics of the forty-four ICSOM orchestras
showed a total of 1,150 female and 2,731 male orchestra members, compared with approximately 109 women in the major orchestras four decades
before. ICSOM would have a large role to play in determining how women
would be regarded and treated as symphony and union members.

At the 1980 ICSOM Conference in Portland, Oregon, where women
constituted one-third of the total number of delegates, a women's caucus of
the conference took on some of the major issues. One of the women sum-
marized the position of her colleagues: "More and more women *have* to
work, and we must not accept that we are being *allowed* to hold a job. The
fact that women bear babies and men don't does not mean that working is
a privilege for women and a right of men. The problems of raising the next
generation are the concern for all society and not just of females."

On this occasion, forty-two years after the 150 female musicians of
the New York Local had met for a relatively inconsequential discussion
of their concerns, the ICSOM representatives of a new generation acknowledged that discrimination with regard to pregnancy and child care
was a serious problem. For the first time, they addressed concerns specifically related to their professional lives and their status as symphony

musicians. In discussion after discussion, they raised many important issues and questions reflecting their belief in the necessity of improving contract language for maternity and paternity leave, child care, tours, auditions, and committee and ICSOM representation. Neither the AFM nor ICSOM had ever formally addressed these issues. It was only then, in 1980, that the concerns of increasing numbers of women began to receive attention at the negotiating table.

In 1960, no U.S. symphony orchestra paid its musicians a full-time salary; by 1976, eleven U.S. orchestras paid all of their musicians on a fifty-two-week basis. In major orchestras the proportion of women increased from 18 percent in 1964 to an average of 25 percent just ten years later. In 2001 the American Symphony Orchestra League survey of major orchestras counted a total of 1,116 women, which constituted approximately 36 percent of the member musicians, or an average of thirty per orchestra. (The ICSOM orchestras that did *not* participate in the League's survey were the Charlotte Symphony, Chicago Lyric Opera Orchestra, Kennedy Center Orchestra, Metropolitan Opera Orchestra, New York City Opera Orchestra, Saint Louis Symphony, San Diego Symphony, San Francisco Ballet, and San Francisco Opera Orchestra.)

The Other Half of Humanity

Berlin Philharmonic

> One year after ICSOM delegates to the Milwaukee convention passed a motion opposing the discriminatory hiring practices of the Vienna and Berlin Philharmonic Orchestras, comes a report that the latter has, for the first time in its 100-year history, accepted a woman musician. Madeleine Carruzzo, 26, was chosen over 12 men who also auditioned for the first violin section position.
>
> *Milestone: November 1982,* Senza Sordino

Until the 1970s, when American orchestras began to advertise for candidates outside the United States, the composition of European orchestras has been more international—and more male—than that of their American counterparts. Two major European orchestras, the Berlin Philharmonic and the Vienna Philharmonic, fearing the collapse of the all-male club, resisted opening their ranks to women until the late twentieth century.

Violinist Madeleine Carruzzo broke the barrier in 1982 when she became the first woman admitted into the Berlin Philharmonic.

> Gynophobia, a dread disease that once was rampant in the world's symphony orchestras, is no longer common among the educated classes in this country. Vaccines, available in most urban centers, have been found to counteract it. However, fear of women still is endemic in many of the great European orchestras, including those in such relatively enlightened places as Vienna and London. (Donal Henahan, *New York Times*, January 1983)

One year later, twenty-three-year-old clarinetist Sabine Meyer was offered a one-year contract as first clarinetist by conductor Herbert von Karajan of the Berlin Philharmonic. When the orchestra vetoed the offer and threatened to strike in protest of this appointment, Karajan's response was to announce cancellation of performances, concert tours, recording sessions, and Salzburg Festival concerts. He continued to insist that he had the right to select players, but the orchestra would not acquiesce to his demands and refused to grant him the power that traditionally had been shared among all the members of the orchestra. After her temporary contract expired, Ms. Meyer resigned.

According to Norman Lebrecht in *The Maestro Myth*, "No one doubted Sabine Meyer's excellence, but players said her tone clashed with the rest of the section and her personality did not fit."

In 2003 there are approximately sixteen women in the Berlin Philharmonic, a positive change from the early 1980s, but still not comparable to an average of thirty to thirty-three women in major American orchestras as of this writing.

The Vienna Philharmonic

The all-male Vienna Philharmonic ended its 155-year-old exclusion of women on February 27, 1997, when it admitted a woman as a full member of the orchestra. Harpist Anna Lelkes broke the men-only barrier in 1971 when she was hired to play full-time. She was not, however, allowed membership in the orchestra, which would have meant a voice in policy regarding concerts, conductors, and recordings. Twenty-six years later her name appeared on a program for the first time. When interviewed by the Associated Press in 1995, Lelkes considered the mention of her name on a Carnegie Hall program a small but significant triumph along the way to full recognition. The Vienna Philharmonic's discriminatory policies had been under public scrutiny throughout Europe and were the subject of a public symposium held in Vienna in early December of 1997.

A meeting by the musicians in February of 1998 resulted in postponing a decision about hiring women in spite of the pleas of the new chancellor, Viktor Klima, to "use the creative potential of the other half of humanity and prove its responsibility for a modern open society." The Philharmonic maintained that as a private, self-governing institution it was not obliged to open its membership to women. However, the *publicly* funded Vienna State Opera Orchestra and the Philharmonic have virtually identical personnel, because the Philharmonic draws all its members from the Opera Orchestra. As the parent organization, the State Opera provides the overwhelming number of services for Philharmonic musicians, with at least three hundred performances a year. The Philharmonic plays just eighty-five concerts annually, plus a residency at the Salzburg Festival. Its musicians depend on the indirect subsidy and support of the state-funded Opera.

Pressure to grant membership to women came from all fronts—the Austrian government, the international music community, and feminist groups worldwide. In the United States, boycotts and protests were organized to take place during the VPO 1996 tour, largely due to the efforts of William Osborne, an American composer and journalist. In January of that year, Osborne had posted documented information on the Internet about the exclusion of women from the Vienna Philharmonic. Bitter personal experience had inspired him to wage a campaign against sexism in the European music world.

Osborne's wife, trombonist Abbie Conant, had been fighting a number of court battles with the Munich Philharmonic over her arbitrary demotion by the orchestra, which ended in precedent-setting legal victory. When she finally won the legal battle, she left the orchestra.

In the first of several essays from the *Journal* of the International Alliance for Women in Music (IAWM), posted on the Internet and titled "Art Is Just an Excuse," Osborne contended that "the VP's [Vienna Philharmonic] belief in male supremacy was gender bias of the worst sort, an exclusionary policy that was part of an intolerable racist heritage, which was the shame, not the pride of Western civilization." His articles ignited a debate in cyberspace and attention from the international media. Reaction to the controversy from Vienna Philharmonic chair Werner Resel was to threaten to disband the orchestra rather than admit women, and he suggested that "if the ensemble admitted women it might be unable to perform due to potential simultaneous pregnancies."

In the meantime the IAWM began to use the Internet to disseminate information and begin advocacy; the group also established a Web site, "Zap the VPO." ICSOM musicians and the locals of New York, Boston, and Los Angeles sent some of the 120 letters received by the VPO urging inclusion of all qualified musicians without regard to gender or race. The National Organization for Women (NOW) and IAWM helped organize peaceful protests and distribute leaflets outside the concert halls in California and New York where the Vienna Philharmonic was scheduled to perform. NOW's participation in the demonstrations was crucial and drew extensive media attention to this issue.

The deeply entrenched attitudes were challenged on all fronts, and the VPO made a historic decision on February 27, 1997, the same day the orchestra departed Vienna for the American tour. Fifty-seven-year-old Ms. Lelkes was admitted as a full member of the VPO, having performed as second harpist for the orchestra for more than twenty years. She was the first woman musician ever to become a member since its founding in 1842. Applications from women were subsequently accepted for the first time, although a photograph and final audition without a screen is still a requirement as of this writing.

The public debate over allowing women in the orchestra coincidentally occurred at the same time a woman was already conducting the male enclave of the Vienna State Opera. Simone Young, seven months pregnant with her second child in 1997, reported: "I conducted 'Lohengrin' on the very day that the Vienna Philharmonic was going to take the vote on admitting women or not. I like to think I had a little bit to do with it" (*New York Times,* September 9, 2003).

Ms. Young had conducted twenty-six different operas over the period of several years. She was assistant to Daniel Barenboim at the Berlin Opera in 1992, and this position opened doors for her. In 2003 she became conductor of the Hamburg State Opera in Germany, the first woman to hold a leading position in a major European opera house.

In order to write an accurate and fair assessment of the situation, the author sent an e-mail to the Vienna Philharmonic to inquire about their current hiring practices and received the following response on Tuesday, February 27, 2001, from Professor Wolfgang Schuster, press officer:

This is the situation since 1997: The orchestra of the Vienna State Opera is open to all musicians male or female to any race and nation who belongs to the special Viennese style of making music ("Wiener Klangstil"). This is the first step to become a member of the private society of "Wiener Philharmoniker." In the beginning two years, only few women tried to come to our auditions. In the last year the situation has improved. Due to artistic reasons we refuse to hire a candidate who has not won an audition. We try to invite more female candidates than male candidates to these auditions. Two women won the following positions: Julie Palloc (France) second harp and Ursula Plaichinger (Austria) viola. Every candidate has to wait three years to become a member of the Wiener Philharmoniker after having a one year audition in the Wiener Staatsoper ("Probejahr").

The Vienna Philharmonic Orchestra has members from 11 nations including Australia, Canada and the United States.

More than two years later, the author asked the same questions regarding the numbers of women and the audition procedures. This was the response from Professor Schuster on May 19, 2003:

Dear Ms. Ayer,

The Vienna Philharmonic Orchestra (VPO) is open for all musicians, male or female, of all nations and races since five years. The only condition is, to play the Viennese style of making music. You have to be a member of the Orchestra of the Vienna State Opera after having succeeded in a blind audition. After one year the jury confirms the engagement or not. After two more years, you can become a member of the VPO. Of course it's possible to play as a substitute before. We try to increase the percentage of women who are invited to the blind auditions, but unfortunately the level of quality of the young ladies isn't still the expected one, this might become better in the following years.

In 2001 Ursula Plaichinger, Viola, got the second place of the audition and was engaged at the Vienna State Opera September 1st, 2002.Charlotte Balzereith, Harp, won the audition in spring 2002, and started her engagement in September 2002; therefore both ladies can become regular members of the VPO at 2005. Both musicians are involved in the "Arbeitsgemeinschaft" [study group] of the VPO; this means they get the same fee, the same privileges, but are not able to elect or be elected at the general assembly. Ursula Wex, Cello, got a first place ex aequo and will be engaged at the Vienna State Opera at Sep 1, 2003, so she can become member in 2006.

Yours Sincerely,
Wolfgang Schuster, VPO Press Officer

The Vienna Philharmonic Orchestra appears to be the last bastion of the exclusionary hiring practice in Europe. Despite improvements since the mid-1990s, the relative proportions of most European orchestras remain less than 10 percent female compared to 36 percent in the United States and 30 percent in the United Kingdom. The most current data for several other major European orchestras, published in March 2001, is as follows:

ORCHESTRA	TOTAL	WOMEN	PERCENTAGE
Berlin Philharmonic	120	7	5 (in 2003 there were 16)
Czech Philharmonic	120	6	5
Dresden Philharmonic	117	6	5
Gewandhaus Leipzig	193	13	7
Staatskapelle Dresden	144	5	3
Vienna Philharmonic	149	1	1 (in 2003 there were 3 in the Opera, as previous letter explains)

Further discussion of present-day European orchestra internal procedures, structures, and unions continues in the next chapter.

In a June 1997 gathering at Ravinia, summer home of the Chicago Symphony Orchestra (CSO) for many years, five of ICSOM's founders—retired members of the CSO—recall their stories. Left: Raymond Niwa. Right: Sam Denov, Walfrid Kujala, Joseph Golan, Rudy Nashan (Collection of the author).

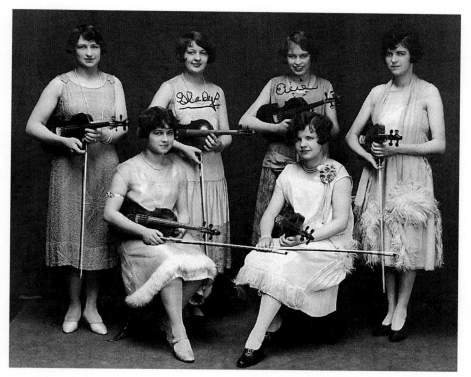

In the 1920s, Gladys Anderson (standing second from left; later Gladys Gingold) and Evelyn Sparlin (standing third from left; later Evelyn Ayer, the author's mother) performed in many Eastern Washington State College ensembles together, including this violin sextet (Collection of the author).

Walter Damrosch strolls down Fifth Avenue, New York City, at the height of his fame as an influential young conductor in American music circles, c. 1890 (Musical America, *February 10, 1942*).

Union Local president, James C. Petrillo (right), Chicago Symphony Orchestra president, Dr. Eric Oldberg (left), and Chicago mayor, Richard Daley (center), meeting to decide on a new Chicago Symphony Orchestra contract, September, 1962 (Chicago Tribune *photo*).

The Chicago Daily News *headline for the article that ran with this November 17, 1962, photo read: "Petrillo Assailed By Symphony Men." At a press conference, the musicians announced that they were filing unfair labor practice charges against the powerful Local 10 president, James C. Petrillo. Among the identified musicians are (seated, from left) Joseph Golan and Rudy Nashan; center standing, William York, and second from right, Sam Denov.*

From the December 6, 1962, Chicago Sun-Times, *flashing victory signs at Sherman House are some of the winners in the musicians union election. Celebrating are (left to right, front) John B. Durant, examining board; Mary-Kay Motherway, board of directors; Bernard (Barny) Richards, president; Rudy Nashan, vice president; Dom Geraci, board of directors and (rear) Anthony Hurcik, trial board.*

"Weeping Petrillo Bows Out After 40 Yrs. As 'Boss' " is the headline that ran in the Chicago Sun Times *with this photo of James C. Petrillo in tears after he lost the election for president of Local 10, Chicago Federation of Musicians, January, 1963. The photo on the right is his swan-song speech to the membership.*

Kurt Loebel, Cleveland Orchestra violinist, 1947–1997, and 1970 committee chair. In 1961, Loebel received notice that Cleveland Local 4, AFM, had filed charges against him and 15 others for union violations, which were later dismissed. Cleveland musicians were the last to achieve ratification rights, in 1971, after many years of acrimony with Local 4 (Photo courtesy of Kurt Loebel).

George Zazofsky (standing), first chairman of the International Conference of Symphony and Opera Musicians (ICSOM), here in his capacity as chair of the Boston Symphony Orchestra Players Committee, celebrating a successful contract negotiation. Conductor Charles Munch, sits at the table, second from right, c. 1955 (Courtesy of Erika Zazofsky).

In 1956, during a hearing before a House Un-American Activities subcommittee in the Los Angeles Federal Building, pianist Edith Rapport stated, "I will not cooperate with this committee." Here, she confers with her attorney, Daniel G. Marshall. Several musicians invoked the First and Fifth Amendments to the U. S. Constitution and refused to testify. The April 17, 1956, Los Angeles Examiner captioned the photo "Woman Pianist Balks at Quiz."

"Friendly witnesses" Albert Glasser, 41, and Katherine Glasser, 36, testified at HUAC hearings and named more than a dozen musicians.

"Pickets at Red Hearing" in front of Los Angeles Hall of Justice, April 21, 1956.

Inside the Los Angeles Federal Building, many people attend hearings led by Representatives Clyde Doyle (D-California), Morgan Moulder (D-Missouri), Donald Jackson (R-California), and Gordon Scherer (R-Ohio) (Photos on this and the previous page courtesy University of Southern California, on behalf of USC Specialized Libraries and Archival Collections).

Local 47 Rhythm Club president Marl Young (seated middle) signing final document transferring Local 767 Rhythm Club assets to the Local 47 Musicians Club of Los Angeles. Looking on are Musicians Club secretary Maury Paul (left), NAACP secretary Lester Bailey (standing), and Rhythm Club secretary Estelle Edson (right). (From March 1999 Overture; Local 47 AFM, Hollywood) (Photo courtesy of Marl Young).

Under the headline "LINE UP TO JOIN INTEGRATED UNION" is the following caption: "All musicians must pay union dues, but Red Saunders (at the window) and 200 other members of his group did more as they lined up to pay their first fees with formerly all-white Local 10 of the American Federation of Musicians. They destroyed a color barrier that had existed for 62 years. The move could lead to the eventual merger of Local 10 and Local 208. The latter is all-Negro." From the Chicago Defender *for March 23–30, 1963.*

From the Chicago Defender, *March 23–30, 1963, "HANDSHAKE OF PROGRESS." The caption reads: Band leader Theodore "Red" Saunders, left, shakes hands with Barney Richards, president of Local 10, American Federation of Musicians, as some 200 Negro musicians from all-Negro union, Local 208, join up with the previously all-white unit. Saunders is head of a rebel faction which is known as the Chicago Musicians for Harmonious Integration.*

The pianist and composer Dame Ethel Smyth conducting an all-male police band and chorus in 1929, before an outdoor audience and newsreel camera, at the unveiling of the statue of suffragist Emmeline Pankhurst by British prime minister Stanley Baldwin (Hulton-Deutsch Collection/Corbis).

Catherine Pickar (left) and other members of the International Alliance of Women Musicians (IAWM) demonstrated in New York City before a Vienna Phil- harmonic Orchestra concert at Carnegie Hall in 1997. They were protesting the VPO's 155 years of exclusion of women and on behalf of the acceptance of harpist Anna Lelkes as a member of the Vienna Philharmonic Orchestra (Photo courtesy of Monique Buzzarte).

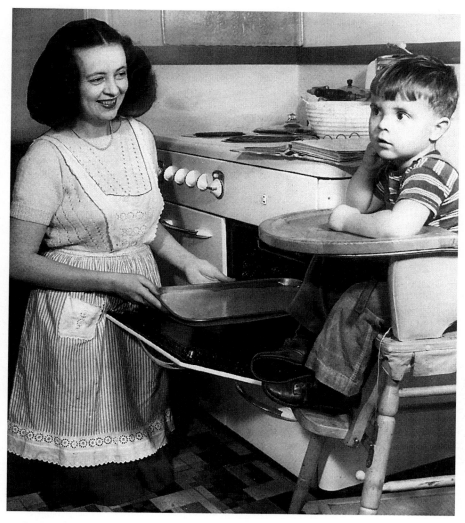

In October 1944, the Minneapolis Sunday Tribune *ran four photos of women whom conductor Dimitri Mitropoulos had hired to perform with the Minneapolis Symphony in the new season. This photo of "Mrs. Henry Denecke, Jr." (identified by her first name, Julia, in the accompanying article), shows her kneeling with her son, Eric, who "likes her in the role of cook." The caption notes that "Mrs. Denecke returned to her music career as a flutist as a wartime project."*

Minneapolis Symphony Orchestra personnel manager Glen R. Cooke and bass player Arthur Gold examine instruments and instrument trunks that had been damaged in a train mishap in the winter tour of February 1957 (Minneapolis Tribune).

In 1958, four new members of the Minneapolis Symphony Orchestra examine the "autograph wall" backstage at Northrop Auditorium on the campus of the University of Minnesota. Looking at the signature of the famed violinist Zino Francescatti are Ronald Hasselmann (pointing), trumpet; James Clute (left), double bass; Anthony Gilombardo, first violin, and Barrett Smith (right), violin (Minneapolis Tribune).

Noted comedian and avid amateur violinist Jack Benny with two of his friends in the Minneapolis Symphony Orchestra, musicians Eddy Blitz and Cynthia Britt, on the occasion of Benny's surprise visit to an orchestra rehearsal at Northrop Auditorium in April 1965 (Minneapolis Star).

Conductor Klaus Tennstedt in a pensive moment during an interview with Michael Anthony in November of 1989, when he returned to conduct the Bruckner Symphony No. 8. Tennstedt was Minnesota Orchestra principal guest conductor from 1979 to 1982. Audiences as well as musicians warmly welcomed him back as a guest conductor with the greatest enthusiasm (Minneapolis Star Tribune, *November 3, 1989*).

The 1970 Minnesota Orchestra Negotiating Committee poses for a rare photo opportunity: standing (left to right) Paul Thomas, Philip Sipser, Carl Holub, Ross Tolbert, Gene Wade; seated (left to right) Kensley Rosen, Carl Nashan, Alan Gerstel (Collection of the author).

*Minnesota Orchestra Musicians Committee chair Carl Holub, ICSOM labor counsel I. Philip Sipser, and orchestra manager Richard Cisek celebrate successful contract ratification in September 1970 after a one-week lockout (*Minneapolis Tribune *photo by Pete Hohn).*

In this 1994 photo, Carl Nashan and Julie Ayer filled hundreds of orders for the famous/infamous Minneapolis Symphony Orchestra sweatshirts. They designed the shirts to protest the name change that had occurred in 1968 (Collection of the author).

ICSOM Conference gathering, 1997 Governing Board (left to right) Charles Schlueter (Boston Symphony), member-at- large; Marsha Schweitzer (Honolulu Symphony), editor Senza Sordino; Lucinda Lewis (New Jersey Symphony), secretary; Mary Plaine (Baltimore Symphony), member-at-large; Leonard Leibowitz, counsel; Robert Levine (Milwaukee Symphony), chair; James Clute (Minnesota Orchestra), member-at-large; David Angus (Rochester Philharmonic), president; Stephanie Tretick (Pittsburgh Symphony), treasurer; and Michael Moore (Atlanta Symphony), member-at-large (Photo by Mark Schubert).

Five members of the New York Philharmonic negotiating committee celebrate ratification of a pacesetting master agreement, just two days before the opening of the 1967 season. Left to right: Bert Bial, Ranier De Intinis, Ralph Mendelson, Lorin Bernsohn, Morris Borodkin. (February 1968 Senza Sordino, *ICSOM monthly newsletter)*

Thirty years later the New York Philharmonic ratified another landmark six-year master agreement, one year before the expiration of its current contract. Left to right: committee members Kenneth Mirkin and Newton Mansfield, attorney Phil Sipser, committee chair Dawn Hanney, committee member Fiona Simon, Local 802 president Bill Moriarity, and committee member Robert Botti. (Photo by Walter Karling, January 1998 Allegro, *AFM Local 802 monthly publication)*

Eight

Current Issues

The musician is expected and agrees to render his services at two full periods each day on Sundays or weekdays without extra compensation . . . If the musician missed both subscription concerts for two or more weeks in succession as a result of illness or for any other reason, the Company could terminate the contract by giving the musician one week's notice of such intention. All liability by the Company under the contract would then cease.

from the 1923–1924 personal contract of
Cincinnati Symphony Orchestra cellist Herbert Weis

*A*S AMERICAN SOCIETY ADJUSTS to new conditions, the members of its symphony orchestras continue to contribute to the enrichment of its cultural life, while meeting the challenges of such issues as musicians' physical and mental health, involvement in orchestra decision making (such as conductor selection), audition procedures and costs, and other matters of contemporary concern.

Fiddler's Neck and Other Maladies

Article XII, Section 12.1, 1998
Minnesota Orchestra Master Agreement
In the event that an Eligible Musician becomes sick or disabled during the Symphony Season, Employer shall pay such Eligible Musician's full salary or half pay for each period of absence due to illness according to the following scale . . .

The long-sought goal that many major orchestras finally achieved in the 1970s, full-time employment of musicians and concomitant benefits, brought to professional orchestra musicians the status and respect they deserved. Achieving that goal inevitably brought with it serious and unforeseen consequences that would affect the entire symphony orchestra profession, from individual musicians to orchestras as a whole. Along with the fifty-two-week contract has come an increase in physical stress. Employing the same number of musicians—and, in some cases, fewer—orchestras have added significantly to the numbers of programs and activities required of their musicians, compared to major European orchestras, for instance, which have greater numbers of musicians on their rolls to allow for substitutions and sick-leave covers. Overplaying and overuse have led to repetitive stress injuries. Furthermore, musicians have become even more susceptible to hearing damage.

In the April 1978 issue of its newsletter, *Senza Sordino*, ICSOM tackled what it called the "Decibel Dilemma." Henry Shaw, a member of the Cincinnati Symphony, wrote an in-depth essay in which he identified "one of the most serious occupational hazards of musicians: sound—noise—music. Stage noise can cause physical and psychological problems, while also manifesting itself as the cause of behavioral patterns, the reasons for which we are often not aware."

ICSOM continued to work on the issues of musicians' health. A multistage project—studying health issues, searching for specialists to design a members' survey, distributing a questionnaire, and analyzing responses—provided a great deal of new information. According to the results of the May 1986 questionnaire distributed to ICSOM members nationwide, 76 percent of the responding musicians had experienced medical problems severe enough to interfere with their performances and to necessitate taking time off from work.

Unfortunately, the affected musicians had not always recognized the symptoms of such medical problems until it was too late, when pain and a resulting injury caused the musician to require use of sick leave or even being placed on disability. Some injured musicians tried to continue playing full time in spite of severe pain, because they feared repercussions from the conductor and management. These fears were not baseless: symphony orchestras did not make allowances for musicians' illnesses or injuries until the mid-1960s, when negotiations began to include sick leave provisions. Playing through their pain, the musicians aggravated their stress both physically and emotionally. Even with this new contract provision, musicians still hesitated to admit that they experienced any physical problems related to their profession.

In September 1987, Janet Horvath, the associate principal cellist of the Minnesota Orchestra, together with the University of Minnesota, organized the first of several conferences on the subject of the physical health of musicians. Horvath invited medical professionals in the fields of sports medicine and performing arts medicine to address the causes of injuries and the strategies for preventing problems due to performance stress, unhealthy practice habits, environmental influences, and overuse. More than five hundred people from twenty-three states attended, and well-known guest artists related their own experiences. The first "Playing Hurt" conference, a great success, introduced to the public the hazards of being a professional musician.

The *Minneapolis Star Tribune* of September 19, 1987, quoted one of the experts, Dr. Robert Leffert, head of the Upper Extremity Rehabilitation Unit of Massachusetts General Hospital in Boston. Explaining that musicians are like athletes and that their profession requires a great deal of physical stress that must be recognized, Dr. Leffert told the conference attendees that he thought of musicians as "super athletes . . . Pro athletes very often get paid to destroy themselves physically in a relatively short period of time. A musician, on the other hand, might start and play until he/she is 67. So, conserving the resources is a far more important consideration in the performing artist than the athlete."

Even now, nearly twenty years later, few people outside the symphony orchestra world have considered Dr. Leffert's point of view. As a patient, I once had a well-intentioned doctor ask me, "Are you having fun this year in the orchestra?" Startled by this remark, I went on to explain that this profession is demanding and often enjoyable, but it is not a question of "fun." It is far removed from the hobby an amateur musician enjoys who plays with community orchestras or chamber ensembles. Life in a professional orchestra requires an extraordinary amount of dedication, commitment, and hard work, and is physically demanding in ways that are just beginning to be understood. It also is a fulfillment of an enduring passion for music and performance.

At the time of the first "Playing Hurt" conference, even doctors had rarely considered the physical requirements of performing on a musical instrument, nor did they have particular sympathy with or knowledge of musicians' ailments. One of the first specialized clinics for musicians opened its doors during this time—the Medical Program for Performing Artists at Chicago's Northwestern Memorial Hospital—and word quickly spread in the musicians' community that they might find help there. Dr. Alice Brandfonbrenner, director of the clinic, at that time saw an average of sixty patients a month, treating everything from tendinitis to stress.

"Arts medicine is a specialty that has been slow to come," Brandfonbrenner said in 1986, in a *Chicago Sun Times* interview. "The average doctor sees one violinist every six years and doesn't put two and two together when the performer comes in with a pain that may be occupation related. Like athletes, performers are terribly competitive with the next guy and themselves. They're obsessed with improvement, always want to get better. Violins come in standard sizes, but people's arms don't, and that leads to shoulder problems. People come with different sized legs, but the cellists' chairs are all the same, causing back strain for some."

In an article she wrote for the journal *Your Health* in February 1986, Dr. Brandfonbrener explained: "All of the physicians must have at least some background in music . . . it's essential, [because] if you don't understand the physical requirements of playing a musical instrument, you really can't know why a particular problem may develop or how you can provide workable solutions. Furthermore, you have to understand the lifestyles and pressures that musicians are under in terms of auditioning and performing. They have a special set of risks and pressures that go with their lifestyle."

Ideally there should be a warm-up and cool-down session before and after every performance, not unlike what an athlete does. Physical therapists and other professionals in the performing arts medicine field have developed exercises that enable performers to minimize the repetitive strain that results from playing an instrument. Today, common backstage preparations for concerts include not only practicing the instrument, but also warming up arms, fingers, and hands away from the instruments, chair massage, neck rotations, doorway stretches, and other such exercises.

Like professional musicians, instrumental students may experience injuries, even before they get to a conservatory or school of music. Some statistics have indicated that as many as 80 percent of students suffer pain and injury. Hours of daily practice, intense competition, demanding schedules, and difficult repertoire all contribute to injuries at an early age. Some schools have begun to offer training in exercise and practice techniques, as well as in human physiology, in order to prevent injury.

The Manhattan School of Music, for instance, offers "Biomechanics and Ergonomics for Performers," a course that teaches basic anatomy, muscle structure, and the elements that contribute to injury. It teaches that the musician is an athlete and applies the expertise developed in the sports medicine field to musicians. The course also addresses general health issues and teaches portable exercises. A physical therapist trains students to exercise correctly. The biomechanics portion of the course addresses such topics as refitting the instrument or selecting a proper chair to maintain health or to prevent reinjury.

Each instrumental group brings its own stresses and strains; performers on the smaller string instruments are particularly at risk. Playing the violin involves an unnatural posture, which the larger, heavier viola can intensify. The musician's neck is bent and turned at an angle, shoulders are curved forward, the right arm is raised with the fingers curved in, and the left arm and shoulder are twisted and raised to accommodate the chin. Overplaying can cause pain and tightness in the neck, shoulders, arm, hands, and lower back.

Woodwind and brass players suffer from other types of maladies such as lower back problems; carpal tunnel and TMJ syndrome (locked jaw) commonly occur in performers on woodwinds, violins, and violas. Anyone who sits in front of the brass and/or percussion section suffers from the sheer volume of sound coming from those sections, which ultimately can cause tinitus and hearing loss of various degrees.

Chiropractic care, massage therapy, shiatsu, yoga, Alexander technique, physical therapy, and a number of other approaches also provide important means of decreasing tensions in the musician's neck, upper and lower back, shoulders, arms, hands, and fingers. Some U.S. medical doctors now understand the benefit of referring a professional musician for both massage therapy and chiropractic care, both as preventive and curative measures.

Many orchestra musicians have had the frustrating experience of long searches for the cause(s) of their pains or injuries. Shoulder pain, for example, common among string players, may not show up on the standard MRI or CT scan, and even today, many doctors do not understand the particular stresses of the musician's daily work in reaching their diagnosis. If the injury becomes severe, therapy can include cortisone shots, acupuncture, ultrasound, physical therapy, chiropractic care, and sometimes even surgery.

Because of the vast amount of attention paid in the past twenty years to the field of musicians' health, many resources, products, and programs now contribute to injury prevention. In addition to physical therapy and healthy warm-up routines, musicians have access to ergonomically designed chairs, lumbar support pillows, acoustic shields, ear plugs, risers, on-site massage therapists, and other resources that help prevent injuries. Master contracts in orchestras throughout the United States have begun to reflect the new awareness of these concerns. In 2001, for example, the Minnesota Orchestra members committee negotiated a precedent-setting agreement whereby management agreed to pay a portion of the cost up to $120 for custom-designed ear plugs for all orchestra members who wished to use them. Designed specifically for musicians, and custom-fitted by an audiologist, the earplugs reduce noise levels by fifteen to twenty-five decibels.

Dr. Frank Heller, doctor of chiropractic medicine in Minneapolis, has worked with many musicians. "The orchestra player has unique stresses and demands," Dr. Heller explains, "and all hold positions and maintain fixed postures that can cause static loading, which causes fatigue and leads to strain, dysfunction or lesions to the spine. Chiropractic adjustments restore motion to a joint that has built up waste products by stimulating the nervous system.

"An ergonomic assessment of the musician, including pictures and video of posture when playing, enables both the patient and me to determine the source of the problem and lessen the strain. The treatments may work, but if the mechanism of the injury remains, you're back to where we started. The insurance industry does not address the kind of unique stresses imposed upon musicians and the frequent care needed to prevent injury. Managed care does not look at individuals, and patients suffer as a result. Athletes often require chiropractic care before playing a game; the same should be true for musicians. The stress of performance is unique—the conductor adds to the stress in ways that the public just doesn't get."

According to a survey of 1,639 musicians in fifty-six orchestras of Europe, Asia, North America, and Australia, reported in the *Erie Times* on March 18, 1997, conductors emerged as the number one cause of stress among musicians. "The questionnaire gave musicians a voice to air problems that they dare not speak about," said Dr. Ian James, founder of the British Performing Arts Medicine Trust, whose aim is to make medical care available to actors, singers, dancers, and musicians. In addition to developing stress from conductors, especially incompetent conductors, 58 percent of musicians reported feeling pain while performing.

Are we having *fun* yet?

Conductor Evaluations and Selections

> If it would change the situation, if the conductor would learn something from it—make him stick to the beat, for instance—it might be healthy. The conductor is supposed to know everything better than the musicians, but on the fingers of one hand you can count the real conductors. Before the first downbeat, the musicians know. Some conductors oppose written evaluation because they believe their swindle might be discovered. Conducting is a grazing ground for lack of talent!?!
>
> *William Steinberg, Pittsburgh Symphony conductor*

Not so far removed from the topic of musicians' health issues (as the 1986 survey results reported above indicated), the subject of evaluating conductors and music directors has naturally accompanied the other significant proposals for changes in working conditions that have emerged in recent decades. Not only weary of the capricious and high-handed behavior on the podium, the musicians have also sought to raise the standards of music making by recording their professional opinions about conductors' abilities and making those opinions available within the symphony orchestra world in a responsible manner.

Henry Fogel, former president of the Chicago Symphony Orchestra, tells an anecdote from his personal experience working with Sir Georg Solti during Solti's tenure as music director of the CSO (1969–1991). When Fogel passed along to Solti the musicians' reaction to a guest conductor, Solti's response was, "Who the bloody hell do they think they are, telling you what they think of conductors?" Particularly in his later years, Solti was an extremely humane conductor, who did not abuse players and, in fact, treated them warmly. However, Fogel cites this remark as typical of the traditional paternalistic attitude of conductors toward musicians.

Solti was not the only one who doubted the validity of musicians' opinions in rating his colleagues; many conductors dreaded the reality of such a rating system. The topic had been a matter of much discussion within ICSOM until 1967, when the proposal for a universal rating system became reality. There had always been informal gossip, stories, and jokes among orchestra players about conductors, but never before had the collective professional knowledge been tapped in this manner. The development of a written form (see Appendix E, p. 248) was painstakingly examined by ICSOM members and legal counsel. The delicate legal issues remain the same to this day as outlined by ICSOM lawyers in 1968: confidentiality, leaks to the press, and proper use of information. That year, ICSOM orchestras tabulated the first conductor evaluation surveys by hand and conveyed them to a Rapid Communication Center for dissemination.

When ICSOM established the conductor evaluation procedure in the 1960s, musicians, critics, and conductors wrote to the editor of the ICSOM newsletter. The following are a few of their opinions, from the April 1967 *Senza Sordino*:

Symphonic and operatic maestros, long known for their autocratic attitudes toward the musicians they direct, will now have to be on their best behavior. They will never know when . . . musicians may be filling in a questionnaire whose results may be considered in deciding [conductor] futures. (Sam Denov, former

Chicago Symphony timpanist, *Senza Sordino* editor, ICSOM vice-chairman and chairman)

The trouble is that the orchestra players frequently have private axes to grind, and their judgments must be modified by awareness of these extra-esthetic considerations. Every orchestra of consequence, regardless who its leader may be, has complaints . . . When the members of ICSOM reach the point where they would recommend the appointment of a conductor known to be a strict disciplinarian because of their respect for his musicianship, they will reflect another and more important aspect of artistic maturity. (Robert Marsh, music critic, *Chicago Sun-Times*)

Musicians have always evaluated conductors. In Europe, they do it constantly. The only question to ask is: To what purpose? It doesn't worry me, but it should certainly worry some people who administer orchestras. Such a poll may tell them some things they don't want to know. (Erich Leinsdorf, former music director of the Cleveland Orchestra, Rochester Philharmonic, and Boston Symphony Orchestra)

Since 1982 the musicians' evaluations of conductors have been computerized. Upon request by carefully screened and authorized applicants— member orchestra players' committees and managements—ICSOM makes available to specific member orchestras, for purposes of evaluation, the confidential results of the musicians' appraisals, which now cover more than six hundred conductors. In 2000, the program provided more than 1,110 sets of evaluations. At the 2002 ICSOM Conference, a committee was formed to review the current form for possible improvements. ICSOM delegates are cautioned and notified of the importance of these conductor evaluation procedures. Ongoing discussions and self-evaluation among ICSOM representatives probe the importance of the evaluations in the selection of guest and permanent conductors. The union and its members, because of legal liability and out of ethical considerations, strictly limit access to the information and *do not post it or make it available to orchestras at large.*

On a related topic, musicians have experienced a slight change of practice and process in the selection of principal conductors, or music directors, as they are now known. In only three decades, the process by which U.S. orchestral organizations choose a new music director has undergone a procedural change. Formerly under the control of a small coterie of orchestral benefactors, most of whom had little background for judging candidates' qualifications, the process has not been without controversy.

By the beginning of the twenty-first century, U.S. musicians have begun to have a voice in the selection of the music director. One example will suffice to illustrate the shift in expectations. In 1970, upon the death of George Szell, the Cleveland Orchestra board of directors acceded to the musicians' wishes to be included in naming his successor and appointed two orchestra members to the selection committee. However, when the time came, in 1972, Lorin Maazel received the appointment, against the opinions and advice of the musicians. Ironically, thirty years

---

♪ Otto Klemperer was a conductor of exceptional talent and temperament, an avid promoter of contemporary music of the day who was often referred to as a "New Age" conductor. He championed many new composers of that era, Gustav Mahler being perhaps the most notable. However, as much as he favored some composers he was equally disdainful and outspoken of those he thought not worthy of his ear, or anyone else's ear for that matter. He had been in ill health for many years and suffered a mild stroke that had left one side of his face with a decided sag, and gave him a profound lisp.

Klemperer's contempt for certain composers reared its head after a *Vorlesung* (lecture) in Salzburg during the late 1940s or early '50s in a class on contemporary music given by the esteemed violist and composer Paul Hindemith. After the conclusion of what was a rather lengthy discourse on the subject, Hindemith said that if anyone had a question, he would be delighted to give an answer. A hand immediately shot up in the rear of the auditorium. It of course belonged to Otto Klemperer, who had been patiently listening to Hindemith's lecture. Without missing a beat and with his pronounced lisp, Klemperer asked, "Herr Professor, können Sie mir mal bitte sagen wo die Toiletten sind?"

later, when Maazel was appointed Kurt Masur's successor at the New York Philharmonic, it was with widespread approval from the players. According to a violinist of forty years with the orchestra, it was the first time in the Philharmonic's history that its musicians had, to a good degree, chosen their own music director.

Reform of the Audition Process

Before the restructuring of audition procedures, which now include international advertisements for position openings, conductors (and sometimes managers) held most of their auditions in New York City, and some in Chicago. In the 1940s and '50s, a musician would learn about auditions through the musicians' grapevine, postings in major music schools, and union boards in different cities, or by writing directly to the orchestras. Depending on the conductor's whim, women and minorities, as described in previous chapters, were usually excluded from this process in the major orchestras. Until the blind audition (behind a screen or curtain) became established audition policy in the 1970s, orchestras remained segregated and mostly male. The Los Angeles and New York City AFM locals would not allow musicians to audition for an orchestra unless they belonged to the local union (NB: the *white* local, as musician unions were still segregated); most other orchestras would hear local union musicians before the conductor heard auditions in New York and Chicago.

Union regulations were not standardized; some unions required that the orchestra could not hire outside of the local, if a local musician was qualified. (Conductors, of course, found many ways to circumvent such regulations.) Other locals required a three-year waiting period for a nonlocal musician to join the local union. This meant the symphony musician was excluded from any outside work for three *years*, a long wait to make desperately needed money in those days. Ironically, if a local player won an audition, the starting salary would be ten dollars lower than for the imported player, in spite of the preference given to hiring from the area.

According to legend, conductor George Szell listened to a violinist tune up for his private audition and dismissed him before he played a note. Szell did not like the way he tuned!

Auditions Trilogy Symphoniphobias by Glen Morley, c. 1950.

"The trilogy . . . was typical of auditions of past eras," the artist, Glen Morley, wrote. "The four photos [wall portraits] are Toscanini and his favorite watch (gift from the NBC Orchestra), Stokowski, Leinsdorf, and Jascha." Note that Jascha Horenstein, one of the great European conductors of the mid-twentieth century, sits imperturbably under his own portrait (autographed and given to himself "mit Loff") while the cellist, Morley himself, wreaks havoc in the sight-reading portion of his audition. (Courtesy of Morris Secon).

Joan Mainzer, retired harpist of the Minneapolis Symphony (now Minnesota Orchestra), has recalled those days: "Local players were financially discriminated against, and the best players were in the largest cities—New York, Philadelphia, Boston, and Chicago. The conductor would sometimes transplant many of his favorite players to a new orchestra, yet another example of no job security. The local unions did not back the symphony musicians, but throughout the country the unions were happy that benefactors were forming orchestras in their respective community. Unions were in no position to dictate terms to the orchestra managers. It was an honor to be in this great orchestra. It was enormously respected, and the Minneapolis Symphony was beginning to carry its own weight as it gained international stature."

The reform of the audition process in major American orchestras took place in the late 1960s, as musicians began to be more involved in all aspects of the workplace. Nepotism and favoritism by conductors ended with the establishment of audition procedures, which guaranteed the participation of musician committees, negotiated into each orchestra's master agreements in the 1970s. Since that time, job openings in the top orchestras have been filled through open, international auditions that are designed, literally, to screen out prejudice on the basis of gender, race, age, or physical appearance.

According to a study published in the 2001 September–November issue of the *American Economic Review,* which called it the "democratization of the hiring process," the data showed that blind auditions increased by 50 percent the probability that a woman would advance from the preliminary rounds. Although there are basic guidelines for audition procedures, each orchestra uses a slightly different screening method. Some orchestras use screens for the entire process, including finals; others use it for only the finals; and some do not use screens at all. If screens are used, candidates are asked not to speak or make any sound. In some cases they are asked to remove their shoes, and women might be asked to wear flat shoes. The audition space might be carpeted so that gender cannot be identified by the musician's gait or kind of shoes worn.

Other aspects of the audition process vary, as well, but they all aim to give candidates an equal chance at securing the position based on their musical skills and talents. In the real world, some auditions will last only a few minutes. It is an almost impossible challenge to create the crucial first impression, with appropriate musical expression, accuracy, and sensitivity in five minutes. Whether in Europe, Canada, or the United States, auditions are grueling and in some ways unrealistic representations of one's actual playing ability—particularly one's *ensemble* playing. Some teachers prepare their students for auditions by teaching the orchestral repertoire and holding master classes in which the students perform the standard symphonic excerpts that they could expect to encounter in auditions. Sometimes the preliminaries and finals are held on one long day; in other cases, the finalists must return, at the expense of the orchestra, for the final round. In some cases, a finalist may rehearse and perform with the orchestra during a trial period. Once they are accepted, they play with the orchestra on a one- to three-year probationary period, depending on each orchestra's contract language.

In 1984, the Code of Ethical Practices for National and International Auditions was unanimously approved by ICSOM delegates, the Major Orchestra Managers Conference, and the AFM. It was a major achievement and was the first time the musicians and managers worked together to address such a major issue. It was emphasized that this document is not a contract but is to be used as a guideline for the review of local policies and practices.

The code does not presume to tell orchestras they will run auditions a certain way; for example, it contained no mention of screens, because orchestras have and continue to be divided on their use. Sometimes tapes are also required, and often auditions are held behind a screen for the preliminaries and sometimes finals, depending on the choice of the committees. But the code articulates that "there should be no discrimination on the basis of race, sex, age, creed, national origin, religion, or sexual preference; steps ensuring this should exist in all phases of the audition process."

Openings in American orchestras are advertised internationally in the American Federation of Musicians trade magazine. "Highly qualified applicants" are asked to send a detailed résumé including educational and professional background, but no one is prohibited from auditioning.

Carry-on Baggage, Tools of the Trade

Wherever the candidates travel, whether it be to or from Europe, Asia, Eastern Europe, or the United States, they must pay for their own transportation to the auditions, including the cost of the instruments, if they are not considered carry-on baggage. An extra seat must be purchased for a bass or cello on all flights, usually equal to or more than the cost of the person occupying a coach seat. In the aftermath of the terrorist attacks in America on September 11, 2001, the issue of carry-on baggage has had a direct impact on professional musicians. As Congress deals with the

♪ Code of Ethical Practices for National and International Auditions
(excerpts)

Purpose and Scope of Code

It is of utmost importance to musicians, managers, and conductors that auditions be conducted in accordance with guidelines ensuring competition that is fair to all who audition while providing the best results for orchestras seeking musicians.

Therefore, the American Federation of Musicians (AFM), the International Conference of Symphony and Opera Musicians (ICSOM), and the Major Orchestra Managers Conference (MOMC) [of the American Symphony Orchestra League] propound the following ethical and fair audition practices to which all parties should adhere, subject to local contractual considerations.

I. Preparation for Auditions

1. Notices of auditions should be given only for genuine vacancies . . . which the management intends to fill . . . with no predeterminations having been made as to who will be hired. Musicians taking such auditions should only do so with the intention of accepting the position if it is offered.

2. Auditions should be advertised in appropriate places . . . Notices should be clear and complete . . . and should appear far enough in advance of auditions for interested musicians to apply and to adequately prepare.

3. All applicants should be sent written responses . . . clear instructions setting forth the date, time and place of the audition, the complete audition repertoire . . . legible and identical parts for all candidates.

4. Applicants should be given notice that if they choose not to attend the audition they should promptly notify the personnel manager or other designated person.

II. Conduct of Auditions

1. In preparing for and conducting auditions, all participants should be aware of policies and procedures governing those auditions, including this code.

2. Although the existence and composition of an audition committee and the nature and extent of its participation in auditioning and hiring are determined locally, musicians' involvement should at least include the initial screening of applicants.

3. Applicants should not be disqualified from auditioning on the basis of information about them obtained from current or previous employers or from other institutions to which they have applied.

4. Auditionees should be given sufficient time and . . . adequate private facilities in which to warm up and practice.

5. Parts supplied . . . should be in good condition, legible, clearly marked . . .

6. There should be no discrimination on the basis of race, sex, age, creed, national origin, religion, or sexual preference . . .

7. There should be reasonable accommodation for the handicapped.

8. Auditionees should be given opportunity and encouragement to comment, anonymously if desired . . . about the audition process.

9. Auditionees should be notified of their status in the auditions process immediately upon such determination . . .

10. Auditionees should be informed prior to auditions of the orchestra's policy regarding reimbursement of auditionees' expenses for additional stay or travel incurred at the request of management.

Administration and Review of Code

A joint committee of representatives of the MOMC, ICSOM, and the AFM Symphony Department shall be established to oversee and review this code periodically.

complex problems and issues of airport security, including much more restrictive carry-on rules, musicians continue to travel and to carry on board irreplaceable musical instruments that cannot be shipped with ordinary luggage. Musicians must be recognized as professional workers who carry with them the tools of their trade. In November 2001 their unique needs were brought to the attention of the U.S. Senate. There have been numerous reports of confiscations by airport security personnel of some essential equipment musicians carry, which have been arbitrary and inconsistent depending on individual airline gate agents. Since January 2003, airline operators have been instructed to allow musical instruments as carry-on baggage and have specified that AFM members experiencing problems with security should speak to a screening supervisor. This change is in large part due to extensive lobbying by the AFM, and President Thomas Lee, who in 2003 received an official memo from the U.S. Department of Transportation assuring him and his AFM members of their rights to carry on their instruments, exclusive of the normal carry-on allowance of one bag and one personal item, and to seek the assistance of a screening supervisor in case of any problems.

Other Cultures

> ICSOM musicians have long been envious of the government-sponsored incomes, pensions and other benefits enjoyed by European orchestras. It is no coincidence that these orchestras take a far more active role in their own affairs than do American orchestras. When the taxpayer's money becomes involved in significant amounts, it is neither proper nor prudent for the use and benefits of those monies to be controlled completely by a privileged few. The more successful the Partnership for the Arts becomes, the greater will be the necessity for a true partnership between the orchestra and all elements of management.
>
> Senza Sordino *(April 1971)*

Many American orchestras were established concurrently with their major European counterparts. The Vienna Philharmonic and the New York Philharmonic were founded in 1842; the Boston Symphony and the

Saint Louis Symphony in 1881, one year before the Berlin Philharmonic; the Chicago Symphony in 1891, thirteen years before the Amsterdam Concertgebouw and the London Symphony in 1904. Many conductors immigrated to America and brought with them musicians from France, Germany, Belgium, Italy, Czechoslovakia, Holland, and London. In spite of American union prohibitions to import foreign musicians, the composition of American orchestras became truly international. The performance and teaching traditions that began with these Europeans have influenced generations of musicians. American orchestras founded in the classic European traditions are comparable in terms of preeminence, quality, and stature. But that is where the similarities end. American orchestras are all nonprofit organizations that depend primarily on private contributions for their survival. Professional European orchestras have traditionally received most of their support from their respective governments, although in Germany this is changing since the fall of the Berlin Wall in 1989. Twenty-six radio symphonies provide employment for 1,700 musicians of Germany. No other nation in the Western world has so many orchestras funded entirely by public broadcasters. In Berlin, unification meant there were suddenly two of everything, including two radio symphonies and two choruses.

Europe's system of medical care is much more liberal regarding patients than the U.S. insurance industry, and the employer/employee–patient/insurance relationship leans toward employee's rights. Requests by a musician for performance-related illness or injury are granted without question by the employer, and often a doctor will recommend a spa for treatment and relief. Insurance must cover all expenses, and the affected musician does not have to convince the insurance company or the employer of the treatment's value. Although each musician pays into the health insurance each month, and since the 1990s small co-pays have been required in Europe, the salary level is high enough to be unaffected by these costs.

American orchestras also faced co-pay issues in the negotiations of the 1990s. The reality of the rising costs of health care was affecting all employees, and musicians were no exception. Part of the negotiating committee's job was to convince their colleagues of the necessity to share with the employer the increasing health insurance costs. For the first time, co-pays were negotiated as a part of the health insurance packages for many American orchestras.

Insurance/health issues notwithstanding, the structure, working conditions, and contractual and union issues of European and American orchestras also present interesting comparisons.

The audition process in German orchestras contrasts sharply with the American ICSOM orchestras. The candidate for a German orchestra is heard by all the orchestra members without a screen, and only the orchestra votes, by secret ballot. The music director and general manager may not vote; they may speak if they so choose, but they can be overruled by a majority vote of the orchestra. The candidate must win by a two-thirds majority.

In contrast with this, according to the Minnesota Orchestra master agreement, the seven- or nine-member audition committee vote may be overruled by the sole decision of the conductor, after a secret ballot vote is taken by the committee. In most cases, the conductor probably would not overrule the committee's vote, but technically it is possible.

According to Thomas Turner, Minnesota Orchestra principal viola since 1994, and former principal viola of the Deutsches Symphonie Orchester Berlin, formerly Radio Symphony Orchestra Berlin, the process of screening candidates is handled very differently than in American orchestras:

> After the opening is advertised in the trade magazine *Das Orchester*, which is available internationally, the candidates must send a complete résumé, including photo, age, and religion, the last being optional. Then the section in which the opening occurs reviews each résumé and votes upon whom they will invite to audition. The employer then pays second-class round-trip train fare within Germany, according to federal law, with the stipulation that if you win, you are obliged to take the job. In the rare case a candidate refuses to accept the offered position, the candidate must reimburse the orchestra for the expenses of holding a new audition.

Openings in American orchestras are advertised internationally in the American Federation of Musicians trade magazine. "Highly qualified applicants" are asked to send a detailed résumé, including educational and professional background, but no one is prohibited from auditioning. Sometimes tapes are also required, and often auditions are held behind a screen for the preliminaries and sometimes finals, depending on the choice of the committees.

German musicians are government employees and belong to a union, but unlike the American Federation of Musicians, which represents only musicians, *all* government employees of Germany belong to the same union, including sanitation workers, and bus and taxi drivers. Every two or three years the union negotiates overall salary issues with the government, which covers all German orchestras' base salary.

Health insurance and sick leave are established by a fixed government standard, but working conditions are negotiated by elected musician representatives and are applied uniformly to all German orchestras. Strikes by German musicians are virtually unheard of.

The orchestras of France, Italy, Holland, and Switzerland are also subsidized by both federal and local governments, and their salary structure is tied to that of the civil service or government employees. In most of the major European orchestras, artistic policy decisions, such as repertoire and selection of guest conductors, originate with the musicians, as well as personnel decisions including hiring, tenure, and termination. The music director may have an equal vote in personnel decisions, or may have no vote.

The Berlin Philharmonic was founded as its own company in 1882, a self-governing organization whose members are shareholders and engage their own conductors. Its service structure (rehearsals and concerts) is based on an extensive rotation system. Each player accumulates credits for each service performed, and the work is distributed equally. The Philharmonic employs 125 musicians, as compared with 95 to 105 by most major American orchestras.

Thomas Turner explained the situation of the Deutsches Symphonie Orchester Berlin's 110 players this way:

> Each section has double principals who split the forty-week season of actual work, which means the co-principals work a total of about eighteen weeks a year. However, if you were to tell German symphony musicians that they could negotiate their

own individual contracts, they would be shocked at this privilege. There are no individual contracts except in the rarest of cases. [The members of American orchestras are able to negotiate personal contracts if they so choose.]

In regard to duration of rehearsals, schedule changes, and efficiency of music preparation, I appreciate the way it is done here. It saves so much time during rehearsal. Very rarely would a conductor [in Germany] send a score ahead with specific requests, so all markings would occur during rehearsal. My orchestra had no librarians, and few European orchestras have the kind of resources of a typical U.S. orchestra, especially an extensive music library.

The staffs of typical European orchestras do not come close to the size of those of their American counterparts. European orchestras do not have development, publicity, or marketing departments, and most have an office of fewer than ten people, which was typical of most American orchestras until the 1960s. Being heavily subsidized by the government, with few sponsors involved or necessary, European orchestras are unfamiliar with the trials and tribulations of U.S. orchestras' fund-raising, marketing, and publicity departments, although they are becoming less so with reduced public funding available.

The orchestras of London are in another category altogether. The London Philharmonic, the Royal Philharmonic Orchestra, the Philharmonia, and the London Symphony are self-governing, which means their boards are staffed entirely by musicians, who are elected by the entire orchestra. Each player in the four major orchestras of London has a share and therefore a vote. Artistic and personnel decisions originate with the players, as they do in the Berlin Philharmonic. London musicians are paid as freelancers rather than having a contracted salary. Musicians must work as many dates as possible, ranging from classical concerts and film scores to recordings and advertising jingles. There is a great deal of competition for the available commercial work, and the schedules are grueling and irregular, with few limits on the hours of daily work.

All of the Australian orchestras have a relatively short history compared to U.S. orchestras. They were founded in the 1930s in Sydney and

Melbourne, and soon after in other states by the Australian Broadcasting Company. The ABC was created because public demand grew for a more national system of broadcasting, similar to the BBC in England. The ABC first went on the air July 1, 1932, and in 1936 six network core orchestras—each composed of permanent professional players—were established in Sydney, Melbourne, Queensland, South Australia, Western Australia, and Tasmania. According to Charles Buttrose, the author of *Playing for Australia*: "The ABC does not play favorites in building orchestral strengths. Numbers, to a degree, depend on the financial co-operation of State Government and municipal authorities. The ABC's problem for some years has been to find the players to keep the orchestras up to growing strengths. The Musicians' Union has been co-operative in permitting the ABC to engage any musician available, (regardless of nationality) and to import players from other countries."

At one time, the Musicians Union negotiated for all the ABC orchestras without musician input—similar to the situation with U.S. symphony musicians before ICSOM in 1962. One of the oldest unions in Australia, it was dominated by freelance and part-time musicians who regarded permanently employed symphony musicians as elite and well off, not unlike the situation in America's unions before the founding of ICSOM.

The Australia Musicians Union did little to improve the pay and conditions of symphony musicians over the years, which was aggravated by a "closed shop" agreement between the union and the ABC, who refused to employ nonunion members. This meant that as long as the union received its dues from the players, it had little interest in doing anything that might upset the ABC. Infighting between local and federal unions necessitated committees to provide services to their orchestras that the union was not able or chose not to provide. Relationships continued to deteriorate between the musicians and their union.

Symphony musicians eventually seceded from the Musicians Union of Australia and joined with other arts workers in an organization known as SOMA, Symphony Orchestra Musicians Association. SOMA represents most of Australia's orchestras, and also covers actors, journalists, and theatrical workers. Like America's ICSOM, it functions as a communication network made up of delegates from various orchestras.

Similar to their American colleagues, Australian orchestras elect a players committee, which is a forum for the day-to-day concerns of players and represents the musicians in consultations with management. The terms and conditions of employment are negotiated between the company and the musicians' representative union every few years. The orchestras of Adelaide, Melbourne, Queensland, Sydney, Tasmania, and Western Australia are currently being formed as independent subsidiary companies of the ABC, along with a national umbrella organization, Symphony Australia. Although all receive government support, they are nevertheless faced with the daunting task of creating endowments and tapping into private funds. Like Europe, there is no real tradition of private and corporate donations to the arts in Australia.

The More Things Change . . .

This chapter's title, "Current Issues," suggests that symphony musicians in 2005 face challenges that their antecedents did not know. To some extent, that may be true. What did the musicians of 1932 know about buying an extra airplane seat for their cellos? When he sold Fuller Brush products door-to-door in the 1950s, what did the Cleveland Orchestra concertmaster know about the stresses of performing under a fifty-two-week contract? Still, some things never change, and even the questions of airplane seats and performance stresses require answers informed by centuries-old knowledge and understanding of a musician's life.

The American symphony orchestra system, grounded as it is in the local communities that provide the support necessary to maintain their orchestras, has grown from the particular social and educational needs of these United States. ICSOM itself arose during a period in which symphony orchestra musicians began to find their own voices and to define the importance of their roles in this society. The founders of ICSOM provided guiding principles that have served its members, and American society, throughout a period of great social changes, and will no doubt continue to do so, no matter what "current issues" arise.

♪ *Issues Addressed by ICSOM*

Many topics have been addressed *in Senza Sordino* and at ICSOM conferences by guest speakers, in workshops, and in floor discussions. The following list suggests the number and range of topics:

Communications among orchestras

Wages and working conditions

Artistic advisory committees and musician artistic input

Relations with the AFM and with local unions

Relations with other organizations: American Symphony Orchestra League (ASOL), Symphony Orchestra Institute (SOI), Major Orchestra Managers Conference (MOMC), Conductors' Guild, Organization of Canadian Orchestras (OCSOM), Regional Orchestra Players Association (ROPA), Recording Musicians Association (RMA), and Theater Musicians' Association (TMA)

Relations with management

Audition policies, procedures, and ethics

Concert halls, lighting, and acoustics

Condition and legibility of printed music

Conductors and conductor evaluation

Copyright laws, piracy, home taping, and royalties

Music critics and criticism

Discrimination on the basis of age, gender, race

Dress codes

Selection and bargaining unit status of extra musicians (subs)

Education and training of classical musicians

Orchestra finances and fund-raising

Conditions in foreign orchestras

Insurance coverage: medical, musical instruments

continued on next page

continued from previous page

Legislative action affecting the arts and unions

Tax rulings affecting orchestras and musicians

Role of the personnel manager and union steward

Occupational health problems, high sound levels, stage fright, overuse injuries

Encouragement of minority programs, Music Assistance Fund

Techniques and procedures in negotiation and arbitration

Orchestra splitting

Pensions, retirement funds, tax-sheltered annuities

Benefits for retired members

Job security: probation, tenure, and dismissal

Job satisfaction and quality of work life

Media: Phonograph/CD recording; radio, television, and Internet broadcasting and taping

Rotations of the work load, revolving seating

Special concerts, activities, and programs

Educational concerts and audience expansion

Time away from work: leave, vacation, sabbaticals, pregnancy

Tours and run-outs

Transportation of musical instruments

Tom Hall in *ICSOM: Forty Years of the International Conference of Symphony and Orchestra Musicians*

Nine

. . . And Other Untold Stories

The Minneapolis Symphony/Minnesota Orchestra: A Case in Point

"The new attitude among symphony musicians is for year-round employment and security through pensions. They have taken up the general attitude of laboring people. This I consider social progress. The unsettled conditions in music are not any worse than any other field. But we expect it less in music because we like to have the men looked upon as artists. It is disconcerting to look upon the men as having the problems of wages, hours, and weeks of work."

> *Erich Leinsdorf, music director, Boston Symphony*
> *(quoted in* Chicago Daily News, *November 29, 1962)*

*I*N SPITE OF THE DIFFERENCES that exist among the regions and communities of this vast country, the symphony orchestra world in the United States comprises, in the end, a network of musicians whose similarities are much more striking than their differences. Reviewing the history of American symphony orchestras, particularly since the founding of ICSOM in 1962, I have marveled repeatedly at the similarities in the stories that musicians in such diverse cities as Cleveland, St. Louis, Los Angeles, Seattle, and Atlanta had to tell.

Documenting each Minnesota Orchestra/Minneapolis Symphony contract negotiation since 1960 is essential to this labor history, because it represents the struggles, conflicts, and progress of a major American orchestra. Not only does it mirror the growth of ICSOM, it tells the real drama of behind-the-scenes-pounding-on-the-table events that are an inevitable and often valuable part of the negotiating process.

The following year-by-year Minnesota Orchestra documentation might also serve as a resource to future committees, when inevitable questions arise about language in the master agreement, and somebody asks in exasperation, "How in the hell did that get in there?"

Orchestra on Wheels—And Other Conveyances:
An International Reputation

The first tour of the Minneapolis Symphony Orchestra in 1907, financed by Emil Oberhoffer, the orchestra's founding conductor (as the music director was titled in those early days), established an important precedent, contributing quickly to the good reputation that the orchestra established first in the United States and later internationally. Extensive touring became an essential part of the orchestra's concert seasons, a way of life that continued until the mid-1960s, keeping the musicians on the road and away from their families for weeks and sometimes months at a time.

The tradition for touring started in the Minneapolis Symphony's fourth season, 1906–1907. Oberhoffer took the orchestra to Moorhead, Duluth, and Grand Forks, North Dakota. He initiated and financed the first three tours (1907, 1908, and 1909) with his own money, because the Orchestral Association was wary of the financial risk. He, however, had several passionately held beliefs about the importance of touring and was willing to underwrite the ventures to convince the board of directors of his reasoning. An idealistic and visionary musician recently arrived from his native Bavaria, Oberhoffer wanted to bring symphony orchestra concerts to people throughout his new land. Furthermore, he knew that the experience of touring would sharpen the performance skills of his musicians, spread the reputation of the Minneapolis Symphony, and prove financially viable.

A tradition of winter and spring tours began in these early years, including two weeks in Ravinia Park in Highland Park, Illinois, and regular visits to Carnegie Hall beginning in 1912. John Sherman, a Twin Cities music critic and author of *Music and Maestros: The Story of the Minneapolis Symphony Orchestra*, coined the nickname "Orchestra-on-

FEBRUARY—
23—Lv. Birmingham, Seaboard No. 6 . . . . 7:50 A.M.
     (Diner serving Luncheon)
   Ar. Atlanta, Seaboard No. 6 (E. T.) . . . . 1:35 P.M.
     (EASTERN TIME FROM ATLANTA)
24—Lv. Atlanta, N. C. & St. L. No. 90 . . . . 10:00 A.M.
   Ar. Chattanooga, N. C. & St. L. No. 90 (C. T.) 12:55 P.M.
     (CENTRAL TIME FROM CHATTANOOGA)
25—Lv. Chattanooga, N. C. & St. L. No. 90 . . 1:05 P.M.
   Ar. Nashville, N. C. & St. L. No. 90 . . . . 5:15 P.M.
27—Lv. Nashville, L. & N. No. 98 . . . . . 12:20 P.M.
     (Diner serving Luncheon)
   Ar. Louisville, L. & N. No. 98 . . . . . 4:45 P.M.
28—Lv. Louisville, Penna. R. R. No. 315 . . . 8:05 A.M.
   Ar. Indianapolis, Penna. R. R. No. 315 . . 10:23 A.M.
   Lv. Indianapolis, N. Y. Central No. 13 . . 11:00 A.M.
   Ar. Urbana, N. Y. Central No. 13 . . . . 2:26 P.M.
   Ar. Champaign, N. Y. Central No. 13 . . . 2:39 P.M.
MARCH—
1—Lv. Urbana, N. Y. Central No. 13 . . . . 2:26 P.M.
   Lv. Champaign, N. Y. Central No. 13 . . . 2:39 P.M.
   Ar. Peoria, N. Y. Central No. 13 . . . . 5:30 P.M.
2—Lv. Peoria, Rock Island No. 502 . . . . 7:00 A.M.
   Ar. Chicago, Rock Island No. 502 . . . . 9:40 A.M.
     (La Salle Street Station)
3—Lv. Chicago, Milwaukee No. 17 (Union Sta.) 9:20 A.M.
   Ar. Madison, Milwaukee No. 17 . . . . . 12:30 P.M.
4—Lv. Madison, Milwaukee No. 28 . . . . . 10:00 A.M.
   Ar. Watertown, Milwaukee No. 28 . . . . 10:50 A.M.
   Lv. Watertown, Milwaukee No. 5 . . . . 12:45 P.M.
     (Diner serving Luncheon)
   Ar. La Crosse, Milwaukee No. 5 . . . . . 3:32 P.M.
4—Lv. La Crosse, C. B. & Q. No. 23 . . . . 8:21 P.M.
   Ar. St. Paul, C. B. & Q. No. 23 . . . . 10:30 P.M.
   Ar. Minneapolis, C. B. & Q. No. 23 . . . 11:00 P.M.
     (Great Northern Station)
NOTE—The party will occupy Pullman Sleeping Cars for the overnight movements from Montreal to Quebec; Quebec to Montreal; Ottawa to Montreal. All other movements will be made in Chair Cars or Coaches.

Hotels
(First Hotel listed for each City is Company Headquarters)
JANUARY
27-28—Chicago Illinois—Hotel La Salle.
29—Lansing, Michigan—Hotel Olds.
30—Battle Creek, Michigan—Post Tavern; Hart Hotel.
31—Toledo, Ohio—Commodore Perry; The Secor.

FEBRUARY
1-2—Utica, New York—Hotel Utica; Hotel Hamilton.
3-4—Montreal, Canada—Mount Royal; Hotel Windsor
6—Quebec, Canada—The Chateau Frontenac.
7—Ottawa, Canada—The Chateau Laurier.
8—Kingston, Canada—Hotel La Salle.
9-10—Buffalo, New York—Hotel Statler; Hotel Touraine.
11—Mansfield, Ohio—Mansfield-Leland Hotel.
12—Columbus, Ohio—Deshler-Wallick Hotel.
13—Bloomington, Indiana—Memorial Union; Hotel Graham.
14—St. Louis, Missouri—Hotel Jefferson.
15—Memphis, Tennessee—Hotel Peabody; Hotel Claridge.
16-19—New Orleans, La.—Hotel St. Charles; The Roosevelt; The Monteleone; The Jung; The New Orleans; The De Soto.
20—Mobile, Ala.—The Battle House; The Admiral Semmes; The Cawthon.
21—Montgomery, Ala.—The Jefferson Davis; The Whitley.
22—Birmingham, Ala.—Hotel Tutwiler; Hotel Bankhead.
23—Atlanta, Georgia—Atlanta Biltmore; Hotel Piedmont.
24—Chattanooga, Tenn.—The Read House; Hotel Patten.
25-26—Nashville, Tenn.—Hotel Hermitage; The Andrew Jackson.
27—Louisville, Kentucky—Hotel Seelbach.
28—Urbana, Illinois—The Urbana Lincoln; Hotel Inman (Champaign)
MARCH
1—Peoria, Illinois—The Pere Marquette; Hotel Jefferson.
2—Chicago, Illinois—Hotel La Salle.
3—Madison, Wis.—The Wisconsin Union; Hotel Loraine; Hotel Belmont.

GENERAL INFORMATION
Official Mail and Messages for the Manager and Conductor should be addressed to them personally at Headquarter Hotels listed above. Personal mail for other members of the party should be addressed: "Care of Minneapolis Symphony Orchestra, General Delivery," and telegrams for individual members should be addressed to them "Care of Minneapolis Symphony Orchestra; Western Union Agent at... Merle Adams will serve as Postmaster, calling for and distributing mail and telegrams and leaving instructions for forwarding. No other member of the party is authorized to handle Company mail or messages.

Itinerary...

WINTER TOUR
Season 1944-1945

•

MINNEAPOLIS SYMPHONY ORCHESTRA

DIMITRI MITROPOULOS
Conductor

•

Tour Under the Personal Direction of
ARTHUR J. GAINES, Manager

•

YVES CHARDON . . . Assistant Conductor
GLENN R. COOKE . . Personnel Manager
HERMAN G. BOESSENROTH . . Librarian
MISCHA BREGMAN . Assistant Librarian
SAM GRODNICK . . . Stage Manager
DR. CARL PETERSON . . Health Officer

Itinerary for Minneapolis Symphony Orchestra Winter Tour, 1944–1945 (Archives of the Minnesota Orchestra, Performing Arts Archives, University of Minnesota Libraries).

Wheels" to describe the importance of touring, which even by that time had taken the orchestra on more miles of concerts outside their home city than any other symphony orchestra in the United States.

From the beginning, bad weather, primitive concert hall accommodations—including tents, churches, gymnasiums, lodge halls, and cattle barns—and the uncomfortable modes of travel in railroad coaches and Pullman cars made touring arduous, to say the least. An immigrant German orchestra musician once said about long tours, "Auf Tour kommt der Charakter heraus" (True character emerges on tours). Those are true words in any language.

Exotic Weight Loss Program

By the mid-1950s, tours had taken the orchestra to almost every state in the Union, as well as to many cities of Canada and to Cuba. Although the ensemble had not yet traveled in Europe, its international reputation, firmly established through recordings and broadcasts, led the U.S. State Department to sponsor a 34,000-mile tour of the Middle East. The Minneapolis Symphony became not only the first Western orchestra to perform in that area of the world, it was also the first symphony orchestra to be sent abroad by the State Department. Music lovers in 175 communities, whose sole previous experience of hearing an orchestra had been through a loudspeaker, now attended concerts of the Minneapolis Symphony as it performed on famous stages and in other historic venues throughout the Middle East. The forty-day odyssey would lead them to cover more than 200,000 miles through Greece, India, Lebanon, Yugoslavia, Iraq, and Iran.

On September 4, 1957, the Mideast Tour set out from Minneapolis for a performance in the Herod Atticus Theater in Athens—which would be followed by concerts in Salonika, Bombay, Beirut, Belgrade, Zagreb, Baghdad, and Tehran. In many of these cities the audience had never experienced a Western orchestra. Over the course of the five weeks, the orchestra performed at least six different concert programs, all conducted by its principal conductor, Antal Doráti, and audiences everywhere responded with overwhelming ovations.

Groups of the musicians traveled to the Mideast in two four-engine planes chartered from a British airline. Because the airplanes could not hold the entire orchestra at once, one group would travel while the others waited, resulting in a lot of free time for the musicians. Other inconveniences and holdups included a nonscheduled stop in Damascus (because flying over Syrian territory required airplane inspections) and the necessity to compensate for the nonpressurized planes. Flying over mountains, some people required supplemental oxygen. (In an unnerving twist, several years later both planes crashed because of age and poor maintenance.)

Some people estimated that each member of the orchestra arrived back home ten to twenty pounds lighter because of the many gastrointestinal problems that they suffered along the way. Bassist Arthur Gold, well known for his droll sense of humor, was asked by someone what was the first thing he intended doing once he returned home. "Well," he said, "the second thing I'm gonna do is put down my suitcase."

Clement Volpe, trumpet player from 1956 to 1997, summed up the Mideast tour and that era: "The late fifties were good times for the Minneapolis Symphony. The season was short and pay was low, but morale was high. Antal Doráti had a knack for putting the symphony on the map, and our recordings of that time on the Mercury label were recognized worldwide. I would have to say this was one of the most exotic tours any orchestra had made."

Back to the Non-exotic

Before 1965 (see contract negotiations for that year, below), the musicians' mode of travel was less than first class. The hotels were primitive and uncomfortable, and room assignments depended upon gender and ranking within the orchestra. All principal players received a private Pullman berth, while the others had to share an upper and lower Pullman, many times without toilets. Untitled players could find showers at the local YMCA—if, upon arrival at a designated city, they could find time before the concert.

"A" hotels served the principal players, managers, and conductors, and the remaining musicians—again, based upon ranking within the orchestra—made do with "B" hotels, or worse. The size of the room key and the speed of the ceiling fan told you more than you needed or wanted to know about the quality of the "accommodations."

Cooke's Tour

Glenn R. Cooke was tour and personnel manager for many years in the 1940s through the early '60s. He would hire a local bus for the musicians to ride in case of bad weather or extensive distances between the hotel and the concert hall. Cooke wore a money clip coin changer and charged the musicians twenty-five cents going to the hall, and another twenty-five cents for the return trip to the hotel.

Stuck on the Ice

The Minneapolis Symphony toured more than two months of the 1962–1963 season, including two weeks in Canada and two weeks in the Midwest, plus many other parts of the country. At an ice hockey arena where one of the concerts took place that summer, some of the musicians found their shoes stuck to the ice. Adding to the bone-chilling cold indoors on the rink, the unlucky players found themselves with refrigerated summer footwear and no means of escape.

So Much for Warming Up

During one of the orchestra's tours in the middle of a frigid Canadian winter, the instrument truck arrived at the gymnasium where the performance was to take place. One of the trumpet players, Clement Volpe, pulled his instrument out of the case to warm up before the concert only to realize the valves on the trumpet were completely frozen.

In the late 1960s and early '70s, the orchestra administration finally acquired steamer trunks for the tours. This long-overdue "luxury" allowed for a safer environment for concert dress and personal articles. (For those who are unfamiliar with "steamer trunks," the Marx Brothers' movie *A Night at the Opera* offers one of the classic American examples of their use.) Violinist Carl Nashan discovered an abundance of these trunks in the Twin Cities and received authorization from the orchestra's

Itinerary for Minneapolis Symphony Orchestra Winter Tour, 1962–1963 (Archives of the Minnesota Orchestra, Performing Arts Archives, University of Minnesota Libraries).

management to buy the best available, with a strict budget not to exceed ten dollars apiece.

Stories of touring over the orchestra's first century include both humorous adventures and misadventures by the hundreds, as well as an anecdotal record of serious issues, hardships, and problems that became central issues in negotiations over the years. Once again, present-day musicians owe a huge debt to their predecessors for enduring the difficult conditions and working assiduously to change them.

Touring in the Postmodern Era

Three Mile Island: Partial Meltdown and the Lancaster 23

As part of a two-week Eastern U.S. tour beginning in April 1979, the Minnesota Orchestra was scheduled to perform in Lancaster, Pennsylvania, on April 26. Approximately one month before departure, radiation was accidentally released from the crippled nuclear reactor at Three Mile Island, or TMI, in Pennsylvania, located twenty-five miles from Lancaster.

Arising from a series of human and technical errors, the first nuclear accident in U.S. history began when a valve opened, unnoticed, to allow thousands of gallons of coolant water to escape from the plant's new Unit 2 reactor. Temperatures quickly rose to exceed 5,000 degrees Fahrenheit, and the fuel core subsequently began to melt. Fortunately, it burned through only one layer of the containment structure. Had it broken through the second, the accident would have reached the proportions of the Chernobyl meltdown in 1986. Instead, in the case of TMI, only a partial core meltdown occurred, averting a potential major steam or hydrogen explosion.

Two days after the accident, the governor of Pennsylvania ordered an evacuation of all pregnant women and young children within an eight-mile radius of the plant. The Minnesota Orchestra committee expressed concern about the wisdom and safety of traveling to Lancaster and asked the managing director of the orchestra to stay in touch with the Nuclear Regulatory Commission (NRC) and Critical Mass, a Ralph Nader nuclear watchdog group. In two meetings with the orchestra before the tour, the manager told the musicians that while there was simply not enough knowledge of radiation to say what was safe and what wasn't, the reactor was cooling down, and he anticipated a cold shutdown by the time of the Lancaster concert. The management told the musicians that it would continue to monitor the situation closely and that "under absolutely no circumstances" would the orchestra travel to Lancaster if there were any danger to the players.

Unbeknownst to the rest of the orchestra, one musician, Jack Moore, timpani, wrote a private letter to the management in which he stated that because of the many unknown factors at TMI, he would not play the concert in Lancaster unless the reactor was in "cold shutdown." He stated he expected to be docked a pro rata portion of his wages for missing the Lancaster concert, and he offered several courses of action to ensure that a substitute musician would be available to perform in his place.

As the tour progressed, it became apparent that the TMI reactor would not be in cold shutdown by the time of the Lancaster concert. Moore then contacted management and stated that he would not perform; they informed him in return that refusal to perform could lead to his dismissal. Moore then told the orchestra committee about the letter exchange and the dismissal threat.

The rest of the orchestra, unaware of these events, was becoming increasingly confused and concerned by the conflicting TMI safety reports appearing daily in the press. The crisis situation had spread from endangering the local community to affecting the whole nation.

As a member of the committee, I was designated to speak during the tour, on a daily basis, with a Nuclear Regulatory Commission representative. The NRC was unable to guarantee our safety because of the risk of possible meltdown and the proximity of Lancaster to TMI. It became increasingly obvious to the committee that the government regulatory agency could not provide us with reliable information; lacking that, we could not make an informed decision on such an unprecedented and hazardous occurrence.

The committee called a full orchestra meeting to inform the members of current events as we understood them. On the morning of the concert, the orchestra met in the large gloomy conference room at our motel in East Brunswick, New Jersey. We told the orchestra everything we knew about the TMI crisis, including a full explanation of the dismissal threats against one of the musicians. We could offer no clear answers to this emotional and troubling subject. The committee encouraged the musicians to express their feelings as much as possible, but we all realized we faced a situation that we were unequipped to evaluate.

After heated discussion, several motions were made. Management addressed the orchestra about an hour into the meeting and said their sources indicated no reason to cancel the concert and that anyone refusing to play the concert could face dismissal for insubordination. By this time twenty-two more musicians said they would refuse to perform. Although some felt we should be "good soldiers" and trust the management, the musicians passed a unanimous motion to support any player who declined to perform in Lancaster. We rejected another motion to refuse to play the Lancaster concert, and to avoid proximity to TMI, we voted to waive a contractual stipulation in order to allow management to make alternate hotel arrangements.

By the time the meeting was adjourned, at least two hours later, many of us felt emotionally drained from the intensity of the discussion and the impact of the decisions. We felt that no one's decision was capricious, and we respected the choices individuals had made. In the end, and after much soul-searching and debate, twenty-three musicians chose not to perform because of the proximity to TMI. The "Lancaster 23," as they became known, chartered a bus from East Brunswick to State College, a seven-hour trip, bypassing Lancaster. The remaining sixty-seven musicians performed the 8 P.M. concert, leaving as soon as possible afterward for the substitute hotel in State College. Most musicians arrived at 2:15 A.M., but a cautious five who took a separate bus after the concert to bypass the TMI area arrived at State College at 3 A.M.

Upon their return to Minneapolis after the tour, the "Lancaster 23" received a letter from management stating that their refusal to play could subject them to disciplinary action, but that due to the "special sensitivity" of this particular situation, none would be taken. Nonetheless, all twenty-three had a prorated portion of their wages docked from their paychecks. None of the orchestra's ninety-five musicians received any travel penalty pay, although all had traveled for an amount of time that exceeded the limits in the master contract.

The committee retained labor lawyer Ronald Rollins to represent the orchestra in general and the "Lancaster 23" specifically. Unable to reach an agreement with management, they submitted the matter to final and binding arbitration. The decision of January 23, 1980, stated that the arbitrator could "find no fault with either party. Each did its best under a difficult and often confusing situation. In this unique situation, beset by the vagaries of radiation, it thus seems fair and equitable that they should share the costs of the impasse in which they found themselves. The dangers inherent in radiation are so vague, so impossible to verify that no one can say for certain what the final results of any exposure will be. Twenty years from now it may be determined that a trip to Lancaster in April of 1979 could result in a genetically damaged child. Simply stated, no one knows."

Postscript

Eighteen years later, in February 1997, the National Institutes of Health reanalyzed data from a 1990 report that had concluded that the nation's worst civilian nuclear accident could not be held responsible for excessive cancer cases, because radiation exposures had been too low. However, the new data indicated that there was a significant increase in cancers downwind from TMI. The study did not offer the entire proof by itself, but constituted part of a body of evidence that was consistent with high exposures.

Minnesota Broadcasts More Than Grain

We cannot overestimate the role that broadcasting and recording have played in the history of the Minneapolis Symphony/Minnesota Orchestra, nor the role that this orchestra has played in the recording and broadcast industries of the United States. Even today, in 2005, when most symphony orchestras struggle to find recording and radio contracts and sponsors, the Minnesota Orchestra continues to record (currently for the Swedish label BIS) and broadcast (live performances from Orchestra Hall heard on more than 250 stations of the Minnesota Public Radio network nationwide and distributed by American Public Media).

Music critic Richard Freed has written extensively about this orchestra's activities in these fields, and I can do no better than to quote Freed's summary as published in the orchestra's twelve-disc CD set issued in

2003, *Minnesota Orchestra at One Hundred: A Collection of Recordings and Broadcasts*. I thank both Mr. Freed and the Minnesota Orchestral Association for permission to use his remarks:

"The Minneapolis Symphony Orchestra—now the Minnesota Orchestra—began broadcasting in 1923 and began recording the following year. As much as recordings and broadcasting played major roles in making the ensemble known to the world, this orchestra itself may be said without hyperbole to have played a similarly important role in establishing and sustaining the validity and importance of those 'electronic media' in the music world.

"Because the Orchestra began broadcasting in March 1923 during a brief interregnum between music directors, the initial broadcast concert was conducted by a guest, the illustrious Bruno Walter, then on his first tour of the United States. It was his own first experience on radio as well as the Orchestra's.

"Recording began in April of the following year, during a concert tour to New York under Verbrugghen. The old acoustical method of recording was still in use at that time, but following the replacement of the acoustical horn by the microphone of the electrical process in 1925, Verbrugghen remade some of the acoustical sides and added several new titles to the Orchestra's embryonic discography.

"It was under Eugene Ormandy, Verbrugghen's successor, that the Orchestra became a major player in the recording world. When he arrived in 1931, the Great Depression had virtually shut down orchestral recording in the U.S. The Boston Symphony Orchestra under Koussevitzky, the Chicago SO under Stock, and even the New York Philharmonic under Toscanini had been suspended by the Victor Company, and only the Philadelphia Orchestra under Stokowski continued active for that label. The same company, alerted to a contract provision that enabled the Minneapolis Symphony to undertake recordings without having to pay its musicians for the extra services involved, sent its production team to Northrop Auditorium in Minneapolis for less than two weeks early in 1934, and again in 1935, and turned out a prodigious quantity of material that was not only marketable but established the orchestra's name throughout the world as symbol of excellence.

"Dimitri Mitropoulos, Ormandy's dynamic successor, had not made recordings before coming to Minneapolis, but one of those he made early in his tenure, the world premiere recording of Mahler's First Symphony, is perhaps the single most significant entry in the orchestra's vast discography. It was the recording through which an entire generation of listeners first became acquainted—and fascinated—with that composer's music. It is still in circulation, on CD, and still unmatched in respect to intensity, drive, and sheer excitement.

"Under Antal Doráti, who followed Mitropoulos, the Minneapolis Symphony became the flagship for Mercury's 'Living Presence' series, ushering in the era of high fidelity on LP and continuing to create landmarks of the early stereophonic years. His recordings with the Orchestra circulated even more widely than Ormandy's, and many of them were splendidly remastered for CD in the early 1990s. Doráti's successor, Stanislaw Skrowaczewski, whose long tenure saw the change of the Orchestra's name, made a memorable series of quadraphonic LPs for Vox; these, too, have been reissued on CD.

"Sir Neville Marriner and Edo de Waart added depth and dimension to the orchestra's discography, on new labels, in new repertory, in new technical developments. Eiji Oue, who stepped down as music director in 2002, made nearly twenty 'sonic showpieces' in HDCD (High Definition Compatible Digital) for Reference Recordings, and Skrowaczewski returned as laureate conductor to record a stunning Bruckner Ninth and several of his own works, also on Reference. Osmo Vänskä, who first established his international credentials with his Finnish orchestra, Sinfonia Lahti, on the BIS label, is scheduled to extend the orchestra's discography."

As Freed predicted in 2003, the Minnesota Orchestra under Vänskä has, indeed, expanded its discography. It is now embarked upon a project with BIS to record the entire nine symphonies of Beethoven. The first disc in the series, containing the Fourth and Fifth symphonies, appeared in January 2005.

A True Identity Crisis: Formerly the Minneapolis Symphony

Many of my colleagues were not even born when the Minneapolis Symphony Orchestra suddenly—from one day to the next in 1968—became the Minnesota Orchestra. Still, the story of the name change belongs to our collective history, and the ramifications of the change, even thirty-seven years after the event, continue to tug at all the musicians, whether new or retired members of the orchestra. Recounting this story, I think not only of them, but also of the many thousands of Minneapolis Symphony Orchestra colleagues and fans who shared in the loss of identity along with the musicians. It is impossible to exaggerate the demoralizing effect it has had.

Sixty-five years of proud tradition seemed to disappear overnight. The unilateral decision made by a few board members at a crucial moment severed the orchestra's international reputation, earned through decades of tours and recordings (including a Mercury Gold Record for the Tchaikovsky *1812 Festival Overture*, which sold more than a million copies during the 1950s, and continues to sell in its transformation to CD). Explaining that the name "Minnesota Orchestra" was more appropriate for its new aspiration to become a "regional orchestra," the board stripped the organization of its internationally respected identity and created a controversy that has had long-term effects on the relationships between the musicians, board members, and its worldwide community.

September 23, 1968

Seventeen months before the musicians and other members of the public learned about the demise of the name "Minneapolis Symphony Orchestra," John Myers, chairman of the MSO board from 1960 to 1964 and president of the Hoerner-Waldorf Corporation, had announced the launching of a $10 million funding campaign for the orchestra. According to an article in the *St. Paul Pioneer Press* (Sunday, April 30, 1967), Mr. Myers explained the board's intention by expressing the hope "that the orchestra can finally become a truly regional orchestra."

By the following year, the board had arrived at the decision for the

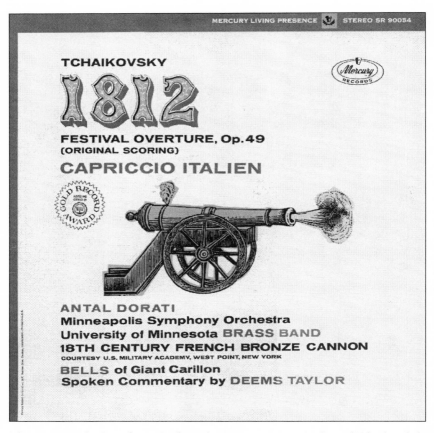

The Minneapolis Symphony Orchestra's Mercury 1958 recording of Tchaikovsky's 1812 Overture, *conducted by Antal Doráti, earned a gold record for sales of more than a million copies within four years and made recording history on a global scale during this era (Courtesy of the Minnesota Orchestra).*

name change. On September 23, 1968, the musicians and the music director, Stanislaw Skrowaczewski, were called to a meeting after a rehearsal at a local high school. Board Chairman Judson S. Bemis was introduced to the gathering. In their wildest dreams they could not have imagined the shock they would receive. "The board intended," Mr. Bemis announced, "to reflect the Orchestra's commitment to the state of Minnesota."

"Due to the desire to expand the performance schedule to include many communities throughout the region, as well as expand program-ming," said Mr. Bemis, "we have decided to change the name of the Min-neapolis Symphony to the Minnesota Orchestra."

After a moment of deafening silence—and in disbelief that the musi-cians had really heard the announcement correctly—one of them asked, "Why can't we do the same outreach with the Minneapolis Symphony name!!??" The board's exact response to that question was not recorded, but the musicians later recalled that the meeting was brought to a quick end, with no discussion allowed.

The musicians reacted with shock, anger, and bewilderment. The board had excluded them from the deliberations and discussions, which had taken place behind closed doors. Their collective feeling of loss—of identity, image, pride, and international reputation—cannot be imag-ined or described. As soon as they could privately gather to express their vehement opposition, they wrote a letter, with a petition that they circu-lated and unanimously signed, which they presented to Mr. Bemis and the Minnesota Orchestral Association.

The musicians' letter said, in part:

> As professional musicians we know that in America today any
> orchestra that uses a state name is synonymous with a semi-
> professional [or] amateur orchestra. We know that the moment
> we appear without our cherished name of 66 years our public
> will speculate that our former orchestra has been disbanded
> and that this is a new venture. Perhaps irreparable damage will
> occur that cannot be rectified. We fear that the present move
> represents complete dislocation from our past and will force
> us out of the ranks of the great name orchestras with whom we
> belong. We feel that it is a mistaken premise to say that because
> we originate from Minneapolis . . . we do not represent the
> region. We are a part of Minnesota just as surely as any other
> organization or business in the state. It might be interesting to
> ask Mr. Ormandy [Philadelphia Orchestra music director] or
> Mr. Szell [Cleveland Orchestra music director] if they would for-
> feit the names of their great organizations because they play in

towns throughout their states. Please give consideration to this, our first and only voice in the matter.

Other phrases the musicians used in the letter were "blow to the future of the orchestra" and "jealous pride for our orchestra, its reputation, history and present development toward increased excellence."

This was the first of three major efforts by the orchestra members to restore the name to Minneapolis Symphony. All three ultimately failed.

The following is the list of reasons for the change that the Orchestral Association gave to the bewildered public and stunned musicians in 1968:

1. Expansion of the Orchestra's performance schedule to
   include appearances in numerous communities throughout
   the region;

The Minneapolis Symphony (MSO) first performed in its "Twin City," St. Paul, in 1914, thus beginning a tradition that continued throughout the twentieth century and into the twenty-first. St. Paul had had its own orchestra for eight seasons, beginning in 1906 (three years after the founding of the Minneapolis Symphony), but it proved to be a truly nonprofitable enterprise. In the fall of 1914, its guaranty fund expired, and the St. Paul businessmen who formed the core of its support decided they had spent enough. Earlier efforts to consolidate the Minneapolis and St. Paul orchestras had come to naught. In August 1914, the Minneapolis Symphony's founding president suggested that the MSO duplicate its Friday night performances on Thursday nights in St. Paul. Eight of these Thursday nights were finally agreed upon for the series across the river.

A contemporary newspaper article reported that although some questioned why St. Paul should support a Minneapolis institution, it was soon accepted "not as an invasion, but as a neighborly loan in time of need," as a local music critic assured his fellow citizens. Soon the MSO's concerts in St. Paul became a symbol of the end of intercity bickering. Still, another controversial suggestion cropped up, according to the same newspaper report: Minneapolis should be magnanimous enough to "change the

2. Diversification in programming to expand the Orchestra's appeal to people of varied age groups and in all economic and cultural strata;

3. To underscore the concept that the Orchestra belongs to all the people of the area and is willing to serve their needs, and to extend itself—both geographically and in its programming—to embrace a larger constituency;

4. This name change is a first. No other established major orchestra has ever dared try it. An orchestra with a tradition and distinguished past such as ours has an obligation to make changes that will ensure an even greater future;

5. Authorities consulted by us say that the future of symphony music in the U.S. will depend upon the ability of a few fine orchestras to serve ever broadening audiences.

---

name of its orchestra to the Minnesota Symphony Orchestra." The idea was not acted upon, because even by 1914, the "Minneapolis" trademark had grown so familiar and famous throughout the country that community leaders considered it a long-term investment that they did not want to diminish. Nine former musicians of the St. Paul orchestra were folded into the Minneapolis Symphony in 1914, bringing to twenty-one the number of onetime players from the disbanded St. Paul Symphony who now belonged to the Minneapolis Symphony Orchestra.

Forty-five years later, another orchestra was founded in St. Paul, and the orchestral connections between the two cities had come full circle. "Some of the best orchestra music to originate in St. Paul in years is being provided by the newly formed St. Paul Chamber Orchestra," said John K. Sherman in a *Minneapolis Star* review of the SPCO debut in 1959. At its founding, most of the SPCO's twenty-five players were also members of the Minneapolis Symphony. At that time *both* ensembles were part-time. In 1967, three musicians left the MSO to join the SPCO. Two of them returned within two years, and one of them remained with the chamber orchestra. The SPCO performed five subscription concerts during its first season. In 2004 the SPCO performed a thirty-two-week season and had no players in common with the Minnesota Orchestra.

The unstated expectation, widely articulated by many observers, was that because of the inclusion of "Minnesota" in the orchestra's name, the state of Minnesota would feel more inclined to play a major role in aiding this regional/state organization by increasing public financial support for the orchestra.

Another Sinking Feeling

Setting out on a tour to Mexico City in 1973, just five years after the name change, the dismayed musicians heard an announcement over the public address system at the Minneapolis airport that "boarding would begin immediately for members of the *University of* Minnesota Orchestra." The orchestra experienced further demoralizing events once they arrived in Mexico.

This was the orchestra's first foreign concert tour in sixteen years. Although the government agency that sponsored the orchestra was criticized for not promoting the concerts adequately, the musicians and other observers blamed the poor attendance at its concerts on the unknown name.

The *Minneapolis Star* reported in its edition of March 26, 1973:

> If the concerts were well-received, however, they were not well-attended. Only 379 persons—many of them orchestra members' spouses and individuals who had accompanied the orchestra on a separate tour—attended the opening concert of the series . . . in the 2,000 seat Palacio de Bellas Artes in Mexico City.

A Mexico City music critic remarked later, having missed the concerts, "If only we had known that this was the great Minneapolis Symphony Orchestra!" One of the orchestra musicians said to an orchestra manager, "Perhaps it would have been cheaper to stay home and hire a busload of Mexicans [to attend the concert in the Twin Cities]."

Twenty-nine years after the name change and twenty-four years after Mexico City, one of the sixteen important music agents who heard the orchestra in 1997 in London remarked; "It's extraordinary—where have you been? It's the best-kept musical secret in the U.S."

A Second Try

The second attempt to restore the name "Minneapolis Symphony Orchestra" came in 1974, the same year Orchestra Hall was built. The newly formed artistic advisory committee of musicians presented a letter on March 18, 1974, to the executive committee of the board of directors of the Minnesota Orchestral Association; all ninety-seven members of the orchestra, the personnel manager, stage managers, librarians, staff conductors, former concertmasters, guest soloists, and guest conductors had signed the accompanying petition.

The musicians wrote that the opening of the new Orchestra Hall would present an "opportune" occasion to restore the treasured name. They itemized six major reasons to "reassume the name of the internationally famous Minneapolis Symphony Orchestra," citing the recent, unsuccessful tour to Mexico City, which had drawn such small audiences. Their reasons included:

1. Mistaken for the University of Minnesota Orchestra: major orchestras are named after the city—universities and sports teams are named after states;
2. No recordings with a major label since the name change, and refusal by Mercury Records to release Minneapolis Symphony recordings under the new name;
3. No national tours scheduled;
4. Difficulty booking major artists;
5. Lack of national and international recognition of the new name;
6. Members of the orchestra demoralized by all the above—loss of identity.

The board of directors appointed a committee composed of board members and two musicians to consider the proposal that the original name of the orchestra be restored. On June 19, 1974, the board's chairman, John S. Pillsbury Jr., wrote a letter to the orchestra: "After a considerable discussion in response to the recommendation of the special committee appointed to review the matter, the board voted to retain the name 'Minnesota Orchestra.'"

Third Attempt to Reestablish the Name "Minneapolis Symphony Orchestra"

During the negotiations of 1990–1991, the issue of the name arose many times in relation to other important matters. As a result of those negotiations, the parties agreed to form yet another committee, which would include musicians and board members, to study the issue. A petition to reestablish the name "Minneapolis Symphony Orchestra" was presented. Not surprisingly, the musicians' views in the early 1990s had not changed significantly from those of their colleagues in 1968 and 1973, despite a new generation of players in the orchestra:

1. The Minneapolis Symphony produced 81 recordings during Antal Doráti's tenure as its music director. The remainder of the Mercury contract was completed by the new music director, Stanislaw Skrowaczewski. The CD reissues by Mercury in 1990 were released under the name of the Minneapolis Symphony, with no mention of the current name;

2. Virgin Classics cancelled its intention to record the Mahler cycle;

3. No European tour in the orchestra's history—one of the few major American orchestras *not* to tour Europe;

4. Universal confusion concerning the identity—from Wisconsin to London; including guest conductors, soloists, colleagues of all ages, and general public—always the same questions and surprise that they are hearing/working with the "famous Minneapolis Symphony";

5. A new generation of young musicians who have joined the orchestra are asking the same questions asked in 1968;

6. Still the only top-ten U.S. orchestra not named after its home city and the only orchestra which regularly has recordings reissued under a name different from its current name;

7. Regional outreach virtually nonexistent (as stated in 1968).

After a series of committee meetings, the board announced that the name would remain the Minnesota Orchestra.

♪ *What's in a Name?*

In 1991, the Minnesota Orchestra was scheduled to tour Japan, but the tour was cancelled owing to the "first Gulf War." Other problems also existed, some of which were related to confusion over the orchestra's name—specifically, its lack of recognition internationally as the Minnesota Orchestra. Although he and many others of his generation were accustomed to disappointment, the name change issue and the cancellation of the Japan tour constituted the proverbial straw that broke the camel's back for violinist Carl Nashan. He designed a sweatshirt with the words

MINNESOTA ORCHESTRA
FORMERLY

MINNEAPOLIS

SYMPHONY

ORCHESTRA

prominently displayed on the front. When Carl and I wore matching shirts of his design to rehearsals that week, they caused such an uproar that many of our colleagues requested (actually they *insisted*) we order some for them. We posted a sign-up sheet and quickly sold at least four hundred sweatshirts. Many colleagues and retirees, staff, management, conductors, and soloists were keen to wear them. As the weather changed, they wanted something more lightweight, so we ordered identical T-shirts.

As the shirts began to be seen in public places, other people outside the orchestra wanted to buy them. Eventually, an article appeared in the press (December 1994—on the general subject of labor issues and a musician strike) that mentioned the unusual grass-roots movement. "Buried—but not very deeply—in the musicians' resentment was the issue of the orchestra's name change. It's an old wound that never heals," wrote music critic Mike Anthony.

In creating and wearing the shirts, we were making a statement, to be sure. What surprised us was the overwhelming response not only by our musician colleagues, but also by members of the orchestra's staff, its audiences, and the general public. The shirts served to expose the strong feelings that remained and to irritate and inflame the controversy once again in a very public way—twenty-three years after the name change.

Identity Crisis a Thing of the Past?

Perhaps the consequences of nonrecognition would have been lessened somewhat had the new name "Minnesota Orchestra" been aggressively publicized and marketed at the time of the change, and every succeeding season. This kind of promotion did not occur with any consistency until the orchestra's first European tour, in 1998—nearly thirty years after the event. All of us have cringed with the inevitable questions from the public and even colleagues in other American and (especially) European orchestras: "What happened to the Minneapolis Symphony?" or "Is this the same orchestra as the Minneapolis Symphony?" or "Is this the Minnesota Symphony?" or "Are you with the University of Minnesota?"

In 1990 the Mercury label had reissued recordings made on LPs under the Minneapolis Symphony name without identifying the orchestra for the new CD buyers. It only added to the confusion. Two years later, the Minnesota Orchestra's president, David Hyslop, pointed out that Mercury must make reference to the "Minnesota Orchestra," and he spearheaded a movement to convince the recording company henceforth to indicate "now renamed Minnesota Orchestra" in a prominent place on each CD, along with the old title "Minneapolis Symphony Orchestra."

For decades, the European press and public had known only of the Minneapolis Symphony Orchestra, because of its large catalog of recordings and radio broadcasts. Going into the 1998 European tour (unbelievably, given the orchestra's tremendous history of touring, it would be the first trip to the European continent), the orchestra needed to identify itself for the press and tour sponsors. Acting on this necessity, the public affairs department identified the Minnesota Orchestra as "formerly Minneapolis Symphony" in marketing and promotion, to increase awareness of the orchestra's true identity. When it distributed the tour promotion books to the musicians, the Minnesota Orchestra public affairs department said in a cover letter, "Here is our Minnesota Orchestra European Tour Book created primarily for press and sponsor use in Europe. You will note that the book relates the Minnesota Orchestra to its previous identity as the Minneapolis Symphony Orchestra."

Along the tour, many observers noted their surprise, as they began to make the connection between the "two" orchestras. After waiting ninety-five years, the orchestra's first European tour in the winter of 1998 proved successful beyond even optimistic predictions. Audiences and critics responded with overwhelmingly positive enthusiasm. Some typical examples:

> Don't laugh: under a name that truly smells of the soil (Minnesota is the granary of the United States) is hidden a remarkable group . . . the Minneapolis Orchestra, founded in 1903. In 1968, its custodians had the bad idea to un-baptize it, hoping for financial support from the state and their St. Paul neighbors. Separated only by the Mississippi, the 2.5 million inhabitants of the two towns have not ceased to be envious of each other. The balance sheet of the deal was thus foreseeable: little additional revenue, but a loss of international image. . . .
>
> Meanwhile the orchestra straddles the Twin Cities of Minneapolis and St. Paul, playing 200 concerts a year on a budget recently yanked up to $25 million. United it stands, but divided it very nearly fell in 1968, when the Minneapolis Orchestra [*sic*] reinvented itself as the Minnesota Orchestra. The idea was to emphasize the broader commitment of this "orchestra on wheels." But in focusing on state over city, many followers felt that the orchestra was, paradoxically, contracting rather than expanding its identity.
>
> *from* L'Express, *Paris (October 9, 1997)*

> A name that does register with European music-lovers is the Minneapolis Symphony, the local orchestra's title from 1903 to 1968, when the board changed it in a controversial move. Minneapolis Symphony recordings of the 1950s and early 1960s still sell briskly in Europe on CD. The Minnesota Orchestra's recent CDs face a host of tax and distribution barriers and are available in Europe only by mail order.
>
> *from the* Times, *London (January 22, 1998)*

Postscript 2004

In March 2004, we returned from our third European tour. Finally, it appears the connection is beginning to be made internationally between the renowned Minneapolis Symphony Orchestra and the Minnesota Orchestra. Receiving rave reviews and acclaim in major European cities is the culmination of years of struggle to reestablish and maintain an international reputation that was diminished by the name change (certainly not by the quality of the orchestra).

Ten

It Didn't Just Happen:
Forty-four Years of Contract Negotiations
1960–2004

In Their Own Words

All quotes in this chapter derive from interviews the author conducted with musicians who had been members of each negotiating committee from 1960 to 2004. The "Reviews" of the negotiations come directly from the musicians who took part. My apologies to anyone I may have inadvertently overlooked.

In the following summaries:

"Musicians" = negotiating committees elected by the musicians.

"Union" = musicians union representative, an officer and/or lawyer.

"Labor lawyer" = the musician-chosen legal counsel representing the musicians (beginning with the 1970 contract negotiations).

"Management" = management representative, including board presidents/chairs/officers, administrative staff members, and others (in the early years, not even administrative staff participated in negotiating sessions; board chairmen talked with the union directly and privately).

"Management lawyer" = management/Minnesota Orchestral Association–appointed legal representative.

For other terms, see the lists on pages xxix and 256.

He's Gone, Let's Go Home

Antal Doráti had a high-pitched voice to match his temperament, which evidenced itself in occasional temper tantrums. At one rehearsal in Northrop Auditorium (the University of Minnesota home of the orchestra for several decades), he threw down his baton and left the stage. When he didn't immediately return to the podium, the musicians decided he was not coming back, so they packed up and went home. The scenario was repeated at the next day's rehearsal, but this time after throwing down the baton and stalking off the stage, Doráti abruptly turned on his heels and shouted, "Don't leave! I'll be back!"

He Just Disappeared

In earlier days there was little attention paid to working conditions at home or on tour. Carelessly built stage risers (platforms erected onstage to elevate certain sections of the orchestra) were common in many halls. Without a secure safety strip affixed to the platform edge behind their chairs, for instance, the musicians rehearsed and performed in potentially dangerous environments. On one concert stage, the bass section stood in front of a black curtain. Suddenly one of them disappeared from view. Responding to an energetic cue from the conductor, James Clute had dropped backward at least five feet, as one of his colleagues managed to grab his bass by one string. Clute survived the fall, but his instrument most certainly would not have.

Watch This!

Conductor Stanislaw Skrowaczewski was experimenting with the use of stage risers at Northrop Auditorium. One of the horn players, Chris Leuba, confronted the conductor and insisted he come to his riser and peer over the edge behind his chair. The musician then tipped his chair off the riser to the floor below, a height of at least five feet. As the chair crashed to the floor, the horn player screamed, "That's where I'll be if something isn't done to prevent this!!"

Negotiations of 1960

Participants

Musicians: Fritz Scheuer, Herman Straka, Lester Davis, Steven Zellmer, Frank Winsor.

No labor lawyer for the musicians allowed by the union.

Union: Robert Bigelow.

Management: Charles Bellows, president of the Minneapolis Symphony Orchestra board of directors.

Summary

- Twenty-seven-week season, increased to twenty-eight in the second year
- $125 per week in the first year, increased to $135 in the second year
- Three-hour rehearsal maximum
- No insurance, no disability, no pension
- Nonrenewal notice to be given by the employer for musician on multi-season contract at least eight weeks before the end of the season to be effective at the end of the following season
- Employer allowed noncommercial radio broadcasts of children's concerts without musician compensation
- Road season: not more than nine weeks of touring and not more than nine services per week while on tour; two-hour tour rehearsals
- Expense allowance: when traveling by train on chartered Pullman sleepers, weekly allowance of $52.50; nonchartered Pullman sleepers, a per diem of $7.50; travel by airplane, train or bus, per diem of $13

Review

Although a committee of musician representatives existed, they had little or no input in the negotiations. The union officers met with management, agreed to a settlement, and informed the orchestra. The rumblings had already begun on a national level, and the orchestras were beginning to communicate formally and to organize in order to force the major issues of ratification and representation. This contract was significant in that it was a two-year master agreement; before 1960 it had usually been negotiated year by year.

Lights Out, Light Up

During a tour concert by the Minneapolis Symphony in the early 1960s, the stage lights suddenly went out. The conductor continued to conduct as if nothing were wrong, and the orchestra tried to continue from memory. Inevitably, the musicians dropped out section by section, one by one, until continuing the performance became impossible. Finding this moment to be as absurd as it sounds, one of the violinists reached into his pocket, lit a match, and uttered, "Let there be light."

The Case of the Phantom Janitor

Well into a rehearsal at the cavernous Northrop Auditorium in the early 1960s, the musicians began noticing someone dressed in coveralls pushing a broom across the apron of the stage. Moving deliberately, and doggedly unaware of the circumstances, the house janitor (or someone dressed as such—the musicians never knew for sure), continued his journey across one end of the stage to the other, behind the conductor, but in full view of the orchestra, to the great amusement of the musicians.

Negotiations of 1962

Participants

Musicians: James Clute, Bernice Beckerman, Ronald Hasselmann, Richard Adams, Robert Wirth, Art Freiwald.

No labor lawyer for the musicians allowed by the union.

Union: Robert Bigelow.

Management: John H. Myers, president of the board of directors, Minneapolis Symphony Orchestra; Boris Sokoloff, general manager, MSO.

Summary

- Thirty-week season, increased to thirty-one weeks for the 1964–1965 season
- $140 per week, increased to $155 for 1964–1965 season: $10 increase in salary across the board
- New mandatory contributory pension plan: 5 percent from employer, 3 percent from musicians annually, including employer rights to apply proceeds from pension fund concerts to satisfy its obligation to the pension fund
- Maximum of eight services per week, maximum of one rehearsal per day
- Nonrenewal, no change: eight weeks' notification for musicians on multiseason contract
- Travel/tour: tour season remains at nine weeks maximum
- New: option for musician *not* to travel by plane, on the condition that the musician use another mode of transport in order to "meet the Orchestra at the designated time at their destination"
- New: the employer agrees to discuss suggested changes in tour conditions, specifically:
    1. length of tour season
    2. length of individual tours
    3. number of services on tour
- New: no individual tour to exceed a total of five weeks, or thirty-five days, without the consent of the union, which shall not be unreasonably withheld
- New: rest period required when the orchestra is traveling on tour in chartered Pullman sleepers for a continuous period of more than one week

Review

This year was an important one for many major orchestras, including the Minneapolis Symphony. In 1962, musicians of the orchestra participated in contract ratification for the first time, albeit in a limited way, because the union still negotiated the contract. The contributory pension plan was instituted in this contract. The nationwide orchestral networking had begun in 1962 and the chart that compared contracts for the 1962–1963 season was distributed to twenty-six major U.S. and Canadian orchestras, with efforts to include many others. ICSOM was formally established in 1962.

Per Diem in Room 304

In the "old days," tour per diem was paid in cash on a weekly basis. The tour manager carried all the money in a leather briefcase, and sometimes even packed a gun. Usually, upon arrival at the hotel, he placed a sign in the lobby giving the room number and time: "PER DIEM IN ROOM 304," for the convenience of the musicians and anyone else (wearing a ski cap) who might be looking for some extra cash . . .

> "Employer shall, whenever possible, provide buses equipped with toilets."
>
> *from the master agreement, 1965,*
> *between Local 73, AFM, and the MOA*

This clause, which at first glance might provoke some disbelieving laughter, appeared in the orchestra musicians master agreement as a deeply serious issue. As one of the most toured orchestras in the country, the Minneapolis Symphony musicians felt the urgent necessity for exact wording to address the many challenges of traveling by bus and Pullman sleepers. Negotiating improvements in the lack of sanitary conditions and inequitable sleeping accommodations was an important agenda item in the 1965 negotiations.

Negotiations of 1965

Participants

Musicians: Ronald Balazs, James Clute, Robert Olson, Steve Chenette, Clement Volpe.

No labor lawyer: This was the last committee not to use a lawyer full time; attorney Sam Segal was consulted when needed.

Union: Robert Bigelow.

Management: Judson Bemis, president of the board of directors, Minneapolis Symphony Orchestra.

Summary

- Five-year contract: the first and last time for this length, as the standard would be three-year contracts until 1997
- Thirty-six-week season, increased to forty-five weeks by 1969–1970 season
- New: guaranteed total weeks of employment, from thirty-six to forty-five, including four consecutive summer season weeks, increased to eight by the fifth year
- $165 per week increased to $205 per week for the fifth season, with a cost-of-living escalation
- New: one-week vacation with full salary in the first year, with four services of the one-week vacation week utilized by employer in other weeks without additional compensation. A second full week's vacation with full pay in the third, fourth, and fifth seasons
- Mandatory contributory pension plan continues, same as previous contract: 5 percent from employer, 3 percent from musicians annually, including employer rights to apply proceeds from pension fund concert to satisfy its obligation to the pension fund
- New: retirement age is sixty-five, with option by the management to extend contract on year-to-year basis
- New: "back-to-back" school concerts permitted, no more than one hour in length, to be constituted as one service (see 1991 negotiations "not so new")
- New: employer may designate special YP/school concert weeks
- Unlimited sectional rehearsals allowed
- New: paid sick leave, not more than fourteen days per incident
- New: unprecedented "Economic Rank of Orchestra," which was defined as the relative economic rank of the orchestra compared to twenty-six other major U.S. orchestras, with the right to renegotiate the salary and weeks of employment in the fourth and fifth seasons
- New: "cost of living" clause: based on 1 percent increase per year to be reflected by stated increase in musicians' salary

- Tour days in winter season not to exceed forty-nine; no tour to exceed twenty-eight consecutive days; improved tour conditions, including services, rehearsals, duration of concerts (2½ hours), medical expenses, expense allowance, hotel day-rooms, and rest periods

Review

This contract was groundbreaking as far as working conditions were concerned, and also because the committee was empowered by the right of ratification. Although minor gains had been accomplished by 1965 and ICSOM had been established, working conditions for the Minneapolis Symphony had not improved, especially in regard to tours. One of the most-traveled orchestras in the industry suffered intolerable conditions on the road. Therefore, the 1965 committee members armed themselves with contracts from many major orchestras and were well prepared to address any issues that might arise with management. For the first time, language was established for "procedures in event of non-renewal." Extensive new provisions established guaranteed employment, time and duration of services, overtime, extra services, length of rehearsals and concerts, doubling, extra players, broadcasts and telecasts, sick leave, vacation, rest days, notice of works to be rehearsed, tours, and runouts.

Goddammit, Number 205!

In 1966, the composer Igor Stravinsky came to Minneapolis to conduct the orchestra at Northrop Auditorium in his ballet *The Fairy's Kiss*. Already quite old and infirm, he lost his place during the performance of the Divertimento, a rhythmically complex work. With the composer-conductor at sea, the orchestra was unable to pull it together. Finally, with only the principal clarinetist still trying in vain to get it all back on track, the music came to a halt. The orchestra musicians sat, horrified, as Stravinsky scrambled through the score, peered through his glasses, and screamed, "Goddamit, number 205!" He gave the downbeat, and the concert concluded without further incident.

Who Is This Man?

The beloved comedian Jack Benny was an avid amateur violinist and a great lover of classical music who had already performed with the Minneapolis Symphony Orchestra in a 1963 Pension Fund Benefit concert. A couple of years later, Benny paid a surprise visit to a rehearsal of the MSO at Northrop Auditorium. Music Director Stanislaw Skrowaczewski was conducting a contemporary, atonal work. Suddenly a familiar voice rang out from backstage, "What the hell is all this noise!!!?!??" Skrowaczewski, startled by the interruption, stopped the rehearsal, at first mystified and annoyed by the raving, then amused to recognize Benny. The comedian enjoyed mingling with the musicians backstage and even used the opportunity to pull some stunts.

It's the Thought That Counts

Sometime in the 1960s, the musicians received word that during a rehearsal break, they would find gifts for each member of the orchestra in the Northrop Auditorium foyer. Curious, they went to the foyer and discovered that an orchestra "benefactor" had provided individually wrapped Christmas gifts. To their surprise, they found ninety-five large shopping bags placed on the floor, each marked with a musician's name. The gifts included wrapping paper, Christmas ribbons, and ordinary kitchen gadgets. The most coveted gift was a pop-up toaster given to the second trombonist. One of the musicians, upon receiving a rubber spatula with a sixty-five-cent price tag attached, crossed out the price, wrote "reduced to 25¢," and passed it along to one of his colleagues—thereby emphasizing the old adage that "it's the thought that counts."

Fifteen Resignations

"Fifteen members of the Minneapolis Symphony have resigned or let their contracts lapse. Some of the departures, three times the normal turn-over rate, reportedly resulted from dissatisfaction with the way the orchestra is run. A small number of those who are leaving are unhappy with the orchestra and conductor, Stanislaw Skrowaczewski, and Richard

Cisek, orchestra managing director. The orchestra's season ended Sunday. Cisek said that three persons actually had resigned and that the rest had let their contracts lapse for various reasons—including jobs in other orchestras, the beginning of solo careers and choosing another career" (*Minneapolis Star,* Monday, May 8, 1967).

In 1967, fifteen players suddenly departed from the Minneapolis Symphony, including three musicians who then joined the Saint Paul Chamber Orchestra. Two of the musicians returned within two years, one of them remained with the SPCO, and the others left town or chose different professions. Not knowing whether the departure of the fifteen represented a coincidence of timing, and noticing that news of their resignations did not appear in the city supplement of the Twin Cities newspapers (only the metropolitan papers), some of the remaining orchestra members expressed outrage by the suppression of the news by the orchestral association.

The orchestra members' committee wrote a letter to the members of the board of directors. They said that the board was presenting to the news media an unrealistic picture of serious issues and the musicians would be forced to make public reply. Representatives of the musicians and management held a meeting in Room 5 beneath the University of Minnesota Northrop Auditorium. Several people spoke out about the poor morale that had been generated by some internal problems. The management said the association's board would look into it and try to come up with a resolution that would satisfy all parties.

However, one of the most prominent and influential board members in attendance dismissed the concerns raised by the musicians. He summed it all up by saying, "I choose not to listen to this," and with that he abruptly walked out of the room, and the meeting was over. Case closed.

"First Woman Percussionist"

The press drew attention to a "first" with this headline in the *St. Paul Dispatch,* November 1, 1968. The article by staff writer Carol Fyrand reads as though it had been published twenty years earlier. "Is that a woman in the percussion section? And sure enough, commanding the timpani was a lithe brunette, Paula Culp, who holds the distinction of being the first woman percussionist to become a permanent member of the orchestra." Fyrand continued: "You might expect her male counterparts in the percussion section to express some resentment of female encroachment in their domain. Not so, according to Paula: 'The setup here is just lovely. I have marvelous people to work with.'"

Negotiations for 1970

Participants

Musicians: Ross Tolbert, Carl Holub, Carl Nashan, Kensley Rosen, Paul Thomas, Eugene Wade, Alan Gerstel.

Labor lawyer: I. Philip Sipser; this is the first time the union allowed musicians to hire their own lawyer.

Union: Robert Bigelow.

Management: John W. Windhorst Sr., chairman (formerly called president) of the board, Minneapolis Symphony Orchestra; Howard W. Mithun; Richard Cisek, administrative staff executive director; and David Hyslop, assistant general manager.

Summary

It was not an easy negotiation, as management locked out the musicians for a week—the first work stoppage in the orchestra's history. But in the final agreement, that week was counted as a vacation week, and significant gains were made in length of season, sick leave, dismissals, rehearsal length, tour conditions, and benefits.

- The establishment of a twenty-concert subscription season series in St. Paul, duplicating the programs performed in Minneapolis
- Forty-five weeks in the first season, to be increased to forty-eight in the third (the biggest point of disagreement), including an eight-week summer season
- New: three weeks vacation per season—the first time vacation with full salary was provided "without utilization of such week's services at other times" (language from 1965 master contract)

- From $205 to $234 per week, increased to $254 per week in the third year, plus a cost-of-living increment increase
- Establishment of the first noncontributory pension plan in the industry (see Chapter 5, "Visionary Leaders and Progress of the 1960s"), amounting to not less than 6 percent of the regular salary; previous employee contributions by musicians to pension plan to be refunded to them over a three-year period
- Mandatory retirement at sixty-five with option to continue at employer's discretion on year-to-year basis
- One-week lockout becomes a vacation week
- Paid sick leave: full salary paid, not to exceed fourteen days per period of absence (no change from 1965); employer may require medical exam by employer physician
- New: rehearsals adjusted from three-hour minimum to 2½ hours
- New: for the first time, hospital and medical insurance coverage provided without cost to each musician
- New: "For all rehearsals a *large* clock shall be placed on a wall in plain sight and the personnel manager must rise from his seat and remain standing until he is recognized by the conductor to indicate that the rehearsal is to be terminated."

The clock had become an important issue, because the conductor consistently ran over the allotted rehearsal time, ignoring the visual signal from the personnel manager. The musicians committee had decided that a mutually agreed timepiece, a large clock, could alert all parties to the exact timing for all rehearsals, concerts, and recordings. Subsequently, the clock became the subject of much wry humor. At one point, the clock had ceased running, or as one musician put it, "The rehearsal was so boring, even the clock stopped." Upon removing the clock, the personnel manager accidentally dropped it, necessitating the purchase of a replacement. Some people suggested that the clock's demise was no accident.

- Letter of agreement to assure that stand-by-stand rehearsal technique would *not* be used for the duration of the contract
- Expense allowance on tour:

1970–1971	1972–1973: + 10 PERCENT
Dinner—$5.75	$6.35 (+ 57.5 cents)
Lunch—$4.25	$4.70 (+ 42.5 cents)
Breakfast—$3.50	$3.85 (+ 35 cents)

Review

The most significant development of this contract was that the union allowed the musicians to hire their own lawyer to negotiate the master agreement. They hired I. Philip Sipser, ICSOM lawyer at that time, and he produced the first *noncontributory* pension plan in the country, which required all past contributions, with interest, to be refunded to the musicians in three equal installments. Other orchestras followed in subsequent negotiations. For a more comprehensive description, refer to Chapter 5.

From the 1962 master agreement between Minneapolis Musicians, Local 73, and the Minnesota Orchestral Association, regarding "Salaries, g) Pension Plan—The employer shall contribute annually an amount equal to five percent (5%) of the regular salaries of the full time musicians and staff, excluding the Music Director, to a pension fund, with the understanding that the full-time musicians and staff participating in the Plan will likewise contribute three percent (3%) of the their salaries."

From Pension Plan Summary, September 1, 1971: "Commencing September 1, 1970, the Association makes all of the contributions to the plan. The amount of the contribution for a plan year will be determined after consultation with the Actuary, and it will be at least six percent of the regular salaries . . . Prior to September 1, 1970, employees were required to make contributions in order to participate in the plan. No employee contributions are made after that date. Participants will have their contributions, with interest, as defined in the plan, refunded to them in three equal installments."

The Clandestine Recording

During the period of this contract, 1970–1973, Music Director Stanislaw Skrowaczewski (also a noted composer) wrote and dedicated an English

Horn Concerto to Thomas Stacey, English horn in the Minnesota Orchestra. The committee was asked if this work could be taped. Permission was denied because it would be in violation of the terms of the master agreement. Audio-taping of orchestra performances could take place only under the specified lower union rate for "tapes made for study purposes."

In the case of Skrowaczewski's English Horn Concerto, the committee discovered that someone had arranged a clandestine taping of the performance, without permission from or knowledge of the orchestra, in order to get a clean tape—without bleeping. One of the musicians of the committee had noticed an electronics truck parked near the basement music library at Northrop Auditorium, with large numbers of wires strung from the truck into one of the music library windows. Furthermore, just as the performance was to begin, a committee member discovered a tape recorder in the library. The committee decided this was not only willful disregard of the committee's authority but also a violation of musicians' union rules, to which the orchestral association was bound.

Management admitted that they had attempted to tape and offered to pay, but the committee refused payment for these illegal actions. Had management been forthright and honest in the beginning, this embarrassment could possibly have been avoided.

Standing Room Only

The orchestra rehearsed and performed in Northrop Auditorium at the University of Minnesota from the early 1930s to the early '70s. Before rehearsals and concerts, musicians would take their instruments, coats, and other personal articles to an unsecured storage room on the lower level. The room offered literally no place to sit down, unless one counted an upholstered chair with an exposed spring that made it virtually impossible to use. Sometimes, if they weren't in use elsewhere, one might sit on stored bass violin cases. The space contained no lockers or places to change or hang clothes. Private restrooms for the musicians, male or female, were not available. Everyone tried to make the best of an uncomfortable situation.

During that era, several orchestra board members would attend concerts in some of the major American cities during the orchestra's tours. This presented an opportunity for one of the Minneapolis Symphony musicians to show board members from the Twin Cities what the Philadelphia Orchestra provided for its musicians: lockers, separate dressing rooms for men and women, and smoking and nonsmoking areas. In 1969, clothes lockers were finally installed at Northrop Auditorium, albeit in the same room for men and women. It was the best that could be expected, because the orchestra did not yet have its own home.

When Orchestra Hall was built in 1974 in the heart of downtown Minneapolis, two locker/dressing rooms were built. The men's had eighty lockers, in 1,134 square feet, and the women had twenty-two lockers in 504 square feet, reflecting the approximate men-to-women ratio at that time. Since then, the women's locker room has been expanded twice, and the number of lockers has almost doubled, from twenty-two to forty-three, but the actual square footage has not kept pace. With the increasing numbers of women winning positions in the orchestra, as of this writing, women's dressing facilities in Orchestra Hall have become inadequate in space, available lockers, restroom facilities, and security. Two possible scenarios could improve the situation: either improve the women's dressing facilities, or return to Antal Doráti's suggestion: "No more women!"

Negotiations of 1973

Participants

Musicians: Fredrik Hedling, Robert Feit, David Kamminga, Merrimon Hipps, Jane Thompson, Marvin Dahlgren.

Labor lawyer: Leonard Leibowitz.

Union: Robert Bigelow, president.

Management: Donald Engle, administrative staff CEO (now called "president"); Richard Cisek, executive director; and some board members who were also attorneys—no official lawyer yet.

Summary

- Forty-eight-week season, to be increased to fifty weeks in 1975–1976
- Four weeks' vacation, increased to six weeks in the third season
- $280 per week, to be increased to $320 for the third season—a $66 increase over 3 years
- New medical benefits: dependent coverage available with gradual contribution by employer toward such coverage, excess premium to be paid by musician
- New: paid sick leave raised to maximum of twenty-six weeks based on years of service; in previous contract musician paid full salary for no more than fourteen days per illness
- Pension plan amended to 5 percent, addition of widows' benefit and minimum—$350/month for previously retired members
- Normal retirement age set at sixty-five
- Increase in the number of five-day weeks (guaranteed weeks with maximum of five days of services)
- Elimination of 3-hour rehearsals, which had long been a contentious issue
- Improvement in tour and runout conditions, especially bus travel
- Twenty-two broadcasts/telecasts per season allowable without additional payment, live or by tape delay

Review

During this negotiation, the Mutual Benefit Association (MBA) was dissolved. This was a fund to which musicians had been contributing since the 1940s, created and contributed to by them, which members could draw from in an emergency for illness or disability. With a greatly improved sick leave policy through these negotiations, the MBA was deemed to be no longer necessary, and the money was transferred to the Orchestra Pension Plan, thereby giving up these funds for improvements in salaries and benefits. In 1970 it totaled $100,000. Unfortunately, much of the money was later lost in the stock market. The decision to transfer the MBA funds in this manner was a divisive one, but the results have benefited all musicians since that time.

Negotiations of 1976

Participants

Musicians: Ross Tolbert, James Clute, Carl Nashan, Steven Zellmer, Carl Holub.

Labor lawyer: Ronald Rollins.

Union: Robert Bigelow, president.

Management: Donald Engle, president; Richard Cisek, executive director; George T. Pennock, chairman of the board of directors; Dale Beihoffer (Faegre and Benson) as management lawyer.

The labor lawyer hired and paid for by the musicians was a local lawyer, Ron Rollins, from a large firm in the Twin Cities who had recently worked on a previous matter for the musicians. He later formed his own law firm and has worked with this orchestra since that time.

Summary

- Fifty-two-week season established by the third year of the contract
- $100 raise over the three-year contract—$420 by the third year
- Four weeks' vacation increased to seven weeks with full payment of salary
- Disability insurance program implemented in the third year of the contract
- New: EMG (electronic media guarantee) included in the salary; payments begin—up to $25 per week in the third year, above weekly minimum salary in the third season
- Pension: maintain the formula based on 1.5 percent of earnings as monthly pension at normal retirement
- New: for the first time a guaranteed fixed pension benefit of $900/month at age sixty-five with thirty years of service based on actual earnings from 1969. Earnings were so low prior to 1969 that the committee came to the realization that a minimum benefit must be established.

- Ten years' vesting and full compliance with federal pension law
- Continuation of musician participation on the Pension Advisory Committee
- New: retirement committee established, following guidelines developed by the AAC, including musicians' health, musical performance, and interest
- Pension Benefit Concert established
- Normal retirement age established as seventy, increased from age sixty-five
- New: notice of works to be rehearsed required the Friday prior to next week's rehearsals
- All musicians on call unless formally dismissed
- Limit of five three-hour rehearsals in the season; three three-hour in the second season of the contract
- New: Artistic Advisory Committee, audition procedures established by letter of agreement
- New: string relief established: six services per season, but on call for such services
- Improvements in life, hospitalization, medical, travel, disability insurance
- Musicians' negotiating committee reduced from seven to five people

Review

In this negotiation, a fifty-two-week season was finally established in the third year of the contract, a goal of the musicians of ICSOM orchestras for many years. The precedent had been set by the "big five" orchestras—Chicago, New York, Boston, Philadelphia, and Cleveland—in the late 1960s, and many other orchestras had made the fifty-two-week season a high-priority goal. This contract set the precedent for a $100-per-week raise over the three-year term of the contract, a historic first in the industry.

This was the first time a *fixed* dollar amount was assigned to the pension, an important and long-overdue accomplishment. The previous 1.5 percent of earnings was too low to provide adequate benefits.

The electronic media guarantee (EMG) was established, crediting the musicians payment due for electronic media services. The payment was included in the salary check, but not calculated as part of the total salary. If an amount higher than the established EMG was earned, the balance owing the musician would be paid at the end of the year.

An audition procedure was finally established by letter of agreement, specifying an audition committee of musicians for each position opening. "In order to establish a more uniform, yet flexible and equitable audition procedure, the following guidelines have been established as a means of player selection . . ." (Article XXII, Section 22.3, 1982 master agreement). Before such a clause was established in the contract, the conductor selected the musicians to be hired, and there was no procedure or input from the orchestra.

The Artistic Advisory Committee was implemented in this contract by letter of agreement. The purpose of this committee was to "serve in an advisory and consultative role with the Orchestra Association on musical matters or the artistic aspects of the Orchestra's functions." It became apparent to the musicians at this time that such a committee was needed to at least have a voice in the programming. The Boston Symphony Artistic Committee was used as the model for the Minnesota Orchestra, as Boston had already established many committees and was much more self-governing than other orchestras.

Also new to this negotiation was the use of musicians meeting in sub-committees in order to research basic problems and suggest solutions, before making any commitment to the other side. Some felt that seven people were too many for the main negotiating team; others felt that it was dangerous to form smaller groups. There was great paranoia across the table in those days, and this was an attempt to alleviate it.

Easy, Bergen

Edgar Bergen, the famous comedian and ventriloquist, had just concluded a performance with the Minnesota Orchestra. His entourage included his sidekick dummies Mortimer Snerd, Charlie McCarthy, and Effie Klinger. By this time, the orchestra had moved into Orchestra Hall, its own home on Peavey Plaza in downtown Minneapolis. The artists' dressing room was within view of the musicians backstage, and as Carl and I wandered offstage after the performance, we heard voices coming from a dressing room. Peeking around the doorway, we observed a private moment between Edgar and Charlie. In order to pack his "children" into the large wardrobe case, Bergen had to disassemble various body parts. As he unscrewed Charlie's head, the "dummy" chided him, "Easy, Bergen, easy."

Viennese Sommerfest and Leonard Slatkin

By the 1970s, as symphony orchestra musicians began to work under full-time contracts, boards and managements extended the performance seasons by creating summer programs. Some orchestras—such as Cleveland, Los Angeles, Boston, and Chicago—had special venues (Blossom, the Hollywood Bowl, Tanglewood, and Ravinia) that would accommodate large audiences for true summer festivals. Lacking such a special venue, the Minnesota Orchestra, under the artistic leadership of its principal guest conductor, Leonard Slatkin, still managed to create a popular and successful summer series, "Viennese Sommerfest," which took place in July and August in Orchestra Hall and on the adjacent, city-owned Peavey Plaza. In its heyday, beginning in 1980, Sommerfest was an exhilarating experience for the audiences and for the musicians.

Leonard had succeeded in gaining local respect through his innovative Rug Concerts of the mid-1970s, which had offered distinctive programming in a casual, audience-friendly environment in Orchestra Hall. Continuing this approach with Sommerfest, he engaged audiences and musicians alike with his creativity and enthusiasm. From interesting chamber music to classic film music and piano marathons, and including stories and anecdotes that he told from the stage, Leonard always offered something to look forward to. While the musicians worked harder during those four weeks than any time during the winter seasons, they truly enjoyed their annual collaboration with Leonard, who for many of us defined Sommerfest.

"You Must It—You Can It!"

The intensity of working with a conductor like Toscanini or Mitropoulos must have been similar to the way many of us felt working with Klaus

Tennstedt, principal guest conductor of the orchestra from 1979 to1982. I looked forward to the rehearsals as much as the concerts, because the level of music making was so intense, on the one hand, and unexpected, on the other. He was never satisfied with mediocrity and he would often shout, "You must it—you can it!"—the literal English translation from German, meaning he wanted *more*—expression, dynamics, character, and whatever else the music required. During rehearsals of Bruckner or Mahler, he screamed, "It must be an unbelievable crazy fortissimo!" Together we gave some extraordinary performances, and he demanded 110% from himself and the musicians.

Tennstedt had a unique conducting style, characterized by unconventional movements and an expressive face and hands. He communicated tremendous emotional intensity, and the musicians learned how to read his body language. "It's a personal thing; I try to find in a very short time the contact with the orchestra—so I try to do this with my voice and this with my body. When it is for the music, then I am Mr. Hands and Legs," Tennstedt said in an interview with Jeanyne Bezoier Slettom that appeared in the April 1980 *Minnesota Monthly.*

Tennstedt enjoyed the camaraderie and respect of the musicians and especially the hours of Ping-Pong after concerts. His wife, Inge, accompanied him wherever he went, a stabilizing influence on his intense lifestyle. She had met her future husband in the opera house in Karl-Marx-Stadt (now renamed Chemnitz) in the former East Germany, where he was conducting and she was singing the mezzo role of Amneris in *Aïda.* Tennstedt and his wife escaped from East Germany in 1971 when a careless official stamped their passports "Indefinite Return." His first American appearances, with the Toronto and Boston symphony orchestras, in 1974, created sensational responses, and all the major orchestras sought him out. Audiences loved him, and an informal fan club was formed, the "Klausketeers," which had its own newsletter, circulated by David Grundy of Pittsburgh.

Tennstedt's background in East German opera houses did not prepare him for procedures of the West, including contract stipulations and how to receive a salary. He used a money belt and once asked to be paid *in cash.* But he quickly learned the ways of the American contracts and the procedures of requesting extra time, extra players, or whatever he needed.

Negotiations of 1979

Participants

Musicians: Charles Schlueter, Ferald Capps, Carl Nashan, Basil Reeve, James Clute.

Labor lawyer: Ronald Rollins.

Union: Patrick J. Rian.

Management: Richard Cisek, president; Richard Bass, general manager; Thomas Manion, Jeffrey Prauer, staff; and Dale Beihoffer, lawyer.

Summary

- Fifty-two-week season
- $569 per week by the third year of the contract; $149 increase over three years
- Seven weeks' vacation per season
- Dental insurance implemented in third year of the contract
- Pension $350 per month—reduced by one-thirtieth for each year of service less than thirty—for previously retired
- Pension increased to $1,000 from $900 per month
- Pension benefit concerts expanded to two additional services without compensation, not to exceed a total of four such concerts within the three-year term of the master agreement
- "On call for string relief" language deleted to "shall not be on call for such service"
- New: seniority relief established: one service per season for five full years of service
- New: three clauses added under Article XX—Miscellaneous:
  20.5 Temperature, humidity, and musicians' use of stage—best efforts . . . to provide consistent conditions and access to stage before services/concerts
  20.6 Authorized management representative required at all concerts, tours, runouts
  20.7 Musicians permitted access to personnel files
- New: initial markings incorporated into master agreement: all section

parts marked no later than the beginning of the first rehearsal (this
was an efficiency clause that needed contract language to enforce);
too much time was wasted during rehearsal marking individual parts

Review

These negotiations were notable for ending in the first strike in the
orchestra's seventy-seven-year history. Coinciding with the opening
concerts of the season and the debut of a new music director, Neville
Marriner, the strike provoked great concern for the disruption it caused.
Although the timing was unfortunate, the crucial issue was parity for the
orchestra. After four months of negotiations and eleven months of internal committee negotiations, the orchestra committee members felt they
could not lower their demands—in spite of the fact that the actual dollar amount was one of the smallest in symphonic history: four dollars.
After five days of strike, the association gave the orchestra what it had
originally asked for and enabled it to maintain its ranking among the top
ten American orchestras. Ironically, because the management refused to
accept the original salary proposal, the final agreement cost them more
than it would have had they accepted from the beginning.

The name change of only eleven years previously had proved to be a
demoralizing issue. Recordings and tours had dramatically decreased. In
spite of these problems, it was a crucial negotiation to make important
gains in salary and working conditions. Some of the significant advances
achieved were in increased salary and pension, establishment of a pension advisory committee, hospitalization and life insurance, and institution of a dental insurance plan.

The musicians gave in on their demand for an eighth week of vacation, converting this proposal to establishment of seniority relief. The
contract date was adjusted to begin October 1, rather than the traditional opening of the winter season in September.

Let Me Out of Here

One of the orchestra's only performances inside the Hubert H. Hum-
phrey Metrodome in Minneapolis was to celebrate its opening in 1982.
Reminiscent of the plot of Richard Strauss's opera *Ariadne auf Naxos*, the

concert was to be followed by a display of fireworks outside the Metro-dome. And, just as in the opera, the small matter of coordination ended unfortunately for the musical arts. The concert started out with a few hundred people in the audience, but within about fifteen minutes, many listeners began to leave. The dull roar the orchestra musicians heard was the fireworks, which had begun before the concert was over, and they finished the performance with only a handful of faithful listeners—who could barely hear anything. But, of course, neither could the musicians, who were quickly dropping out due to convulsive laughter.

Negotiations of 1982

Participants

Musicians: Carl Holub, Carl Nashan, Steven Zellmer, James Clute, Merrimon Hipps.

Labor lawyer: Ronald Rollins.

Union: Patrick J. Rian, president.

Management: Richard Cisek, executive director; Robert Jones, general manager; Luella Goldberg, chairman of the board; Tom Manion, Jeff Prauer, and Sam Dixon, staff members; Tom Vogt, lawyer.

Summary

- Fifty-two-week season
- Salary $760 by third year; increase of $191 over three years; EMG remains at $25 per week
- Vacation increased to eight weeks in the third year of the contract
- Pension increase annual benefit to $13,000 by second year: $1,083 per month
- Improvements in life, dental, and health insurance
- New: provision for chamber music distributed equally: $175 for rehearsals and performance
- New: seniority pay based on years of service, one lump sum

- New: leave of absence provisions, including three-month unpaid maternity leave, personal and professional leave, and ICSOM delegate leave for annual conference
- New: Section 22.2 Artistic Advisory Committee established, from letter of agreement in previous contract
- New: Section 22.3 Audition Committee, guidelines established
- Saturday rehearsals reduced from six to three
- Clarification of general language throughout contract, including tours and scheduling
- Management presented a laundry list of grievances at initial meetings
- Musicians requested shorter, more reasonable proposals in order to accomplish mutual goals
- Two new committees are added to the contract: Artistic Advisory and Audition Committee

Review

Chamber music opportunities are now incorporated into the contract, to be distributed on an equitable basis (comparison with many other orchestras' similar clause). There was considerable discussion about the dangers of air travel and lack of sufficient pressurization, which could cause injury: a letter was sent to all air carriers addressing pressurization and other concerns. Longevity (seniority) pay begins, based on years of service.

Great improvement in leave of absence provisions, including deletion of "sole discretion" in regards to granting leave of absence.

A Couple of Big Ones

Diplomatic dignitaries and Scandinavian royalty attended a sold-out Orchestra Hall concert in 1982 of the Minnesota Orchestra, choruses, and soloists, conducted by Music Director Neville Marriner. The "Tonight Scandinavia" concert was also presented as a live television and radio broadcast, with pianist Victor Borge of Denmark, performing. The soprano guest soloist, Madame Birgit Nilsson, was a dramatic presence that evening, in a beautiful gown and medals appropriate for the occasion. In an impromptu onstage exchange at the beginning of the performance, Marriner looked closely at her chest and remarked, "I see you have a couple of rather large ones there!" Without hesitation, Madame Nilsson responded, "Oh, yes, and I have two more just like them at home!"

Another Diva, Another Show

Reminiscent of another live performance many years earlier, this concert mishap had a different result due to a coincidence of repertoire. It occurred in February 1998, when the orchestra was performing at Carnegie Hall with the soprano soloist Kathleen Battle. The house and stage lights flickered several times and then went out altogether. The small instrumentation and repetitive nature of the accompaniment enabled everyone to continue the performance flawlessly—in total darkness—a magical moment!

The Outdoor Experience

Summer outdoor concerts typically begin just before sunset, and with the combination of lights, heat, and humidity, bugs arrive in droves. Bug spray and swatting help somewhat, but often the creatures not only end up in one's hair and face, but also on the music. A squashed mosquito has been preserved and dated on the page of a first-stand viola part—in memoriam. Another memorable experience occurred during one of the daytime outdoor concerts on the grass under the trees. The orchestra performed *Poet and Peasant Overture,* and just as she finished her solo, cellist Janet Horvath felt the distinctive *splat* of bird droppings. On the cello. A commentary of a different sort.

"Gritty Little Rules"

Neville Marriner (later, Sir Neville), music director of the Minnesota Orchestra from 1979 to 1986, spoke often about his irritation with certain work rules of major American orchestras. In an interview with the *Philadelphia Inquirer* in October 1984, Marriner said he preferred to work with musicians who have "absolutely no security. Conducting has become very different," he said. "We lack the ultimate weapon now. Orchestras have become so democratic that it is difficult to make changes."

This and another similar interview created no small degree of ill will between him and the musicians, and the committee wrote a letter of protest. In response, Marriner wrote to the orchestra that the press had misrepresented his views and that he regretted the tone of the articles.

In a letter to all members of the Minnesota Orchestra dated March 31, 1985, Marriner explained: "It was accurate to report my concern over the loss of some of our musicians to other major orchestras; but it was an omission not to report the continuing ability of this orchestra to attract some of the most talented players in the country and not to report the low turnover rate this orchestra enjoys. Similarly, it was accurate to report my irritation with certain work rules of major American orchestras; but it was a distortion to imply that such rules are worse than certain other practices in Britain and Europe that concern conductors. Nor is it fair to conclude that American orchestras cannot or do not achieve greatness because of their labor agreements."

He also asked that we continue constructive communication to resolve problems, and the committee did so. And in spite of the rancor, the musicians also understood and appreciated several aspects about his reputation being linked with ours. Our recordings on a major label, the first in twenty years since the Minneapolis Symphony Mercury LPs, and the two international tours during his tenure, to Australia and Hong Kong, happened primarily because of *his* name recognition.

Marriner had come to conducting from the ranks of the violins in the London Symphony Orchestra, before he formed the Academy of St. Martin-in-the-Fields in 1958. The unique London phenomenon of the freelance life he experienced was, and still is, characterized by the insecurity and stress of irregular hours, no fixed schedule, and no job security. One of the long-sought goals of ICSOM was job security and protection from dictatorial conductors, but American orchestras never have been as "democratic" as our European colleagues, who usually have at least equal power to the conductor, and in some cases, more.

In 2003, all former Minnesota Orchestra music directors were invited back to conduct during the season, the Orchestra's one hundredth anniversary. In an interview in the *Star Tribune,* April 27, 2003, with music critic Michael Anthony, Marriner reminisced about his debut as music director of the orchestra, which had coincided with a five-day strike. "I don't think I ever completely recovered from that; I suppose, as a result of the strike, I was always a little bit guarded with the orchestra, because with the Academy it's such an easy relationship." Marriner told Anthony that he has no regrets about his tenure with the Minnesota Orchestra, except that "it was pure cowardice on my part, really, not having the stamina to fire people. But that's the only thing I regret. Perhaps I didn't behave as a music director should have."

Negotiations of 1985

Participants

Musicians: Ross Tolbert, James Clute, Basil Reeve, David Herring, Hyacinthe Tlucek.

Labor lawyer: Ronald Rollins.

Union: Patrick J. Rian, president.

Management: David Wax, general manager; Tom Manion; Tom Vogt, lawyer.

Summary

- Fifty-two-week season remains
- Salary $960 per week by the third year; increase of $200 over three years; EMG remains $25 per week
- Percentage increases relative to salary increases in other provisions: i.e., doubling, small ensemble, chamber music, insurance, disability insurance, pre-1979 retirees
- Vacation remains eight weeks
- Pension increase in annual benefit for thirty years of service to $17,000 by 1987
- Medical insurance plan offered by carrier as an independent option to musicians who choose to pay the difference

- Section 6.3, sectional rehearsals: increases in use of sectionals from thirty to sixty minutes within 2½ hour rehearsal, six times in winter season; two-hour sectionals scheduled, three times in the winter season, counting as one service
- New: Section 8.3: thirty minutes of scheduled overtime added
- New: Section 12.2: Paternity leave added, two weeks total

Review

There was considerable discussion of and resistance to the music director's requests for more flexibility with sectionals. More language was added to Section 6.3, including addition of one-hour sectionals on six occasions, and two-hour sectionals on three occasions, to be followed by discussion with current music director, Edo de Waart, of the importance to him of such sectionals at the end of the 1987–1988 season. There was a verbal agreement that guest conductors could not use the sectional clause. This agreement has since been violated, all the more reason to have all working conditions in writing.

There was a 26.3 percent increase in salary to cover the life of the contract amounting to $960 per week, placing us among the top ten in salary. Chicago and New York are currently the benchmarks and on the same negotiation cycle. Major gains in health insurance also occurred with this contract. There were initial discussions of excessive sound levels on stage and an agreement to meet with musicians to address such problems.

During the period of this contract, the musicians received a memo from management to inform them of the policy on sexual harassment and a review of federal regulations that make sexual harassment illegal. Among other things, it suggested whom to contact if one had evidence of sexual harassment by anyone in the work environment. In any situation in which sexual harassment had clearly taken place, appropriate action under provisions of the master agreement, Article XVIII, would be taken.

Also during the period of this contract, a work-hardening policy was established. This allows for the rehabilitation a musician would need for full-time employment while under the physician's care, and while remaining on sick leave or disability, until released to return to full-time work. The Members Committee, manager Mark Volpe, and personnel manager Ronald Balazs worked together to institute this program.

Negotiations of 1989

Participants

Musicians: David Herring, Richard Marshall, Charles Pinto, Adele Lorraine, Carl Holub.

Lawyer: Ronald Rollins.

Union: Patrick Rian, Russell Moore.

Management: Mark Volpe, general manager; Richard Cisek, president; Tom Vogt, lawyer.

Summary

- Salary $1,115 per week by the third year
- Vacation eight weeks
- Pension to $23,000 for thirty years of service in the third year, a 35 percent gain
- Seniority pay: beginning in the second year of the contract, a weekly amount to a maximum of $25 per week for twenty-five years
- Sick leave: increase in protection for probationary players to half pay after six weeks
- Termination for tenured musicians, extended service allowed to one additional winter season
- Unscheduled overtime: more language in regard to five- and fifteen-minute unscheduled OT
- Life insurance: employer premium paid up to $50,000 per musician, group term life increased from $50,000 to $60,000
- Medical insurance: employer continues to pay full cost for individual and dependent coverage for each musician, with optional coverage available at musician's choice to pay $25 per month individual; $50 per month family

Review

This negotiation was straightforward and efficient, with good relationships on both sides. The major issues were discussed openly by all. The contract was settled six weeks after its expiration, and concurrent play-and-talk. There was no strike deadline.

Pension increased 35 percent from $17,000 to $23,000. The first significant weekly seniority pay to be included in the paycheck, from an annual maximum of $300 for thirty years of service to a maximum of $1,300 for twenty-five years of service. A small lump sum had been distributed annually before this time.

Sick leave was improved for probationary players, to half pay during the first two seasons after the first six weeks.

Extended season of playing for tenured musicians during termination procedures.

Problematic touring and runout conditions continued to plague musicians and management.

Dissolving Cello

During a week of summer outdoor concerts, the instrument truck arrived earlier than the musicians, in order for the stage crew to set up the stage, sound, and light systems. The heat was oppressive. Some of us had packed our instruments in the truck, instead of carrying them. To her shock and horror, cellist Mina Fisher opened her case to find the entire fingerboard had dropped off from the intense heat. Expensive repair was paid for by the management, and the possibility of this situation has since been remedied by the use of climate-controlled trucks. Thirty-five years earlier, Clem Volpe could have used climate-controlled trucks when he discovered the valves of his trumpet had frozen during one of the winter tours!

Raindrops/Cinders Falling on Our Heads

The orchestra completed a performance at one of the outdoor venues during a Fourth of July week, and, typical of all venues during this week, a fireworks exhibition was on the agenda. The presenters did not wait for the musicians to leave the area before beginning the fiery event, and even though musicians ran with their instruments for shelter, many were not quick enough and experienced the shower of cinders landing on the stage.

The shower of cinders is not the only danger to the musicians. Severe summer weather is always an issue, which can obviously pose a serious threat to musicians and audience alike. It was not until 1998 that "Safe Use of Fireworks" and "Outdoor Playing Conditions" were negotiated into the master agreement and provisions were spelled out to protect musicians and their instruments, including a defined cancellation policy due to severe weather conditions. Nevertheless, the lack of an adequate tent or shelter for the orchestra was (and still can be) a chronic problem. In another instance of imminent danger during a summer evening concert, the threat of a storm hovered, and indeed it began to rain—in torrents—halfway through the performance. The concert was immediately terminated. The bass section had only one canvas case among them, so they sprinted to the truck to try to protect their instruments. Some in the audience booed the drenched musicians—music lovers, by the way, who sat in lawn chairs protected by umbrellas. Many people are not aware that string instruments, unlike brass and woodwind instruments, are not suited to the elements of wind and rain in unprotected outdoor venues.

Negotiations of 1991

Participants

Musicians: Fredrik Hedling, James Clute, Adele Lorraine, Mark Kelley, Julie Ayer.

Lawyer: Ronald Rollins, Jean Boos.

Union: Brad Eggen, president: Russ Moore, secretary-treasurer.

Management: David Hyslop, president; Ward Gill, finance director; Julie Haight, personnel manager; Tom Vogt, lawyer.

Summary

• Salary $1,260 per week in the third year

- Vacation 8½ weeks, including a half week in exchange for double YP (to be counted as one service)
- $27,000 pension: for thirty years of service
- New: health insurance, Section 9.2: co-pays on specific plans with limits on percentage of musicians' costs: a Joint Health Benefit Study Committee is created to "review plan design in an effort to maintain benefits and control costs." Diabetic supplies coverage added at 50 percent to a $750 limit; chiropractic cap raised to fifteen visits
- Unsuccessful attempt to include domestic partner coverage; assurance of affirmative action policy protection of "affectional preference"
- New: Section 3.3: an informal meeting with music director and Audition Committee is established in the first year of musicians' employment
- Not so new: Section 4.7: (Young People) "YP Concert Relief": additional one-half week off (relief services) in exchange for allowing back-to-back YP to be considered as one service, not to exceed two and one half hours. (After many years of "back-to-back" YP being considered TWO services, in this negotiations it was restored again to one service with the "exchange" being for extra relief [time off]. *New in 1965: "Back-to-back" school concerts permitted, no more than one hour in length to be constituted as one service*)
- New: Section 4.8: "Employer shall make every effort to assign relief services to give the musician the entire day off"
- Disability insurance: Removed cap on musicians' regular salary to 60 percent of minimum salary scale
- Instrument insurance increased from $20,000 to $50,000
- Life insurance increased to $100,000, reduced at age seventy by 50 percent
- New: auditions committee is paid $30 per day plus per diem
- New: Section 20.11: Minimum of ninety-five staff musicians, which shall include a minimum of sixty strings and minimum of thirty-five for all other instruments
- Number of sectional rehearsals up to two hours reduced from six to three times

- All pronouns changed from "he" throughout the contract to "s/he" and "his" to "his/her"

Review

This negotiation was notable in that it was the longest "play-and-talk" in this orchestra's history—seven months without a contract, until a strike deadline was finally set.

The biggest obstacle was the co-pay added to the health insurance, and although it was becoming standard throughout the industry and appeared inevitable, it was a complicated issue, and the committee felt it needed limits to the percentage of co-pay required of the musicians. Throughout America in the 1990s, symphony orchestras faced co-pay issues. The reality of the rising costs of health care was affecting all employees, and musicians were no exception. Negotiating committees everywhere had to inform their colleagues of the necessity of sharing with the employer the increasing health insurance costs. For the first time, co-pays were negotiated as a part of the health insurance packages for many American orchestras.

The 1991 Minnesota Orchestra committee tried to maintain unity and support for the play-and-talk while waiting for an offer it could live with. Finally both sides requested a federal mediator to resolve the stalemate. In spite of the problems and frustrations, some important gains were made. The breakdown of communication forced some serious reflection on how to improve relationships, but not before a strike in 1994.

Negotiations of 1994

Participants

Musicians: Ross Tolbert, Marcia Peck, Burt Hara, Michael Gast, James Clute

Labor lawyer: Ronald Rollins

Union: Brad Eggen, president

Management: Steven Ovitsky, general manager; David Hyslop, president; Ward Gill, Doug Kelley; Tom Vogt, lawyer

Summary

- Salary: wage freeze in the first year of a four-year contract, to $1,455 in the fourth year
- Vacation remains 8½ weeks
- Pension increased to $30,000 with addition of Section 10.2, Pension Reopening
- EMG increased from $25 per week to $70 per week in the fourth year
- New: domestic partner health insurance coverage available with full cost paid by the musician
- New: library staff is added to the bargaining unit
- New: Section 6.2: grace period of up to three minutes permitted without overtime to be used "only to complete the work being rehearsed"
- Section 6.3: for all sectional rehearsals, subdivision no smaller than entire string section

Review

These negotiations became one of the bitterest in the orchestra's history and ultimately led to a strike of 2½ weeks. The musicians formed a number of internal committees in anticipation of a possible labor dispute so that they could be immediately mobilized if necessary. Some of the committees formed were social contacts, outreach, audience, speakers, picket, musicians aid, communications, and media.

It appeared that the strategy of management, driven by the management lawyer, was to remain intractable and rigid, no matter how much pressure they might feel from the public and/or the board.

The projected figures needed for an agreement were known by the musicians. The 4 percent salary increase was to come from the capital campaign. But as the strike deadline approached, the figures previously discussed across the table went from a projected 4 percent or 5 percent to a wage freeze, with no possibility of flexibility or compromise. The musicians did not consider an extensive "play-and-talk," because that had proved unsuccessful in the previous negotiations (1991).

The committee felt that maintaining *parity* of ranking in salary and pension with the other major orchestras was and always had been the priority. The salary, the length of the contract (musicians had always had three-year contracts, except for 1965's five-year contract), and the lack of recordings and tours were the major issues. However, the musicians felt that there was very little negotiating with the other side, in spite of accepting a salary freeze in the first year and trying to explore different approaches and ways to reduce costs. The committee also felt that relevant facts were "filtered" from the board. Many orchestras around the country were having difficult negotiations during this period, and in this committee's opinion, there was a clear sense that the hard-line stance was part of a national collusion by managements determined to hold the line against player demands.

The strike was settled with a salary scale that kept the musicians within the ranks of the top ten orchestras in this country. However, the new four-year contract placed the orchestra a year behind in future negotiations. There was a large increase in the EMG (electronic media guarantee), which pays the musicians for broadcasts and recordings.

The ultimate result of the strike and the actions that precipitated it created mistrust, bitterness, and ill will between musicians and management. After the strike was settled, in a unifying decision by the orchestra, the musicians voted to have no contact with board or management on any committees besides those mandated in the contract.

The "no-contact" policy continued for two years, until the pension reopener in 1996. At that time the federal mediator suggested that both sides consider interest-based bargaining. There was nothing to lose, because communication could not have been worse.

Edo Reflections

Edo de Waart, music director from 1986 to 1995, returned to conduct during the 2003 centennial season. Reflecting upon his eighteen years as music director of two major American orchestras, San Francisco and Minnesota (1979–1995), and as conductor of the Rotterdam Philharmonic in 1967, as well as ten years with the Sydney Symphony (1993–2003), he said one of the positive aspects of the U.S. musicians union rules was that they forced the conductor to learn how to manage his time. According to union rules, length and number of rehearsals are fixed, usually four rehearsals of 2½ hours each week, and with some overtime exceptions. This is a fixed schedule and the result of collective bargaining over many years.

De Waart said, "You get used to it, and you learn how to be efficient."

The abuse of power by some conductors in America until the 1960s that had a direct impact on U.S. musicians' working conditions simply "did not happen, at least in Holland or Sydney," according to de Waart. He made the point that conductors have the advantage of working all over the world, which enables them to experience very different situations and "see both sides." An orchestra musician who does not exchange with another musician, or work in Europe before getting a job in the United States (or vice versa), will not experience or be aware of advantages and disadvantages to both.

"It is something I have felt lacking in the U.S.," said de Waart, "and that is, for the musicians to stay motivated and involved, the power must be shared, and surely there are some enlightened managers who understand this."

The idea of a musician exchange was suggested as early as 1965 by George Zazofsky, former chairman of ICSOM and the assistant concertmaster with the Boston Symphony: "You can't imagine how refreshing and stimulating it would be for a symphony player to have that kind of change. Not a year off, but something new and broadening." It was attempted by the Boston Symphony and a Japanese orchestra, but because of the disparity of salaries and living conditions at the time was not considered entirely successful (although the artistic and cultural rewards were great). The Japanese and Australian musicians' unions sponsored a successful exchange program for orchestral musicians in the mid-'80s. Although it may not be the first time between major orchestras, my exchange with Gary Andrews of the Sydney Symphony Orchestra (SSO) was unprecedented in the Minnesota Orchestra's history.

I discussed my idea with the Minnesota Orchestra's former music director, Edo de Waart, who was music director of the SSO at that time. He

continued on next page

continued from previous page

was very supportive of my proposal, which enabled me to proceed. I arranged countless details with the managements of both of the orchestras, the national and local unions, both orchestra committees, and Gary himself, formerly principal second violin of the SSO. Eiji Oue, the Minnesota Orchestra's music director who succeeded Edo de Waart, also approved the exchange.

Not only is it a rare opportunity to exchange artistic and contractual ideas with colleagues, and to observe different working conditions and a different pool of conductors and soloists, it is also a cultural exchange. Both musicians are representing their orchestra, city, and country, and are goodwill ambassadors in every sense of the word. It is also important to absorb the experience with an open mind and without preconceived notions. Unlike conductors, most of us do not have an opportunity to participate in another orchestra after we have committed our professional and personal lives to a particular job and its environment. We can become frustrated in our respective situations, which can lead to anxiety, psychological and even physical stress. An exchange provides a break from one's routine, and although the working conditions are usually similar, there are other differences, which impact upon every orchestra.

All the Australian orchestras have a relatively short history compared to U.S. orchestras, having been founded in the 1930s by the ABC (Australian Broadcasting Corporation). Over the last few years, the SSO and the other ABC network orchestras have undergone by far the most substantial change in the seventy years of their history. Spearheaded by the divestment of the SSO, four of the six orchestras are autonomous corporate entities. It is only in the past 10 years that they have separated from the ABC, and now face the daunting task of creating endowments and beginning to tap into private funds. There is no real tradition of private and corporate donations to the arts in Australia.

As explained to the 1998 ICSOM Conference by Martin Foster, head of SOMA (Symphony and Opera Musicians Association of Australia) and contrabassoonist of the SSO, at one time all ABC orchestras were covered by a single collective bargaining agreement negotiated by the Musicians Union without musician input. (Sound familiar? This parallels U.S. orchestras' experiences until the formation of ICSOM in 1963.) There had been much infighting between local and federal unions, and by the early '70s, committees were providing services to their own orchestras that the union was not able or chose not to provide. Australian symphony musicians were given little opportunity to replace the union leadership, because the union would hold unannounced elections, and relationships continued to deteriorate. The orchestra musicians eventually decided to secede from the Musicians Union of Australia and join with other arts workers in the Media Alliance as SOMA, the musicians division of the Media Alliance. The general feeling is that this has been a positive move, and the complete overhaul of industrial practices has seen an end to the confrontation and divisiveness of the previous two decades.

However, the future of all SOMA orchestras depends on the future of opera and dance, and these companies equally depend on the orchestras. In Australia, it is the responsibility of government to provide sufficient base funding in order to provide a vibrant artistic life for its artists and audiences. Depending on which party is in office, the arts dollar can be quite finite.

From the 1998 ICSOM Conference, Motion #10:

Resolved: "That the delegates of the 1998 ICSOM Conference express their heartfelt admiration to Martin Foster and their colleagues in the Symphony Orchestra Musicians of Australia for their tenacity and courage in their fight for self-determination and union democracy."

Gary and I agree that our exchange was a wonderful experience, and I am happy to say that the exchange was a success for all involved.

———

Julie Ayer, *Senza Sordino* (August 1999)

Negotiations of 1996

Pension Reopener

Participants

Musicians: Marcia Peck, Michael Gast, James Clute, Ross Tolbert, Fredrik Hedling (replacing Burt Hara, who was on leave of absence that year)

The same committee (with only one replacement) that negotiated the 1994 contract continued with the pension reopener. They unanimously agreed that looking at this one issue was as complicated as negotiating the entire master contract. They also agreed that they worked extremely well together, always a bonus when dealing so closely with one another on important issues.

Union: Brad Eggen.

Lawyer: Ronald Rollins.

Management: David Hyslop, Ward Gill, Robert Sayre, Douglas Kelley, and lawyer Tom Vogt.

Ronald J. Bauers and Lal Basham facilitated the implementation of integrated pensions.

Summary

Single Issue: Pension

Integrated benefit effective September 1, 1996, of $36,000 annual pension for thirty years of service; beginning January 1, 1997, the Association contributes 7 percent of scale to be integrated with the MOA benefit.

Two benefits: eligible musicians will receive two pension checks:

- a check from the AFM Plan representing the contributions made to that Plan on behalf of the Musician
- a check from the Minnesota Orchestral Association based on the enhanced benefit formula, offset by the AFM Plan benefit

Interest-based bargaining (IBB) negotiations are different from traditional negotiations in many ways. Participants do not sit *across* the table, but *around* the table. A three-day workshop for all participants is a prerequisite for using this method of negotiations.

Some of the IBB training objectives are:

- understanding the IBB process
- applying IBB to labor negotiations
- acquiring basic IBB skills

- providing practice opportunity
- building rapport with counterparts

Some of the requirements for participation are:

- All parties must be present for all meetings (including both lawyers, the union president, and the musicians' committee and the management's committee);
- Discussions are open and heard by all, and decisions are consensus-based;
- Communication and brainstorming are priorities; common interests and mutual goals are identified; and
- There is a maximum exchange of information.

Interest-based bargaining was unique in that it was a first for this orchestra, and the Minnesota Orchestra was the first orchestra to use IBB to negotiate a pension reopener.

According to Section 10.2 in the 1994 master agreement, "Either party may reopen the provisions of this Article X for renegotiation by giving at least 90 days' written notice to the other party."

Review

The reason for the choice of IBB was that there was the hope that this approach might improve communications, which could not have been worse. In fact, there had been no communication between musicians, board, and management for two years. After the strike of 1994, the musicians had voted for nonparticipation on any committees except those mandated by the contract. Although the musicians approached this new IBB method with skepticism, everyone agreed it was worth trying. They were assured by the IBB facilitator that a return to traditional negotiations was possible at any time, which is in fact what happened at the end of this process.

In the end, drawing from the union pension was the key. The old pension was paid in full, and all future contributions went into the existing union pension. For many players, their pension would remain split between the two until such time that the MOA benefit has been frozen at the annual pension of $36,000, and the union pension continues to grow.

How parties often view their issues.

Among the materials given to participants of interest-based bargaining (IBB) workshop before negotiations of September 1996 (Federal Mediation and Conciliation Service).

Upon reflection, the committee felt IBB was a positive experience and that it had been worth the effort to bring board members into the process. One of the most important aspects of IBB is that the "filter" could not exist in this kind of negotiation, which had been such a hard-line position from the previous negotiations.

"The best contract is the goal of any negotiations," Leonard Leibowitz, ICSOM lawyer, reminded the 1999 ICSOM conference. He stated that there is nothing wrong with an adversarial relationship, if improving the contract is the combined goal. He warned that orchestra musicians should not enter into IBB in the belief it would get them a good contract or develop a good relationship with management. He also stated that IBB usually will apply to non-economics, but becomes more difficult when financial issues are raised. In any case, it is only a tool, and the obligation is to bargain, however it is done.

David J. Hyslop, president of the Minnesota Orchestra, compared traditional and IBB negotiating styles in this way: "ICSOM's growth was driving the challenges to raise money and to fund longer seasons, and at the same time the musicians developed much better informed leadership in the orchestras. Never before ICSOM, in their networking among orchestras, did the musicians have that kind of information. As far as bargaining styles are concerned, forty years ago, traditional bargaining was probably necessary. IBB (interest-based bargaining) only happens when the parties are in sufficient pain, and it does make it easier to get board participation in the negotiations. In reality, 80 percent of our goals (musicians and management) are the same, but we still have to argue over money and working conditions."

A Senior Moment

During the orchestra's 1997 European tour, the musicians had a free day in Vienna. One of the senior members of the orchestra looked forward to visiting the famous Schloss Schönbrunn. When he arrived to purchase admission for a tour, he asked about a senior citizen pass and was promptly told by the tour guide in typical Viennese fashion, "In Vienna, you haf to be at least vun hundret years old!"

Negotiations of 1998

Participants

Musicians: Kathy Kienzle, Anthony Ross, David Kamminga, Richard Marshall, Norbert Nielubowski.

Labor lawyer: Ronald Rollins.

Union: Brad Eggen, president.

Management/board: David Hyslop, president; Robert Neu, general manager; Ward Gill, chief operating officer; Julie Haight, personnel manager; Beth Kellar-Long, staff member; Nicky Carpenter, board chair; Charles Zelle, Doug Kelley, and Robert Sayre, board members; Tom Vogt, lawyer.

Summary

- Salary from $1,455 in 1998 to $1,700 per week in the fourth year, including $70 in EMG. No change in EMG
- Pension: AFM/MOA integrated benefit, which insures $36,000 annual pension for thirty years of service; 7 percent of scale contributed by MOA to AFM and Employers' Pension Fund, beginning September 1, 1997
- An enhanced pension of $42,000 per year provided to any musician of age sixty-two on or before August 31, 1999 (including August and September of 1998)
- New: Any working musician who is not age 70½ as of September 1, 1999, cannot receive their pension and continue to work
- Vacation/relief: Nine weeks effective the first year of the contract; New: second-chair wind and brass players to receive seven relief services per season
- New: insurance: dependent portion of same-sex domestic partner to be paid by employer
- New: instrument insurance paid by employer increased to $100,000
- New: "members of" services paid at a rate not less than one-eighth of weekly scale (less EMG) for all musicians who play outside of their regular service schedule

- Rates in Article 8 overtime, doubling, small ensembles increased according to percentage of minimum scale increase; chamber music fee increased from $261 to $350; Audition Committee pay increased to $50 per day
- Maternity leave extended from six to eight weeks; unpaid medical leave extended from one to two years
- New: MOMC shall appoint a Tour Committee, and an orchestra representative will accompany management for each major tour or festival advance
- New: outdoor playing condition clause adopted; refusal to play under serious health hazard, and consultative language regarding managing fireworks display
- New: at least four days' prior notice will be given of works to be added in concert or recording session
- Other working condition language regarding tardiness, force majeure, missed services deductions, Sunday services start times, calculation of probation period
- Kinder Konzert pay increased, conditions added

On May 1, 1998, the musicians received a notice from management that the sexual harassment statement had been expanded to an unlawful harassment policy, effective immediately. Two orchestra services were dedicated to discuss this topic, conducted by a lawyer with the Felhaber, Larson, Fenlon and Vogt law firm. Attendance was mandatory.

Review

Interest-based bargaining (IBB) was used again for this negotiation. There was some concern in the beginning that the musicians would be outnumbered by the management/board group, but in reality it was not an issue.

The musicians felt that the "other side/around the table" expressed great interest in continuing with this method from two years before, and all participants were trying to maintain the good relationships and success of the 1996 single-issue IBB pension reopener. They hoped that would translate into multiple issues and felt that substantive changes and improvements were made. The process evolved into an IBB/traditional hybrid that suited this particular group. It was essential for the participating board members to hear the issues directly from the musicians. The process worked well on the non-economics, but the dynamics of bargaining changed when financial issues were raised. In spite of potential for a serious stalemate, better relationships had been established, and at the very least, everyone was listening to each other and respecting their differences.

The issue of the music director became an important factor in discussions pertaining to "earned income," that is, revenue from ticket sales. The musicians insisted that the MD's problems were crucial and relevant to this issue, and it was an essential element to be discussed openly in the presence of the board. Concurrent with these negotiations was an internal MOMC/AAC evaluation among the musicians verifying the negotiating committee's position by a clear majority, including the question of contract renewal for the MD.

The summer venue was also a large part of the discussion, although the Association did not have the money in hand and there was no "Plan B." A side letter to the master agreement "acknowledged that there is a definite likelihood for a summer performing arts center, owned and operated by the Employer, to be built during the period of this Agreement, and agreed that if specific contract language is needed, it will be addressed and if necessary, negotiated at the appropriate time prior to the opening of the center."

A side letter to address the "changing world of electronic media with a particular emphasis on potential internet possibilities . . . agree[s] that Musicians and Association should jointly work together, to explore these opportunities and find ways to take advantage of them." The committee emphasized that the skills of Ron Rollins, labor lawyer, facilitated the process, controlled the tempo, and established respect among all participants.

At this time there was a trend among many major American orchestras to ratify longer contracts. The negotiating committee's view was that a four-year master agreement would be the maximum length they could recommend to their orchestra colleagues for approval. In 1998, the New York Philharmonic signed a groundbreaking six-year contract, settled one year before their current agreement expired. The contract included a substantial economic package, with a 26 percent wage increase that brought the scale to $2,000 a week by 2004. The pension was increased to $53,000 per year and there is a 50 percent increase in seniority pay over the six-year length of the contract. Although they did not identify it as IBB, the New York Philharmonic 1998 negotiations were a sharp break from the confrontational tone of the past. "These talks were dignified, speedy, and honest . . . we were all at the table trying to accomplish the same thing," said one of the musicians who negotiated their contract.

I. Philip Sipser was the New York Philharmonic's labor lawyer for this negotiation. In the January 1998 issue of *Allegro*, Local 802 AFM musicians magazine of New York, he spoke about the groundbreaking contract. "I have no doubt that it [this contract] will affect negotiations for the next decade," Sipser said. "To what degree the contracts achieved will be comparable will depend on a lot of factors. In this case, we got a fairly decent money package, including the $53,000 pension, which was a quid pro quo for accepting a six year agreement."

Sipser was asked how it was possible to begin negotiations so early. "As you may remember, the former president and vice president resigned three months after the last negotiations were concluded, because there had been a great deal of acrimony and things were going badly. And management saw what was taking place in terms of the strikes through-out the country. We sat down and asked our committee whether they thought it was possible to have a negotiation without a laundry list of demands, to which they answered, 'yes.' This made it possible to talk to the other side and to set the negotiations up.

"There was new ground in the $2,000 week, and the elimination of the laundry list. There was a major improvement in the pension provision. And there was new ground, conceptually, in sitting down with management and working in a cooperative, rather than a confrontational, fashion."

Negotiations of 2002

Participants

Musicians: Norbert Nielubowski, Richard Marshall, Aaron Janse, Paul Gunther, Robert Anderson.

Labor lawyer: Ronald Rollins.

Union: Brad Eggen, president.

Management/board: David Hyslop, president; Robert Neu, general manager; Ward Gill, chief operating officer; Nicky Carpenter and Doug Kelley, board members; Tom Vogt, lawyer.

Summary

- Salary: wage freeze in year one and a 3 percent increase in year two to $1,756 in 2003–2004, and a $5 increase in EMG to $75 per week. Two-year contract; fifty-two-week season remains
- Pension: pre-1979 retirees' pension increased from $1,200 to $1,400 per month.
- Contributions to AFM-EPF remains at 7 percent of scale
- Vacation: increased from nine to ten weeks
- Insurance: instrument insurance increased from $100,000 to $200,000 for strings and from $50,000 to $75,000 for nonstrings
- Working conditions: major reorganization concerning scheduling of concerts and rehearsals beginning in 2003–2004, including no limit on double rehearsal days beginning in 2003–2004; no double concert days during subscription weeks beginning in 2003–2004
- New: revolving and rotating strings established: voluntary for current musicians, mandatory for new musicians; new language for personal days; consecutive free days reduced from twenty-five to twenty-one in 2003–2004

Review

We recognized that the next twenty-four months would represent an exceptional moment in the history of the orchestra, with both the centennial and the introduction of the new music director, Osmo Vänskä, on the horizon. We wanted to do everything we could during this time period to assist the organization's continued growth and its long-term artistic excellence. We felt that the new leadership group who presented themselves to us was far more responsive and, we hoped, capable, than the business-as-usual group with whom we'd been working for a decade.

Our argument was that, in terms of professional quality, level of playing, Midwest location, metro area size, and annual budget size, there should be every reason to be considered completely comparable with Cleveland. We reminded management that, in order actually to reach this position, three things must occur. Two of these we borrowed from their own then-current long-range plan, and the other from Mr. Vänskä himself: the highest artistic achievement, sound fiscal management, and parity of musician compensation. No one or two would be able to work alone; all three legs of this tripod would have to be present in order to support and achieve this shared vision. And it was our great hope that a shared vision might prevail.

Negotiations of 2004

Participants

Musicians: Kathy Kienzle, Anthony Ross, Norbert Nielubowski, Marcia Peck, Paul Gunther.

Labor lawyer: Ronald Rollins.

Union: Brad Eggen, president.

Management/board: Anthony Woodcock, president; Robert Neu, vice president and general manager; Holly Duevel, vice president, finance; Paul Zech, lawyer; Ronald Lund, board chairman; Gwen Pappas, director, public affairs; Esther Saarela, human resources; board members Paul Grangaard, Merlin Dewing, and Doug Kelley.

Summary

- Salary: wage freeze in the first year, with a total 4 percent increase by 2007 to weekly salary of $1,827, with no change in EMG. Three-year contract; the fifty-two-week season remains
- No change in pension and vacation
- Seniority pay increases $5/weekly for each increment
- Insurance: the health plan changed to a less expensive plan from the same provider, requiring slightly higher co-pay and deductible amounts from employees

- Instruments: becomes a $12 million pool for all string instruments, with maximum of two bows and two instruments per player (total represents $200,000 per each of sixty string players)
- Pension: no change in current plan for musicians; for previously retired, an increase from $1,400/month to $1,600/month
- New: employer is allowed to use one concert per year permitted by the pension letter for the Symphony Ball or a season preview concert
- New: "hiring slowdown": Attachment 2, application of Sections 20.11 and 22.3 that pertain to timelines for filling vacancies in the orchestra. There will be a schedule of filling eight vacancies over the three years, from 2005 to 2008. Until these positions are permanently filled they will be filled by substitutes as dictated by programming needs
- New: new minimum conditions were set for all touring, both foreign and domestic
- Working conditions: revolving/rotating strings will continue on year-by-year basis; rehearsal intermission increased to twenty minutes; double concert days—sole exception will disappear by the end of this contract; maximum of fifteen Sunday services notification deadline; paternity leave increased to two weeks paid, of six allowed; unpaid leave during K–12 child's spring break

Review

Ours was decidedly not a great contract, not even a good one, but one that reflects these concessionary times. After eight months of bargaining, we accepted an unprecedented second consecutive contract with a wage freeze in the first year; containing an overall salary increase significantly below the cost of living; major concessions in the cost and quality of our health insurance; as well as reductions in other areas. All in all, the Minnesota Orchestra will save $1.2 million in musician costs this season as compared to last.

We made some incremental progress in touring, paternity leave, rehearsal and concert scheduling and seniority. In the end, our committee unanimously recommended this agreement for ratification, because we believed it was the best we could have achieved under the circumstances.

Eleven

Reflections

To my colleagues I give the last word. It is my hope that their legacy of commitment will inspire us all. I hope, also, that these reflections will remind us of the continuing pertinence of their story and the necessity for ongoing vigilance.

Julie Ayer, May 2005

The growth of ICSOM has helped the individual player to the degree that the younger players will never understand. It was an incredible effort made in those days. Informing the new members of the hard-won battles of the last three decades is of paramount importance. If they are not given the knowledge of how things came to be, and that the wages, pension, and benefits they now enjoy were not given to them by the employers, they will not be equipped to continue making progress. None of these achievements occurred in a vacuum. The musicians and their counsel now negotiated with managements that were willing or had no choice but to acknowledge their presence at the table. And with the shift in power came the responsibility of representation and ratification that accompanied it.

Very early, pensions were a big issue because at that point, twenty-five or thirty years ago, contributions by the players were required. Elimination of those pension contributions was critically important, and ultimately that came to pass. Another very important area was in winning the fifty-two-week season, which was present in very few orchestras at that time. Seniority pay came into play at another time. All of these items, plus others, were critical points that presaged a sweep across the country.

I. Philip Sipser, ICSOM labor lawyer, 1968–1985

Without a union and without an orchestra committee and advice of labor attorneys, orchestra musicians would still be in prehistoric times. Working conditions, remuneration, and even employment would still be decided by the whims of an absolute dictator. We can all be truly thankful that the efforts and sacrifices of so many have brought musicians the respect and the stature they enjoy today.

Carl Holub, second oboe,
Minnesota Orchestra Committee chair, 1970

When I joined the Chicago Symphony in 1954, I noticed a new contract posted on the bulletin board. It was the announcement to the orchestra players by the union of what had been negotiated for them. The musicians had nothing to do with the drafting of that contract. There was not even an orchestra committee. At that time problems were addressed by the statement, "Why doesn't the union . . . ?" Now the question is at least phrased in the first person. ICSOM was the first response to that new and daring question. Orchestra musicians began to think "we," not "them." There is now more of the players' voice. Though not perfect, this is better than it was.

Wayne Barrington, retired Chicago Symphony
Orchestra hornist; Chicago Symphony Orchestra
Committee and ICSOM representative

It was most important for him [George Zazofsky] to make sure management and the public viewed the musicians as professional workers. The misconception is that musicians don't "work," they "play." [When my] husband first approached management for more money, their reaction was, "That's a lot of money you're asking for," to which he replied, "You didn't give up your childhood to practice." His main goal with ICSOM was to have an organization where if orchestras have to go on strike, there would be supportive and informed people that they could talk to.

Orchestras had to have financial support and had to learn how to handle disagreements. If these kids who walk into $60,000 jobs don't think to give anything back, if nobody does anything, there's going to be a division and conquer. They're going to have to take cuts, or else. This is what my husband tried to prevent.

Edith Zazofsky, on her husband, George Zazofsky,
one of ICSOM's founders and Boston Symphony
Orchestra assistant concertmaster, 1941–1960

I went to work for the AFM in January 1982 and left in May 1994. I was an assistant to the president for Symphony Matters. At the time it was just the Symphony Department. It was several years later that it became the SSD (Symphonic Services Division). Perhaps the most important contribution I made was to convince players that there was a body of knowledge about committee administration and negotiating from which they could draw so as not to reinvent the wheel every day. In many situations I was able to convince the AFM and locals that it was worthwhile to support the symphony folk in terms of good unionism as well as self-interest. When the New York City Opera committee was fired, there was an extremely plantation-mentality contractor who simply did not stand for any opposition. He thought firing the committee would solve his problems with "uppity" musicians. Not a novel story, but as often happens, in this situation it didn't work. The committee was reinstated and the resultant contract (the first) changed the status from single engagement to contracted job status.

Lew Waldeck, former tubist and ICSOM delegate
with the New York City Opera, and director emeritus of AFM's SSD

As a former chairman of the Chicago Symphony Orchestra Members' Committee, member of the board of directors of the Chicago Federation of Musicians, first president of the Chicago chapter of the Recording Musicians of America, and the chairman of the first meeting of the International Conference of Symphony and Opera Musicians, I have been active in the labor movement involving professional musicians from the 1950s well into the 1960s. During the last forty-five years, much has changed in the nature of issues, priorities, communications, internal as well as external circumstances, and policies. But certain things still remain constant. Among them is the fact that no matter what progress the professional musicians have achieved over the years, the "struggle" continues to protect their interests. Also, the battle for the "many" is fought with the blood of the "few." While it is gratifying to have been among the leaders working for the betterment of our colleagues, it is disappointing that so few seem to appreciate the sacrifices made on their behalf. In addition, the younger generation of musicians coming into the business haven't a clue as to how the benefits they enjoy came about. That is why it is so important that they know the history of this amazing journey.

> *Joseph Golan, retired principal second violin*
> *Chicago Symphony Orchestra; first chairperson of ICSOM,*
> *and Chicago Symphony players committee*

Looking back at the days before ICSOM, I remember how our local union president informed us about the contract he had just signed "for us." He had the attitude that we were lucky just to have a job. I will be forever grateful to the founders of ICSOM, for their vision and courage and hard work. They gave symphony and opera musicians a voice and, eventually, control over our own destiny. Before that, we had had to fight our own union for that right, even before we could convince the orchestra's management that the musicians' negotiating committee truly spoke for us. The help of Phil Sipser was vital to that process. Whether they know it or not, all of today's musicians are deeply indebted to those founders.

> *Bernice Beckerman, retired violist,*
> *Houston Symphony Orchestra; former chairperson,*
> *Minneapolis Symphony Orchestra Members Committee*

ICSOM has been an integral part of my life for the last thirty-four years—more than half my lifetime. In 2002 I missed my one and only annual conference, but only because the doctors would not let me leave the hospital.

It has been, and continues to be a remarkable experience. I literally don't know of another labor organization like ICSOM (except, of course, its counterparts which sprung up in its wake, i.e., ROPA, OCSM, RMA, and TMA). That is, a labor organization for rank-and-file musicians, organized by and run by other rank-and-file musicians, virtually all of whom work full time at being professional musicians, and none of whom get paid for their [ICSOM work]. How they find the time, energy, and devotion to do what they have done and continue to do is a constant source of amazement to me. While the heart of the organization is communication, the soul is the devotion of those musicians who, over the years, were and are willing to treat their ICSOM roles as almost a religious calling. In a recent piece for *Senza Sordino* (the major artery of that "heart of communication"), I named some of the men and women to whom I refer. (I needn't mention them again—especially since whenever I do, I invariably, but unintentionally, omit the names of some who should be included.)

Originating as a dissident group of disgruntled symphony musicians in 1962, ICSOM has become perhaps the single most powerful force in the AFM. I sometimes wonder how James Petrillo would have dealt with them. In any event, the lot of symphony, opera, and ballet musicians, and, I believe, all union musicians, has been immeasurably improved by the existence and influence of ICSOM. Despite the problems of the field in recent years, symphony, opera, and ballet jobs are still among the steadiest, highest compensated, and most respected in the music business. This alone is vivid testimony to ICSOM's achievements.

I cannot end these reflections without pointing with pride to the role my late partner, father-in-law, and mentor, Phil Sipser, played during the formative years, and continued in one form or another until his death. He was a committed trade unionist (and troublemaker) all of his life, and his spirit continues to be the motivating force behind the accomplishments and aspirations of ICSOM.

Leonard Leibowitz, ICSOM labor lawyer

Appendixes

A. Comparative Growth in Orchestra Annual Salaries, 1952–2000

CPI (base 1967=100):	1952	79.5 1952	1962	90.6 1962	Real Sal Growth	1972	125.3 1972	Real Sal Growth
ORCHESTRA	Minimum Annual Salary	Salary Adj to 2000 $	Minimum Annual Salary	Salary Adj to 2000 $	prev 10 years % change (adj for inflation)	Minimum Annual Salary	Salary Adj to 2000 $	prev 10 years % change (adj for inflation)
Alabama								
Atlanta	1,210	7,806				9,553	39,104	
Baltimore	1,400	9,032	3,185	18,031	100%	9,660	39,542	119%
Boston	4,830	31,161	8,880	50,271	61%	16,640	68,114	35%
Buffalo	1,882	12,142	3,388	19,180	58%	9,975	40,831	113%
Charlotte						3,875	15,862	
Chicago Lyric						4,340	17,765	
Chicago	4,505	29,064	7,500	42,459	46%	16,640	68,114	60%
Cincinnati	2,660	17,161	4,185	23,692	38%	11,960	48,957	107%
Cleveland	3,270	21,097	6,120	34,646	64%	14,820	60,664	75%
Colorado (Denver)	1,660	10,710				8,600	35,203	
Columbus								
Dallas	1,600	10,323	4,500	25,475	147%	11,700	47,892	88%
Detroit	3,040	19,613	4,940	27,966	43%	12,855	52,620	88%
Florida Orch								
Florida Phil								
Florida Sym	720	4,645						
Grant Park	704	4,542						
Honolulu						5,280	21,613	
Houston	2,560	15,516	3,998	22,633	37%	11,180	45,764	102%
Indianapolis	1,400	9,032	2,250	12,738	41%	7,980	32,665	156%
Jacksonville								
Kansas City	1,560	10,064	3,474	19,667	95%	5,300	21,695	10%
Kennedy Center								
Los Angeles	3,050	19,677	5,011	28,368	44%	14,790	60,541	113%
Louisville								

Organization								
Met Opera						17,595	72,023	
Milwaukee	2,600	16,774	4,350	24,626	47%	9,020	36,922	103%
Minnesota (Minneapolis)						12,192	49,906	
Nashville	2,080	13,419	4,480	25,362	89%	13,500	55,261	118%
National (Washington)								
New Jersey								
New Orleans	1,300	8,387	2,830	16,021	91%	7,828	32,043	100%
NYC Ballet								
NYC Opera								
New York Phil	4,200	27,097	8,720	49,365	82%	17,160	70,242	42%
North Carolina	1,054	6,800				4,495	18,400	
Oakland								
Oklahoma City	1,331	8,587	976	5,525	-22%			63%
Oregon (Portland)	1,100	7,097				2,200	9,005	
Philadelphia	4,995	32,226	7,770	43,987	36%	17,180	70,324	60%
Phoenix								
Pittsburgh	2,500	16,129	5,230	29,608	84%	13,500	55,261	87%
Rochester	2,640	17,032	4,125	23,352	37%	9,225	37,761	62%
St. Louis	2,214	14,284	4,380	24,796	74%	10,965	44,884	81%
St. Paul Chamber								
San Antonio	1,470	9,484						
San Diego						5,760	23,578	
SF Ballet								
SF Opera								
San Francisco	2,200	14,193	4,010	22,701	60%	13,720	56,161	147%
Seattle								
Syracuse						6,800	27,835	
Toledo						3,960	16,210	
Utah	892	5,755						
Virginia								
AVERAGES	2,221	14,328	4,741	26,840	87%	10,311	42,205	57%

A. Comparative Growth in Orchestra Annual Salaries, 1952–2000, *continued*

CPI (base 1967=100): 1982 = 289.1 | 1992 = 420.3 | 2000 = 512.9

ORCHESTRA	1982 Minimum Annual Salary	1982 Salary Adj to 2000 $	Real Sal Growth prev 10 years % change (adj for inflation)	1992 Minimum Annual Salary	1992 Salary Adj to 2000 $	Real Sal Growth prev 10 years % change (adj for inflation)	2000 Minimum Annual Salary	2000 Salary Adj to 2000 $	Real Sal Growth prev 10 years % change (adj for inflation)
Alabama	9,486	16,829					23,575	23,575	
Atlanta	26,260	46,589	19%	52,000	63,457	36%	62,504	62,504	-2%
Baltimore	22,540	39,989	1%	53,560	65,360	63%	62,400	62,400	-5%
Boston	37,400	66,352	-3%	63,960	78,052	18%	88,920	88,920	14%
Buffalo	18,200	32,289	-21%	33,000	40,271	25%	31,650	31,650	-21%
Charlotte	11,648	20,665	30%	22,210	27,103	31%	25,650	25,650	-5%
Chicago Lyric	11,050	19,604	10%	27,005	32,955	68%	41,875	41,875	27%
Chicago	37,440	66,423	-2%	65,000	79,321	19%	88,400	88,400	11%
Cincinnati	31,980	56,737	16%	57,250	69,863	23%	78,910	78,910	13%
Cleveland	34,320	60,888	0%	66,144	80,717	33%	85,280	85,280	6%
Colorado (Denver)	21,190	37,594	7%	25,350	30,935	-18%	34,356	34,356	11%
Columbus				32,550	39,721		44,666	44,666	12%
Dallas	28,600	50,740	6%	54,600	66,629	31%	71,760	71,760	8%
Detroit	32,500	57,659	10%	61,672	75,260	31%	80,834	80,834	7%
Florida Orch				23,700	28,922		26,730	26,730	-8%
Florida Phil				26,950	32,888		36,400	36,400	11%
Florida Sym	10,013	17,764		out of business					
Grant Park	4,636	8,225		8,359	10,201	24%	10,699	10,699	5%
Honolulu	13,090	23,223	7%	27,616	33,700	45%	25,740	25,740	-24%
Houston	28,600	50,740	11%	51,480	62,822	24%	69,940	69,940	11%
Indianapolis	21,045	37,336	14%	43,290	52,828	41%	61,872	61,872	17%
Jacksonville				20,646	25,195		30,005	30,005	19%
Kansas City	12,000	21,290	-2%	28,200	34,413		39,932	39,932	16%
Kennedy Center							29,805	29,805	
Los Angeles	38,360	68,055	12%	66,480	81,127	19%	89,880	89,880	11%
Louisville	11,466	20,342		26,158	31,921	57%	28,564	28,564	-11%

Met Opera	32,510	57,677	-20%	62,712	33%	76,529	77,792	77,792	2%
Milwaukee	22,095	39,199	6%	46,080	43%	56,232	52,008	52,008	-8%
Minnesota (Minneapolis)	32,708	58,028	16%	62,790	32%	76,624	79,950	79,950	4%
Nashville	8,800	15,612		19,490	52%	23,784	24,916	24,916	5%
National (Washington)	29,840	52,940	-4%	58,240	34%	71,071	79,690	79,690	12%
New Jersey	8,000	14,193		22,120	90%	26,993	33,000	33,000	22%
New Orleans	20,494	36,359	13%	to Louisiana Phil					
NYC Ballet	14,375	25,503		35,483	70%	43,301	45,750	45,750	6%
NYC Opera				29,750		36,304	34,957	34,957	-4%
New York Phil	40,319	71,531	2%	63,960	9%	78,052	88,920	88,920	14%
North Carolina	16,200	28,741	56%	26,650	13%	32,521	35,670	35,670	10%
Oakland	7,896	14,009		to Oakland/East Bay					
Oklahoma City	11,342	20,122							
Oregon (Portland)	13,118	23,273	158%	29,791	56%	36,355	36,716	36,716	1%
Philadelphia	38,940	69,084	-2%	65,980	17%	80,517	88,400	88,400	10%
Phoenix	11,095	19,684		24,500	52%	29,898	31,210	31,210	4%
Pittsburgh	23,150	58,812	6%	65,260	35%	79,638	82,940	82,940	4%
Rochester	23,520	41,727	11%	35,210	3%	42,967	32,400	32,400	-25%
St. Louis	28,600	50,740	13%	53,560	29%	65,360	72,280	72,280	11%
St. Paul Chamber				46,400		56,623	58,162	58,162	3%
San Antonio	15,010	26,630	13%	22,698	4%	27,699	28,548	28,548	3%
San Diego	13,335	23,658		26,730	38%	32,619	25,200	25,200	-23%
SF Ballet	9,580	16,996		24,580	76%	29,995	31,950	31,950	7%
SF Opera				47,241		57,649	57,740	57,740	0%
San Francisco	35,620	63,194	13%	65,780	27%	80,273	88,400	88,400	10%
Seattle	19,580	34,737	25%	out of AFM					
Syracuse	12,684	22,503	39%	21,715	18%	26,499	24,659	24,659	-7%
Toledo	11,080	19,657		16,640	3%	20,306	20,226	20,226	0%
Utah	23,400	41,515		31,980	-6%	39,026	42,380	42,380	9%
Virginia				15,990		19,513	21,697	21,697	11%
AVERAGES	21,173	37,563	-11%	39,970	30%	48,776	50,312	50,312	3%

NOTES: 1) Inflation adjustments are based on the Consumer Price Index for All Urban Consumers (U.S. city average, all items, not seasonally adjusted). Different regions of the country may have experienced inflation rates that differ widely from the national averages at various times. Thus, the figures in this chart are approximations only, for general comparative purposes, and should not be relied upon to assess the progress of a particular orchestra. CPI data specific to a particular city may be obtained from the U.S. Bureau of Labor Statistics: www.bls.gov. 2) Sources: Annual ICSOM Wage Charts as published in Senza Sordino, and AFM Symphony Wage Charts (ICSOM and ROPA), supplemented with data provided by ICSOM Delegates. Special thanks to Sara Honen of the SSD and several Delegates who rummaged through attics and garages to unearth data 30 to 40 years old.

B. The Delegates to the Founding Meetings of ICSOM

May 12 and 13, 1962, Chicago, Illinois
"Symposium of Symphony Orchestra Delegates"
Joseph Golan, acting chair

Boston: George Zazofsky
Chicago: Joseph Golan, Wayne Barrington, Sam Denov,
　　　　　Walfrid Kujala, Richard Lottridge, Rudolph Nashan,
　　　　　Gordon Peters, Laurence Thorstenberg
Cincinnati: Henry Shaw, Harold Roberts
Cleveland: Gino Raffaelli
Indianapolis: John Kitts, George Rhodes
Los Angeles: Vance Beach
Met Opera: Jacques Rubenstein, Leonard Grossman
New York: Bert Bial, Robert Gladstone
Philadelphia: Leonard Hale, Edward Arian, Michael Bookspan,
　　　　　Santo Caserta, Ernest Goldstein, Alan Iglitzin,
　　　　　Carl Torello, Jerome Wigler
Pittsburgh: Charles Hois
St. Louis: Joe Bluck
Toronto: Roy Cox

September 6 and 8, 1962, Cleveland, Ohio
(Formal establishment of ICSOM)
George Zazofsky, chair
Sam Denov, vice chair

Boston: George Zazofsky
Chicago: Walfrid Kujala, Rudoph Nashan
Cincinnati: Henry Shaw, Jack Wellbaum
Cleveland: Elden Gatwood, Gino Raffaelli
Detroit: Harold Laudenslager
Indianapolis: John Kitts, Harald Hansen
Met Opera: Jacques Reubenstein, Clarendon Van Norman
Minneapolis: Andre Speyer
New York: Ralph Mendelson

Philadelphia: Leonard Hale, Michael Bookspan
Pittsburgh: Murray Feldman, Louis Paul
Rochester: N. Harold Paley, Herbert Brill
St. Louis: Henry Loew
Toronto: Roy Cox
Baltimore: Bonnie J. Lake (nonvoting observer)

C. ICSOM Member Orchestras by Year of Entry (Courtesy ICSOM)

Sixty-four orchestras have been members of ICSOM since its founding. There are currently fifty member orchestras.

1

The following orchestras, active in the formation of ICSOM and represented at meetings which preceded the formal adoption of bylaws establishing membership in 1963, were accorded charter member status in the bylaws. They are arranged in order of first meeting attended; within that classification they are listed alphabetically.

Boston Symphony Orchestra (May 1962)
Chicago Symphony Orchestra (May 1962)
Cincinnati Symphony Orchestra (May 1962)
Cleveland Orchestra (May 1962)
Indianapolis Symphony Orchestra (May 1962)
Los Angeles Philharmonic (May 1962)
Metropolitan Opera Orchestra (May 1962)
New York Philharmonic (May 1962)
Philadelphia Orchestra (May 1962)
Pittsburgh Symphony Orchestra (May 1962)
Saint Louis Symphony Orchestra (May 1962)
Toronto Symphony Orchestra (May 1962–1971) (withdrew)
Baltimore Symphony Orchestra (September 1962)
Detroit Symphony Orchestra (September 1962)
Minneapolis Symphony Orchestra (now Minnesota Orchestra)
   (September 1962)

Rochester Philharmonic Orchestra (September 1962)
Buffalo Philharmonic Orchestra (June 1963)
National Symphony Orchestra (June 1963)
San Francisco Symphony Orchestra (June 1963)

2

The following orchestras became members in the years indicated. Before current policy was instituted, an orchestra could be granted membership in mid-season and was not required to send a representative to the annual conference at the time it joined. Hence some orchestras listed were not represented even long after becoming members, while some orchestras sent observers to conferences before becoming members.

Houston Symphony Orchestra (1965)
Kansas City Philharmonic (1966–1983)
   (folded; superseded by Kansas City Symphony; see below)
Seattle Symphony[1] (1966–1989)
   (formally notified of loss of eligibility on 27 March 1989)
Honolulu Symphony Orchestra[2] (1967)
Dallas Symphony Orchestra (1968)
Denver Symphony Orchestra (1968)
   (became Colorado Symphony Orchestra in 1989)
Montreal Symphony Orchestra (1968–1975) (joined OCSM)
New Orleans Philharmonic (later New Orleans Symphony) (1968–1992)
   (folded; superseded by Louisiana Philharmonic)
New York City Ballet Orchestra (1968)
San Antonio Symphony[3] (1968–1970, rejoined 1978)
Vancouver Symphony (1968–1975) (joined OCSM)
Lyric Opera of Chicago (1969)
Milwaukee Symphony Orchestra (1970)
   (joined during preceding season)
New York City Opera Orchestra (1970)
   (joined during preceding season)
Syracuse Symphony Orchestra (1970)
New Haven Symphony (1970–1977) (not listed after 1977)

Atlanta Symphony Orchestra (1971)

Oregon Symphony Orchestra (1971)

Winnipeg Symphony (1971–1975) (joined OCSM)

North Carolina Symphony (1972)

New Jersey Symphony Orchestra (1973)

Florida Symphony Orchestra (1974–1992) (folded)

Phoenix Symphony Orchestra (1974)

San Diego Symphony Orchestra (1974)

Birmingham Symphony (later Alabama) (1975–1995)
(folded; reconstituted in 1997; rejoined in 1998)

Nashville Symphony Orchestra (1975–1977)
(not listed after 1977; rejoined in 2000)

Oakland Symphony Orchestra (1975–1990)
(reconstituted, joined ROPA as Oakland East Bay)

Grant Park Symphony Orchestra (1977)

Hartford Symphony (1977–1980) (voted in December 1980
to discontinue membership)

Oklahoma Symphony Orchestra (1977–1989) (folded)

San Francisco Ballet Orchestra (1977)

Toledo Symphony Orchestra (1977–1987) (joined ROPA)

Kennedy Center Opera House Orchestra (1978)

Utah Symphony Orchestra (1979) (became Utah Symphony
and Opera in 2002)

Louisville Orchestra (1980)

San Francisco Opera Orchestra (1983)

Saint Paul Chamber Orchestra (1984)

Florida Orchestra (1987)

Columbus (Ohio) Symphony Orchestra (1990)

Philharmonic Orchestra of Florida (now Florida
Philharmonic Orchestra) (1990)

Jacksonville Symphony Orchestra (1997)

Kansas City Symphony[4] (May 1998)

Charlotte Symphony Orchestra (1999)

Virginia Symphony (2000)

Fort Worth Symphony Orchestra (2001)

(1) The Seattle Symphony became ineligible to remain a member of ICSOM during the 1988–1989 season, when it decertified its local and a majority of Seattle Symphony members ceased to be members of the AFM.

(2) The Honolulu Symphony became the Hawaii Symphony Orchestra in 1994. The name was restored to Honolulu in 1996.

(3) The San Antonio Symphony sent an observer to the September 1963 meeting at which bylaws were drafted and, having been present at a formative meeting, is listed in earlier bylaws as a charter member. However, San Antonio did not formally join ICSOM until 1968.

(4) At the 1995 ICSOM conference, the Kansas City Symphony was ensured membership once it negotiated a union recognition clause into its contract. This happened in May 1998, and membership was immediate at that time.

The Chamber Orchestra of Philadelphia was provisionally granted membership in 1968, and the orchestra's name appears in the *Senza Sordino* listing of orchestras that season. However, the orchestra doesn't appear again in the minutes, presumably because the orchestra membership did not subsequently confirm intent to join.

The Chautauqua Symphony was accepted as a member at the beginning of the 1979 conference, but the action was reconsidered a few days later. Although perhaps technically a member for that brief period, the Chautauqua Symphony has never been listed as a member and is not considered one in this compilation.

Several orchestras retained membership in ICSOM during difficult periods of transition as members attempted to keep their orchestras extant: The Oklahoma Symphony, which folded following a long strike in 1988; The Oakland East Bay Symphony, an incarnation of the Oakland Symphony following that orchestra's bankruptcy in 1986; the Denver Symphony, whose musicians formed the cooperative Colorado Symphony in the face of bankruptcy proceedings in 1989; and the Louisiana Symphony, which succeeded the New Orleans Symphony and was briefly an affiliate member of ICSOM.

D. ICSOM Member Orchestras, 2004

Alabama Symphony

Atlanta Symphony

Baltimore Symphony

Boston Symphony

Buffalo Philharmonic

Charlotte Symphony

Chicago Lyric Opera

Chicago Symphony

Cincinnati Symphony

Cleveland Orchestra

Colorado Symphony

Columbus Symphony

Dallas Symphony

Detroit Symphony

Florida Orchestra

Florida Philharmonic

Grant Park Symphony

Honolulu Symphony

Houston Symphony

Indianapolis Symphony

Jacksonville Symphony

Kansas City Symphony

Kennedy Center Orchestra

Los Angeles Philharmonic

Louisville Orchestra

Metropolitan Opera

Milwaukee Symphony

Minnesota Orchestra

Nashville Symphony

National Symphony

New Jersey Symphony

New York City Ballet

New York City Opera

New York Philharmonic

North Carolina Symphony

Oregon Symphony

Philadelphia Orchestra

Phoenix Symphony

Pittsburgh Symphony

Rochester Philharmonic

Saint Louis Symphony

Saint Paul Chamber Orchestra

San Antonio Symphony

San Diego Symphony

San Francisco Ballet

San Francisco Opera

San Francisco Symphony

Syracuse Symphony

Utah Symphony

Virginia Symphony

E. The Original 1967 Conductor Evaluation Sheet

Part I

Musicians first gave their personal yes/no reactions to two broad questions:

1. Do you, or would you, like to play under this man as a guest conductor?

2. Do you, or would you, like to play under this man as a permanent conductor?

Musicians were also invited to "make comments on reverse" side of the questionnaire. NB: In the 1960s, when this questionnaire first made its appearance, few people considered the possibility that a conductor would be other than a man.

Part II

Musicians had the opportunity to rate the conductors with whom they worked on a four-level scale—Exceptional, Good, Mediocre, Inferior—in response to thirty questions about the conductor's leadership, musicianship, and technique. In addition to instructing the musicians to "answer the following questions as OBJECTIVELY as you can," the questionnaire repeated the request to "make comments on reverse" side of the page.

Leadership

1. Is he able to convey his ideas clearly and in a way that gets a willing response from the musicians?
2. Does he command respect as a person?
2A. Does he maintain self-control under pressure?
3. Does he have the necessary self-confidence?
4. Does he make the orchestra feel secure during performance?
5. Is he inspirational to the musicians?
6. Does he consistently treat the musicians with courtesy and respect?

Musicianship

7. Does he understand the emotional content of the music?
8. Is he sensitive to good playing rather than just errors?
9. Is his ear keen enough to hear clearly many parts being played simultaneously?
10. Does he have a good sense of pitch and intonation?
11. Does he have a strong sense of rhythm?
12. Is he able to achieve good orchestral balance?
13. Does he demand the best performance of which the musicians are capable?
14. Does he know what he wants musically, that is, a definite interpretation for each piece?
15. Does he communicate the proper mood for his interpretation?
16. Does he know the score well?

Technique

17. Is his beat clear most of the time?
18. Does his beat have a clear inner rhythm?
19. Does he give proper cueing?
20. Can he conduct complex modern rhythmic passages without error?
21. Does he accompany soloists well?
22. Does he show his interpretation with the baton, keeping talk in proper perspective?
23. Does his beat communicate proper character, mood, and intensity of the passage?
24. Does he avoid stopping for mistakes that will correct themselves?
25. Is he efficient with his rehearsal time?
26. Does he conduct performances essentially as he rehearsed them?
27. Is he familiar with the capabilities of the various instruments?

For Regular Conductors Only

28. Does his programming indicate a well-rounded knowledge of the symphonic repertoire?

29. Is he concerned with the working conditions of the musicians?
30. Have the new musicians chosen by the conductor proven satisfactory? (Does he audition well?)

The questions above continue to provide the basis for the (now computerized) evaluation sheet still used in symphony orchestras today. However, in 1986 ICSOM condensed the form and reduced the number of questions to thirteen. Today's questionnaire also asks players to indicate their instrument, and the form provides a section for optional use by individual orchestras to ask questions relevant to their local needs.

F. Kurt Loebel Summons Text (September 21, 1961)

(As discussed in Chapter 3, in the section "Endless Battles in Cleveland")

You are herby notified that you have been charged with the following violations of the Constitution and By-Laws of the American Federation of Musicians and the Constitution and By-Laws of the Cleveland Federation of Musicians, Local No. 4, A. F. of M., in the manner and particulars hereinafter set forth:

Violation:

Article II—Constitution of the Cleveland Federation of Musicians, Local No. 4. "The object of this local is to unite the instrumental portion of the musical profession . . ."

Charge:

Promoting disunity within the Union by engaging in activities individually, or as a member of a group, supporting or participating, directly or indirectly, through committees or representatives;

- Attempting to supersede the authority of Local No. 4 and set up the Cleveland Orchestra as a separate, autonomous unity—dual unionism, by demanding the power of prior ratification of all collective bargaining agreements negotiated between the Local and the Musical Arts Association; and

- Contrary to, "The better protection of its (Union's) interests in general . . ." Jeopardizing the interests and welfare of the Union and its members by issuing false, misleading and deceitful press releases to newspapers of wide circulation, serving to undermine the prestige of the Union in the community, alienate donors to the Cleveland Orchestra Maintenance Fun, and sabotage the Local's efforts and expenditures the years in building and helping to sustain a Cleveland Symphony Orchestra; and
- Contrary to, "The better protection of its (Union's) interests in general . . ." In attempting to upset also the contractual relation presently existing between the Union and the Musical Arts Association, which, if successful, could expose the Local to possible financial loss in a court action by the Musical Arts Association to recover damages for causing its failure to fulfill its own commitments to others.

Violation:

Article II—Constitution of the American Federation of Musicians. ". . . consistency with Union principles . . ."

Charge:

Engaging in activities *inconsistent with Union principles* individually, or as a member of a group, supporting or participation, directly or indirectly, through committees or representatives;

- In defiance and contempt for Union laws and principles, rejecting and refusing to abide by rulings of the Executive Board of Local No. 4, concerning matters of ratification; also, violative of the solemn oath of membership—"to obey all laws of the Federation and the Local and to abide by all rules and regulation emanating therefrom"; and
- In deliberately by-passing of the orderly processes for appeal, provided for under Federation and Local laws for resolving matters pertaining to the internal affairs of the Union, electing

instead to dun, badger and harass the Executive Officers of Local 4, by repetitious demands, by devious illegal motions and resolutions, by applying external social and legal pressures in an attempt to coerce Union officers into yielding to your demands for the power of ratification.

Violation:

Article II—Section 2, By-Laws of Local No. 4 ". . . breach of good faith and fair dealing . . ."

Charge:

Engaging in activities, individually or as a member of a group, supporting or participating, directly or indirectly, through committees or representatives;

- By demonstrated, selfish disregard for the rights and welfare of fellow Union members in refusing to acknowledge and abide by the principle of majority rule, attempting to impose upon fellow members the concept of divided group authority for the benefit of Cleveland Orchestra members only, despite the rejection and repudiation of such concept by the great majority of members at general membership meetings.

Violation:

Article 22, Section 4—By-Laws of the American Federation of Musicians. "The home local shall be the bargaining representative of the members of a Symphony Orchestra. Symphony players and/or Locals shall be free to make contracts with the management of Symphony Orchestras . . ."

Article 13, Section 35—By-Laws of the American Federation of Musicians. "A local of the Federation enters into collective bargaining agreements for its members and for Federation members who perform within the jurisdiction of the local. Each member of such local and each Federation member who performs within its jurisdiction is bound by the terms of the collective bargaining agreements executed by such local."

Article 232, Section 13—By-Laws of the American Federation of Musicians. "A member who signs a contract with the Symphony Orchestra Association must hold all lawful provisions in same inviolate."

Charge:

Through individual or group action, supporting or participating, directly or indirectly, through committees or representatives;

- Attempting, through the device and subterfuge of court action to obtain a release from your contractual obligations under the individual player's contract, which you voluntarily signed with the Musical Arts Association, by petitioning the court to declare the basic Master Contract negotiated between the Union and the Musical Arts Association, and all individual players' contracts executed with the Musical Arts Association, null and void, to the detriment of those members of the Cleveland Orchestra who are not in sympathy, affiliation, and/or in support of such action.

Violation:

Article 13, Section I—By-Laws of the American Federation of Musicians. ". . . placing obstacles in the way of the successful maintenance of the Local . . ."

Charge:

Placing obstacles in the way of the successful maintenance of a Local by acts and published threats attempting to forestall the execution of the Master Contract entered into between the Union and the Musical Arts Association as follows:

- Threatening "Unfavorable consequences," per telegram to Mr. Szell, May 2, 1961.
- Assuring that the Musical Arts Association and Mr. Szell will have "85 bitterly dissatisfied musicians in its orchestra." Telegram to Mr. Frank Joseph and Mr. Beverly Barksdale, May 2, 1961.

- May 5, attempting to persuade the Musical Arts Association to allow the signing of individual player's contract under protest; the same to become null and void in the event the Master Agreement would be declared invalid.
- Attempting to interfere with the arrangements set forth in both Master Agreement and individual player's contract, providing for payments by the Trustee of the Music Performance Trust Fund for some of the regular services rendered by members of the Cleveland Orchestra, violative of your contractual obligation and jeopardizing this source of contributions to the Cleveland Orchestra Maintenance Fund.

G. Memo from I. Philip Sipser and Leonard Leibowitz

Although by 2005, most symphony orchestra musicians' committees have experienced strikes and know how to survive them, three decades ago such labor struggles were new to our profession. This 1970 document was immensely helpful to orchestra musicians of that time—and remains so to this day.

TO: Negotiating Committee
FROM: I. Philip Sipser and Leonard Leibowitz

In connection with a possible labor dispute, the following Committees should be formed and put into action forthwith:

1. *Bulletin Committee*
A bulletin must be prepared which tells the full story from the musicians' viewpoint. It should contain all cost-of-living statistics, comparisons with other orchestras, and basically all of the facts and figures. The aforementioned bulletin should be sent to every member of the Board of Directors, etc. It is the only way we can get our message across to those in a position to help. It is this bulletin which will be used by many of the committees listed below.

2. Media Committee

This is perhaps the most important assignment. This committee must be fully familiar with all of the facts and figures and must be prepared to discuss, debate, etc., at any time. Only its spokesperson, elected by the Negotiating Committee, together with the Chairman of the Negotiating Committee, and counsel should speak to the press.

3. Political Committee

This is the group that must make contact with all of the local, city, state, and federal politicos in an effort to gain their support. Hopefully some of these politicians will make public statements on our behalf, appear at rallys [sic] or benefit concerts, or perhaps even introduce legislation.

4. Audience Association

A Committee must be formed to try to organize a group of interested members of the audience who will hopefully seek to intervene with the management, issue public statements tending to support the musicians, etc. The Audience Association must, at all times, appear to be mostly impartial, consistent however with its main purpose of influencing a rational settlement.

5. Speakers Bureau

This Committee must start to call local organizations of all kinds, to ask if they would like a small playing group from the Orchestra to appear at the next meeting *free*. All we ask is 10 or 15 minutes afterwards to explain our position. If they get any invitations, then this Committee must arrange for these small groups to go and play, together with a spokesperson who will make the most of the 10 or 15 minutes.

6. Benefit Concerts

A Committee must be formed to seek hall rentals, arrange for a famous conductor or soloist, etc., and generally produce a benefit concert or concerts.

7. Music Schools

This Committee should contact the faculty and students at the local music schools to see if it can organize a students committee to Save the Symphony, etc. Hopefully one or two faculty members can be persuaded to make public statements in support. Perhaps the beginnings of the Audience Association can be found here.

8. *ICSOM*
The ICSOM Delegate must start contacting other orchestras for telegrams, letters, etc. of support to be sent to the Board Chairman and the other representatives of management. These letters and telegrams should, at the appropriate time, be turned over to the press.

9. *Picket Committee*
This is the group that must see to it that signs are prepared, that a schedule of picket duty is made up, and that members are notified of their required tours of duty, etc.

The Orchestra Committee alone cannot do all of the above. It is both physically impossible and destructive of morale. As many members of the Orchestra as possible should be involved in the above activities.

Any other ideas should be checked out with I. Philip Sipser before implementation.

H. Glossary of Union Terms

Alligator clause: The "alligator" clause in a collective bargaining agreement provides insurance that, should the audio/visual product created under the specific terms of the master agreement ever be used for any other purpose, you will receive the appropriate compensation for that use.

American Arbitration Association (AAA): Public service, not-for-profit organization offering dispute resolution services.

Arbitration: A method of settling a dispute through recourse to an impartial third party whose decision is final and binding. Arbitration is voluntary when both parties of their own volition agree to submit a dispute to arbitration; it is compulsory when the two parties involved are required by the law to submit the dispute to arbitration.

Bargaining agent: The union that is designated by a majority of the employees in a bargaining unit and recognized by the employer or a government agency as the exclusive representative for the employees for the purposes of collective bargaining.

Collective bargaining: Process whereby representatives of employees negotiate with employers to obtain a signed contract covering salaries, hours, and other terms and conditions of employment mutually agreeable to both sides.

Collective bargaining agreement (CBA): A written contract, between the union (acting as bargaining agent) and an employer, and resulting from negotiations. The CBA covers the terms and conditions of employment, including wages, hours, working conditions, fringe benefits, rights of workers and unions, and procedures to be followed in settling disputes and grievances. In Canada this contract is known as a collective agreement. Others terms for CBA include "master agreement" and "union contract."

Contract: Written evidence of an agreement between two or more persons. Each musician is signatory to an *individual contract*, containing the terms of employment binding on the individual, e.g., from Minnesota Orchestra Master Agreement, Section 3.1: "Employer shall enter into contracts with Individual Staff Musicians comprising the Orchestra, which shall be consistent in their provisions with the terms of this Agreement."

Duty of fair representation (DRF): It is the duty of the union to represent each member without discrimination, hostility, or malice in bargaining, grievance handling, and arbitration. Unions that commit DFR violations are subject to unfair labor practice charges at the National Labor Relations Board or sued in court.

Federal Mediation and Conciliation Service (FMCS): FMCS was established by the Taft-Hartley Law of 1947 to mediate labor disputes; notification must be thirty days prior to expiration of the agreement.

Grievance: A grievance is a dispute between the employer and the union regarding an alleged breach of the CBA or an alleged injustice.

Impasse: An impasse is a good-faith deadlock in negotiations. It is the point at which no further progress toward a collective agreement appears likely because neither side is making movement on major unresolved issues. An impasse can come only after good-faith bargaining breaks down.

Mediation: Efforts of a third party to adjust the differences between employer and employees through interpretation, suggestion, and advice; used interchangeably with the term "conciliation."

National Labor Relations Board (NLRB): Agency created by the National Labor Relations Act of 1935 and continued through subsequent amendments.

National Labor Relations Act (NLRA): Federal law passed in 1935 giving employees the right to join unions, bargain collectively and strike.

Past practice: A standard procedure of operation not written into the collective bargaining agreement. Past practice can be used to clarify ambiguous language if it is shown that the practice was consistent, long-standing, and accepted by both parties.

Ratification: The right of union members to vote on whether to approve a collective bargaining agreement.

Unfair labor practice: To do any acts that would interfere with, restrain, or coerce employees in the exercise of their rights as guaranteed by the NLRA.

Union steward: The steward is the local's representative in the workplace. The steward is protected by labor laws from discipline for reasons of union activity.

Weingarten rights: The rights of employees to request union representation at a meeting with the employer, especially if the employee believes that he or she will be disciplined. The employee must request the union representation at the meeting.

Resources

Books

Ammer, Christine. *Unsung: A History of Women in American Music.* Portland: Amadeus Press, 2001.

Arian, Edward. *Bach, Beethoven, and Bureaucracy: The Case of the Philadelphia Orchestra.* Tuscaloosa: University of Alabama Press, 1971.

Brodine, Russell, with Virginia Warner Brodine. *Fiddle and Fight.* New York: International Publishers, 2001.

Brymer, Jack. *In the Orchestra.* N.p.: Hutchinson, Ltd., 1987.

Burlingame, Jon. *For the Record: The Struggle and Ultimate Political Rise of American Recording Musicians Within Their Labor Movement.* Hollywood: RMA, 1997.

Buttrose, Charles. *Playing for Australia: A Story about ABC Orchestras and Music in Australia.* Netley, Australia: Griffin, 1982.

Dickson, Harry Ellis. *Gentlemen, More Dolce, Please! An Irreverent Memoir of Thirty-Five Years in the Boston Symphony Orchestra.* Boston: Beacon, 1974.

Hall, Tom. *ICSOM: Forty Years of the International Conference of Symphony and Opera Musicians Based on Minutes of the Annual Conferences, Senza Sordino, and Additional Source Material.* New York: Oscar's House Press, 2002.

Hart, Philip. *Orpheus in the New World.* New York: Norton, 1973.

Kelley, Robin D. G. "Without a Song: New York Musicians Strike Out Against Technology." In Howard Zinn, Dana Frank, and Robin D. G. Kelley, *Three Strikes: Miners, Musicians, Sales Girls, and the Fighting Spirit of Labor's Last Century.* Boston: Beacon Press, 2001.

Kirk, Elise K. *Music at the White House: A History of the American Spirit.* Chicago: University of Chicago Press, 1986.

Lebrecht, Norman. *The Maestro Myth*. London: Simon & Schuster, 1991.

———. *Who Killed Classical Music? Maestros, Managers, and Corporate Politics*. Secaucus, NJ: Carol Publishing Group, 1997.

Leiter, Robert D. *The Musicians and Petrillo*. New York: Bookman, 1953.

Levine, Faye. *The Culture Barons: An Analysis of Power and Money in the Arts*. New York: Thomas Crowell, 1976.

Lewis, Thane, with Steven Staryk. *Fiddling with Life: The Unusual Journey of Steven Staryk*. Oakville, Ont.; Niagara Falls, NY: Mosaic Press, 2000.

Millikan, William. *Union against Unions: The Minneapolis Citizens Alliance and Its Fight against Organized Labor, 1903–1947*. St. Paul: Minnesota Historical Society Press, 2001.

Pendle, Karin, ed. *Women and Music: A History*. 2nd ed. Bloomington: Indiana University Press, 2001.

Sadie, Stanley, ed. *The New Grove Dictionary of Music and Musicians*. London: Macmillan; Washington, DC: Grove's Dictionaries of Music, 1980.

Seltzer, George. *Music Matters: The Performer and the American Federation of Musicians*. Metuchen, NJ: Scarecrow Press, 1989.

Shanet, Howard. *Philharmonic: A History of New York's Orchestra*. New Haven, CT: Yale University Press, 2000.

Sherman, John K. *Music and Maestros: The Story of the Minneapolis Symphony Orchestra*. Minneapolis: University of Minnesota Press, 1952.

Solti, Sir Georg. *Memoirs*. New York: Alfred A. Knopf, 1997.

Spivey, Donald. *Union and the Black Musician: Narrative of William Everett Samuels and Local 208*. Lanham, MD: University Press of America, 1984.

Steinhardt, Arnold. *Indivisible by Four: A String Quartet in Pursuit of Harmony*. New York: Farrar, Straus and Giroux, 1998.

Stern, Isaac, with Chaim Potok. *Isaac Stern: My First 79 Years*. New York: Alfred A. Knopf, 1999.

Uscher, Nancy. *Your Own Way in Music: A Career and Resource Guide*. New York: St. Martin's Press, 1990.

Walton, Ortiz M. *Music: Black, White and Blue.* New York: William Morrow, 1972.

Zinn, Howard, Dana Frank, and Robin D. G. Kelley. *Three Strikes: Miners, Musicians, Sales Girls, and the Fighting Spirit of Labor's Last Century.* Boston: Beacon Press, 2001.

Articles

Bezoier, Jeanyne. "Tennstedt." *Minnesota Monthly,* April 1980.

Blum, David. "A Gold Coin." *New Yorker,* February 4, 1991.

Borenstein, Susan. "The AFM: Its History and Its Future." *Allegro* (Newsletter of AFM Local 802), January 1998.

Buzzarte, Monique. "Advocacy: Vienna Philharmonic Orchestra." *IAWM Journal,* June 1997.

Carvajal, Doreen. "Musicians Are Gaining Bigger Voice in Orchestras." *New York Times,* February 6, 2004.

Freed, Richard. "Pathbreaker in Broadcasting and Recording." *Minnesota Orchestra at One Hundred: A Collection of Recordings and Broadcasts.* CD booklet published by Minnesota Orchestra, 2003.

Herman, Jan. "Taking on the Vienna Philharmonic," *IAWM Journal,* February 1997.

———. "Advocacy: Vienna Philharmonic Orchestra." *IAWM Journal,* June 1997.

Fogel, Henry. "Are Three Legs Appropriate? Or Even Sufficient?" *Harmony, Forum of the Symphony Orchestra Institute,* April 2000.

Lunden, Leon. "Bargaining Prospects for Major Symphony Orchestras." *Monthly Labor Review,* May 1966.

Poe, Elizabeth. "Revolt Against Petrillo." *Nation,* May 5, 1956.

Sipser, I. Philip. Letter to the editor. *New York Times,* February 8, 2001.

Velie, Lester. "The Union That Fights Its Workers." *Reader's Digest,* December 1956.

Young, Marl. "The Amalgamation of Locals 47 and 767." *Overture,* December 1988.

Journals and Miscellaneous Collections

Ford Foundation Annual Reports, 1964–1972.

Medical Problems of Performing Artists, the official (quarterly) publication of the Performing Arts Medicine Association (PAMA).

Senza Sordino. The official (monthly) newsletter of the International Conference of Symphony and Opera Musicians (ICSOM). 1963–2005.

Symphony Magazine. Official publication (bimonthly) of the American Symphony Orchestra League.

Electronic Media

American Federation of Musicians Web site: www.afm.org

ICSOM CD-ROM

ICSOM Web site: www.icsom.org (ICSOM was an early adopter of the Internet as a way to communicate and distribute information. The Web site first came into being in January 1995, leading the music field into this area of communication.)

Unpublished Resources

American Federation of Musicians Files (AFM), "Civil Rights in the AFM"

AFM Symphonic Services Department

American Symphony Orchestra League Information Resources

Chicago Federation of Musicians, Local 10-208

Chicago Symphony Orchestra committee newsletters, 1960

Contracts and notes from players committee files

Ford Foundation Symphony Program Archives, 1967–1976

A Labor History of the Houston Symphony Orchestra, compiled by David Waters, July 1994

Master agreements, 1960–2004, Minnesota Orchestra and Twin Cities Musicians Union, Local 30-73

Minneapolis Star Tribune archives

Minnesota History Center Weyerhaeuser Reference Library

Oral history: taped interviews between author and current and retired colleagues, labor lawyers, managers, and union staff and officers
I. Philip Sipser, personal archives
University of Minnesota Manuscripts Division/Performing Arts Archives: Minnesota Orchestra Archives, including personal archives of Steven Zellmer (deceased, former Minnesota Orchestra principal trombone) and Herman Straka (retired violinist, Minnesota Orchestra)
Erika Zazofsky personal archives

Musicians' Health Issues Resources

Horvath, Janet. *Playing (less) Hurt™: An Injury Prevention Guide for Musicians.* Rev. ed. 2004. Kearney, NE: Morris Publishing, 2002. (Contains a resource list of more than thirty pages of books, articles, journals, videos, tapes, and Web sites, as well as lists of clinics, practitioners, and products.)

Medical Problems of Performing Artists, the official (quarterly) publication of the Performing Arts Medicine Association (PAMA).

Norris, Richard, M. D. *The Musician's Survival Manual: A Guide to Preventing and Treating Injuries in Instrumentalists.* St. Louis: MMB Music, 1993.

Paull, Barbara, and Christine Harrison. *The Athletic Musician: A Guide to Playing without Pain.* Metuchen, NJ: Scarecrow Press, 1997.

Sataloff, Robert Thayer, Alice G. Brandfonbrener, Richard J. Lederman, et al. *Textbook of Performing Arts Medicine.* New York: Raven Press, 1991.

Index

To order additional copies of *More Than Meets the Ear:*

Web: www.itascabooks.com

Phone: 1-800-901-3480

Fax: Copy and fill out the form below with credit card information. Fax to 763-398-0198.

Mail: Copy and fill out the form below. Mail with check or credit card information to:

Syren Book Company
5120 Cedar Lake Road
Minneapolis, MN 55416

Order Form

Copies	Title / Author	Price	Totals
	More Than Meets the Ear / *Julie Ayer*	$16.95	$
	Subtotal		$
	7% sales tax (MN only)		$
	Shipping and handling, first copy		$ 4.00
	Shipping and handling, ___ add'l copies @$1.00 ea.		$
	TOTAL TO REMIT		$

Payment Information:

__ Check Enclosed __ Visa/MasterCard		
Card number:	Expiration date:	
Name on card:		
Billing address:		
City:	State:	Zip:
Signature :	Date:	

Shipping Information:

__ Same as billing address __ Other (enter below)		
Name:		
Address:		
City:	State:	Zip: